YOU ARE ABOUT TO FIND OUT:

–How to recognize dependencies that affect your life in ways you probably do not even suspect.

–How to rid yourself of *all* your dependency needs: Physical. Emotional. Social. Sexual. Financial. Intellectual.

–How to learn to act in independent ways that will let you be the 100% boss of you!

GARY EMERY, Ph.D., is Director of the Los Angeles Center of Cognitive Therapy and Clinical Associate Professor in the Department of Psychiatry at U.C.L.A. Dr. Emery is the author of *A New Beginning: How You Can Change Your Life Through Cognitive Therapy* and *Women and Depression.* He lives in San Antonio, California.

OWN YOUR OWN LIFE

HOW THE NEW COGNITIVE THERAPY CAN MAKE YOU FEEL WONDERFUL

GARY EMERY, Ph.D.

FOREWORD BY
JAMES CAMPBELL, M.D.

A SIGNET BOOK
NEW AMERICAN LIBRARY

NAL BOOKS ARE AVAILABLE AT QUANTITY DISCOUNTS WHEN USED TO PROMOTE PRODUCTS OR SERVICES. FOR INFORMATION PLEASE WRITE TO PREMIUM MARKETING DIVISION, NEW AMERICAN LIBRARY, 1633 BROADWAY, NEW YORK, NEW YORK 10019.

ACKNOWLEDGMENTS

Bedrosian, Richard. "Ecological Factors in Cognitive Therapy: The Use of Significant Others." In *New Directions in Cognitive Therapy*. G. Emery, S. Hollon and R. Bedrosian, Editors. Copyright © 1981, The Guilford Press. New York: Guilford Publications.

Berne, Eric. *Games People Play*. Copyright © 1964 by Eric Berne. New York: Ballantine Books.

Elgin, Duane. *Voluntary Simplicity*. Copyright © 1981 by Duane Elgin. New York: William Morrow and Company.

Kiev, Ari. *A Strategy for Success*. Copyright © 1977 by Ari Kiev, M.D. New York: Macmillan Publishing Company, Inc.

Maslow, Abraham H. *Toward a Psychology of Being*. Copyright © 1968 by Litton Educational Publishing. New York: Van Nostrand Reinhold Company.

Missildine, W. Hugh. *Your Inner Child of the Past*. Copyright © 1963 by W. Hugh Missildine. New York: Simon & Schuster, Inc.

Smith, Adam. *Powers of Mind*. Copyright © 1975 by Adam Smith. New York: Random House, Inc.

Wood, John. *How Do You Feel?* Copyright © 1974 by Prentice-Hall, Inc. New York: Prentice-Hall, Inc.

SIGNET TRADEMARK REG. U.S. PAT. OFF. AND FOREIGN COUNTRIES
REGISTERED TRADEMARK—MARCA REGISTRADA
HECHO EN CHICAGO, U.S.A.

SIGNET, SIGNET CLASSIC, MENTOR, PLUME, MERIDIAN and NAL BOOKS are published by New American Library, 1633 Broadway, New York, New York 10019

First Signet Printing, June, 1984

1 2 3 4 5 6 7 8 9

PRINTED IN THE UNITED STATES OF AMERICA

To Pat and Zachary

Acknowledgments

I would like to thank Pat Day, Jill Neimark, Anne Snell and Michael Geller for their help and encouragement in the completion of this book.

I want to give special thanks to Dr. James Campbell for the ideas he shared with me while he was a fellow at UCLA's Department of Child Psychiatry. His ideas about the importance of acceptance, choice and the crucial difference between responsibility and accountability helped me to reshape many of my beliefs about human behavior.

Contents

Foreword

The Author

As his established fans already know and his new readers will soon discover, Gary Emery possesses a number of characteristics that contribute to his success as a writer. In *Own Your Own Life* he deals with the new cognitive therapy in a diverse but practical manner. He is often humorous and always informative. His blend of case histories and personal accounts reveals the depth of his life experience as a therapist.

After nine years of private practice in Phoenix, Arizona, I decided in 1960 to do a two-year Child Psychiatry Fellowship at UCLA. Because of his work in the area of cognitive therapy, I requested Dr. Emery as a supervisor for my second year. That choice led to one of the most satisfactory educational experiences in my life. Unlike a previous supervisor who saw any comment I made about past experiences and therapy techniques as a "resistance to learning something new," he was supportive. When my concepts differed from his he would sometimes take those ideas and try them in his own therapy. The result was that we both had an opportunity to develop new concepts. Some of those ideas appear in this book.

His work at the University of Pennsylvania with Aaron T. Beck, M.D., and others, developing the cognitive approach to therapy, has led to a workable and understandable approach to life's problems. The readers of this book will not be troubled by references to penis-envy, oedipus complexes or other psychoanalytical jargon. This book was written the way the author communicates. I forewarn you that you may carry ideas from this book around with you for a long time.

The Concepts

The surface theme of this book is about unhealthy dependency, how you experience it, and what you can do about it. Through creating an awareness of the many ways dependency sticks its "ugly" head into our lives, we may begin to develop a sense of self and a sense of independence. This allows the emergence of the beautiful side of dependency as it can be manifested in love and trust. Only when we believe in and know ourselves can acts of healthy dependency foster growth.

The deeper themes are related to awareness and choice. These are two of the most misunderstood concepts (along with acceptance, change, responsibility and accountability) that I encounter in the practice of psychiatry. One must have awareness about what is available before a choice can be made. This seems logical, and yet I see people day after day who will assume, because they do not think, listen, look or keep an open mind, that choice does not exist. Perhaps it is this very failure that leads people to attempt to *change* things. Others deny the existence of choice because the particular choices they tell themselves they need are not there. To limit our ability to create our own experience in life because the choices *we think we need* are not available is a tragedy of Shakespearean depth. Because of the compelling relationship between awareness and choice-making, Dr. Emery has spent much of his effort in this book with consciousness-raising ideas.

Once people are willing to open their eyes to awareness there is the problem of what to do next. The single most inhibiting concept I encounter is that of change. Change implies effort, time and transformations. What is ironical is that change is seldom, if ever, what is needed. What is helpful is the making of choices that lead to the desired end product—not attempting, through effort and work, to make changes. People spend countless dollars and hours attempting to create, through change, what they could have obtained effortlessly by more careful choices. Dr. Emery shows the reader some of those choices.

The Serenity Prayer, which directs us to accept what we cannot change, still strikes me as one of the soundest pieces of advice ever written. A few years ago I heard a past president of the American Psychiatric Association discuss the concept of acceptance in a negative manner. He stated that people do not come to a psychiatrist to hear that they must accept something, but to hear how they can change. In my practice I find that the single best predictor of a rapid shift in symptoms is based precisely on a person's ability to be accepting. The act of accepting is a good antidote for the majority of pains and hurts one experiences in life. Acceptance in no way implies a wish for conditions to remain as they are; it is merely an acknowledgment that the world (other people, ourselves, etc.) is the way we find it. If acceptance reflects reality, then choices will become more clear. Dr. Emery's book provides the opportunity to confront many concepts about life and where we really are. The rest is up to you and me. . . .

—JAMES E. CAMPBELL, M.D.,
Medical Director
Cognitive Therapy Institute
Phoenix, Arizona

OWN YOUR
OWN LIFE

CHAPTER ONE

Introduction

"GET MY SOCKS, WOULD YOU, HONEY?" Linda scurried around and brought her husband a pair. "No, not these," he said. "I need the black ones." She rushed off to fetch him another pair.

My wife and I watched similar scenes throughout the weekend. When Pat and I drove home, we talked about Bill and Linda. We both said we didn't like Bill. At first, we weren't sure exactly why. But as we talked, it became clear. His helplessness put us off. Every time he asked Linda to do something he could more easily do for himself, we cringed inside. We also agreed that we didn't have much respect for Linda. We figured she must not have much for herself either or she wouldn't put up with Bill's behavior. We decided not to see them again.

Nearly everyone is put off by full-grown people expecting others to take care of them—like the coworker who can't do anything on his own, the husband who blames all of his unhappiness on his wife or the man whose first thought when meeting you is always, "What can you do for me?"

Pathway to Growth

To overcome dependency and become independent is the main challenge of life; it begins at birth. If you don't cry or fuss too much and if you are relatively pliant, people will call you a good baby. However, if you assert your independence too much or too often, people will start to label you a problem baby. Your first real try at independence is called the "terrible twos." "Let mommy feed you, you're making a big mess" is just a sample of what's to come. The pull toward dependency continues into old age ("Don't you think you'd be much happier in a nursing home?").

The problem isn't all external pull. You also have a strong internal push toward dependency. Your whole life you have to contend with compelling desires and urges to ask someone else to make you feel better, someone to hold you up when you're down, and someone to blame when you don't get your way.

Society today places great demands on you to be independent. You have to depend less on the schools to educate your children, less on political parties and labor unions to protect your interests, less on church officials to define your morals and values, less on relatives to help you when you're in trouble and less on employers to look out for your economic well-being.

The new social realities require that you do more for yourself and rely less on others to take care of you. If you meet these new requirements, you'll reap the benefits of technological advances and the richness of a more self-determined way of life. If you don't, you'll be left behind.

Social Interdependency

I'm not suggesting that you can or should do away with constructive and appropriate dependency. In many areas where you don't have the skills, it's sensible and desirable to depend on others. Medical doctors, mechanics, computer scientists, sausage makers—often their skills and products are more readily available to you, cost less and represent better quality than you could provide for yourself. This is the normal course of social interdependence. Independence doesn't mean you have to do everything for yourself and assume every skill necessary to free you from all reliance on the services of others.

I'm also not advocating that you become a hermit or that you isolate yourself from others. One of the paradoxes of life is that the more independent you are, the closer you can be to others. Spontaneity of feelings and a deepening of intimacy are by-products of increased independence. Self-isolation and loneliness are the results of excessive dependency, not independence.

Attempts at Independence

Self-help Groups. If dependency is undesirable from a personal and social standpoint, how do you go about becoming more independent? In the past you may have sought help through groups and organizations to become more independent. This can be useful, but many groups that masquerade as self-help organizations produce more dependency, not less.

Rick's dependency, for example, led to a problem with excessive drug and alcohol use. He joined a religious cult that promised to cure all his problems. After a year of selling flowers on street corners, he realized he was getting nowhere. He left the group, then became depressed and attempted suicide. It was at this point that he decided he'd better start looking toward himself, not others, to become more independent.

Therapy. If you're suffering, you may have thought of going for therapy. The danger of therapy is that, like a group, it can make you more dependent. When you're overly dependent, you're likely to seek out a therapist who will be like a parent to you—someone who will love you unconditionally. The problem with paying to be loved unconditionally is that it can make you more dependent.

Classical psychoanalysis is the basis of most of the current therapies. While patients are in psychoanalysis, they aren't supposed to begin new love affairs, move, travel much, or get too involved with outside hobbies. The rationale is that this would take away from the therapy. Do you think this kind of behavior is conducive to increasing your independence?

Many people will go to the same therapist for years. They schedule their time around the therapist's time. They usually start attributing grandiose qualities—"He's brilliant," for example—to the therapist. They may begin to adopt the therapist's mannerisms and way of speaking. They often say, "I have a way to go but I've gone a long way in therapy." Often, they're confusing imitation with independence.

A recent article in *Newsweek* reported on what happens to patients when their therapists go on vacation. Some develop stomach pains and other psychosomatic ills. Many become depressed. A typical comment was, "My therapist's vacation left a big gap in my life." Therapists are not immune to this process. One therapist, telling about his vacation, said, "I get the same feeling a parent has when he goes on vacation and leaves a child behind."

This is not to say that you can't benefit from therapy—or even that you can't benefit from long-term therapy. The crucial issue is, *Will you come out of therapy more independent than when you went in?*

If you wanted to learn to whitewater raft, you would probably hire a guide—someone who knows the currents, rocks and rapids, a person who would help you avoid the dangers of the river. You would want a person willing to teach you what he or she knows, preferably as soon as possible, so you could start to run the rapids on your own. Similarly, the most useful form of therapy is one in which you learn how to become your own guide as quickly as possible.

This is a book on achieving independence—in all areas of your life. One of its main goals is to teach you how to think for yourself so you can make better choices. The major reason you have trouble in being independent is that you've let others do your thinking for you.

Clinical observation and research studies have found that you feel and act the way you think. If you think you have to have everyone's approval, you feel constant pressure to please others. If you think you can't make decisions, you ask others to make them for you. If you think others are better than you are, you feel inferior.

By misperceiving and misevaluating your experiences, you end up making poor choices—choices that aren't in your own best interests. You can avoid this and learn to master your problems and lead a more self-directed life.

Choice Points. At certain critical moments you can choose how you feel and act. After you become aware of these moments, they become like windows in time. You can look out the window and see the different outcomes of your choices. With practice, you can learn to recognize and create choice points almost at will.

In and Out of Control. From the standpoint of your own perception, there are only four things in the world: how you *think*, how you *feel*, how you *act*, and *the rest of the world*. You have a lot to say about the first three, and very little about the last. Most people, however, act as if it were reversed. They are more concerned with trying to control how the world treats them than with controlling how they think, feel and act.

As Dr. Jim Campbell points out, when you try to control the rest of the world, you're out of control and when you stop trying, you're in control. The independent person chooses to control him- or herself—not the rest of the world.

You can only affect others indirectly. You can write a letter to your congressional representative about inflation and hope he reads it and takes some action. You can keep your end of a bargain and hope the other person does the same. You can ask others to treat you with more respect and hope they do. In situations with others, you don't have direct control over them; they can always choose to do as they like. But you do have direct control over the elements in the ACT formula: *how you think, feel and act*.

ACT

In *Owning Your Own Life*, I'll talk repeatedly about a three-step formula called ACT.

1. *A*ccept reality.
2. *C*hoose to be independent.
3. *T*ake action.

This formula can be applied to any situation in which you want to increase your independence. I'll expand on it throughout the book. However, I'll go over each step briefly right now. The ACT formula can become your key to leading a more independent life.

Accept Reality. Acceptance goes beyond merely knowing or understanding something. You might know that you would be better off if you were more independent, but this doesn't mean that you have accepted it. Acceptance is a letting-go process. You let go of your wishes and demands that life be different. It's a conscious choice. You choose to let go or you choose not to.

Acceptance of reality isn't passive compliance, nor is it quitting and giving up. On the contrary, acceptance is often the first step toward constructive action. You have to accept that you have a flat tire before you can fix it. When you don't accept something, you become stuck. Pathological grief over the loss of a person or object is an extreme form of nonacceptance. The purpose of emotional pain is to nudge you into accepting reality. Your brain wants you to accept what is, so it signals you with emotional pain. You hurt when you're not accepting what's in front of you. When you say, "Okay, I accept that my husband is gone," or "Okay, I accept that I made a wrong choice," the pain starts to go away.

Self-acceptance is the most healthy and most useful form of acceptance. When you were an adolescent, you probably couldn't accept many aspects of yourself—the way you talked, the way you looked, the way you acted, or even your family. As you matured and became more independent, you started to accept yourself more, flaws and all.

A major obstacle to self-acceptance is *lack of awareness*. You probably aren't aware of all the areas in your life where you're dependent. You consciously and unconsciously block out what you find unacceptable in yourself. Without awareness, you can't have *acceptance*, which is Step One of the ACT formula.

Closing your eyes is only one way to avoid reality. More often, however, your mind takes a devious route: you distort your experience in a way that makes reality even more unacceptable to you.

Your mind can make a difficult job into "it's impossible." The possibility of making mistakes becomes "I'll be a complete failure." Someone giving you negative feedback becomes "I displease him, just like I do everyone else." One woman, Sally, distorted being on her own over the weekend into "It'll be a terrifying experience and I won't be able to handle it." By blowing up the real consequences, she had greater difficulty in accepting the kernel of truth—she could survive being lonely over the weekend.

Choose to Be Independent. Step Two in the ACT formula has to do with consciously deciding to be independent. Once you accept something you don't like, you can choose not to be dependent on it.

Take feelings, for example. Most people don't realize how much choice they have in how they feel. People confuse telling themselves "I don't want to feel bad," or "I shouldn't feel bad," with "I'm not going to feel bad." The former has little to do with how you feel, the latter a great deal.

I've always been amazed how some actors and actresses can have exquisite control over their emotions while playing a scene and yet appear to have little control over their real-life emotions. I once treated an actor who was playing a happy-go-lucky fellow in a movie he was making; in between scenes, however, he would become hysterical while talking on the phone to a woman with whom he was breaking up.

When I told the actor he could choose how he felt, he said, "If I can choose how I feel, how come I feel so bad? I sure don't enjoy feeling like this." I told him that most of the time we don't know we have the choice. For example, you learn as a child that if someone criticizes you, you're supposed to feel bad. In fact, if you don't feel bad, those around you will get quite upset. Eventually, we come to believe we have to feel bad whenever we're criticized. As children, we often don't learn that we have choices in how we feel, think and act.

Take Action. Taking action is the most important part of the formula. You have to act on your acceptance in order to make it stick; and you have to act on your choices to make them real. Without action, the formula becomes an intellectual exercise.

To become more independent, you have to act differently. You have to act when you're afraid, when you feel like a phony, when you know you'll do a poor job, when you think it's stupid and when you don't want to. Action is necessary; without it you can't move out of dependency.

Often just reciting the reason why you should do something isn't enough. You become too good at rationalizing the reasons away. At this point the only strategy that works is to just do it. You don't do it for any reason, you just do it. At the simplest level, action is physical movement. You tell your muscles to move and then they get the job done.

The specific type of action grows out of the situation. One general rule when considering what action to take is to think the reverse: *when you're off track take the opposite tack.* For example, Willard was intimidated by his boss and disliked by his fellow employees. He began by treating his boss with some of the same friendly informality that he used with those under him. And he began to treat those who worked under him with the same respect he had for his boss. His relationships on the job improved greatly.

When you're being dependent, you move away from reality, so when you take the opposite tack, you're moving back toward reality.

One of the facets of independence is the ability to form close, real friendships. You can approach people free of any hidden agendas ("What can you do for me?"). This also applies to working with others. As an independent person, you work well with others because you treat everyone the same and you do your job well. There's no need to get the boss to love you or to get the person in the next desk to finish the assignment.

You're acting constructively when you seek help for a problem you lack the basic skills for dealing with. If you own your own life, you can start choosing what you want to do with it.

Throughout the book I'll talk about specific ways you can recognize your dependencies and ways you can choose to become more independent. To rate your current level of independence overall, you can use the Independence Rating Scale in the Appendix.

CHAPTER TWO

Step One: Acceptance

Lucy wanted to become more independent from her father's influence. Although she was twenty-eight, she continued to seek his advice. She would ask him what kind of apartment she should look for, how she should approach her boss for a raise and what kind of car to buy. She had trouble accepting that she might be wrong if she made her own decisions.

Your first step in becoming more independent is accepting reality.

Beliefs: Barriers to Acceptance

Your dependency-producing beliefs are the major obstacle to acceptance. Lucy, for example, believed that her father *always* knew best and that if she made a wrong decision on her own, it would be a near-tragedy. She couldn't accept that her decisions could be as good as her father's or that a wrong decision is often just the long way around to the same place.

Rigid beliefs are a form of self-imprisonment. Your mind uses them to put you under house arrest—presumably for your own good. While your beliefs lock in on some truth about the world, they exclude much more. For example, suppose you believe you're a helpless person. It's true you may be helpless at times to control events, but it's also true that there are many more times when you aren't helpless.

Your false beliefs keep you dependent. You may believe other people are bigger, smarter or better than you. You may discount your real abilities. You may think it's easier to avoid problems than face them. You may think you can't make it on your own. In short, you believe the world is more hostile, dangerous and difficult than it really is.

In this chapter I'll talk about ways you can correct the faulty thinking and beliefs blocking your acceptance. Once you correct them you can see and accept the world as it is. This in turn frees you for the second step in the ACT formula: you can choose to be independent in the way you live your life.

The World Should Care. You may, like David, believe that the world should care more about you. He thought he should be provided with all the goods and services he wanted. And if getting this required a job, the world should provide a good one.

The world is relatively indifferent to you. David's wishes and demands that the world should be "easier," "fairer," and "different" went unanswered. The more he insisted the world be different, the more frustrated he became. When your satisfaction depends on how the world treats you, you're dissatisfied most of the time.

Suppose you have a plan to go on an outing with a friend on Saturday, and when you wake up on Saturday morning, you find it's raining. You could react in many ways. You might tell yourself that it shouldn't be raining and that it's not fair. You might get angry at your friend for not suggesting you go on Sunday instead. You might feel sad and conclude everything bad always happens to you; or you might feel hopeless and tell yourself that nothing you plan ever works out. While you're thinking this, nothing is happening to the rain. It doesn't care, it just keeps on raining. But once you accept that it's raining, you can then start to make different plans.

Much of the world operates by inflexible rules ("You must breathe, eat and drink, or you die"). Some other rules are nearly as inflexible ("You have to do something to get something"). David's beliefs ("The world should be different" . . . "I'm special") ran counter to the second set of rules.

The World Is Difficult and Dangerous. The other main distortion about the world is that it is more difficult and dangerous than it really is. This was one of Lucy's beliefs. She exaggerated how terribly difficult the world was; it was for this reason that she believed she needed a third party to intervene for her. Dave's response was to give up when the world didn't turn out the way he wished it would. Lucy's was to ask her father to handle it for her.

While you can't change the world by wishes, you can change your own personal world by how you think, feel and act. You need to accept reality before you can start to move into independence.

The Road to Acceptance. Acceptance is on a continuum that runs from not being consciously aware of reality to feeling comfortable with it. At this final point, what was once unacceptable and constantly on your mind is usually forgotten. Just as there is a transition from night to day, there is a transition from nonacceptance to acceptance. You usually have to go through five detours or stages before you reach acceptance. At each stage you'll run into distortions that may keep you stuck there. In *table 1* (p. 31) I've listed the stages you usually have to cycle through to reach acceptance: *nonawareness*, *disbelief*, *anger*, *depression* and *anxiety*. You can cycle through these in a matter of moments or you can take years to do it.

In some areas of your life you may reach acceptance rapidly, in others it may be a slow tortuous process. Dependency has no absolute pattern. Individuals differ in what they find acceptable or unacceptable. Lucy found the fact that you have to work for a living easy to accept, Dave did not.

I've also found great differences in which stage different individuals get stuck in. You may have more trouble with depression than anxiety. Dave was often angry about the way the world was. Lucy was anxious.

You may complete the cycle in many ways each day. Or you may carry over many unacceptable activities as unfinished business for years. You may advance through one stage and then fall back again. For example, you may move from depression to anxiety and back to depression. This example is common with depressed people. They often have trouble tolerating the anxiety they feel after they start coming out of their depression.

Your stay in each stage will be determined by how much you distort reality. If you continue to distort your experiences, you can stay indefinitely. The ticket out is seeing the world more realistically. The more you distort, the more difficulty you'll have in moving through the cycle to acceptance.

Distortions That Keep You Dependent

In each of the stages of nonacceptance, you distort reality in ways particular to that stage. By learning how to recognize and correct the thinking that comes with each stage, you can move much more quickly through them. I'll talk about each of these stages for a moment before getting on to how you can choose to think differently.

Nonawareness. The central message of this stage is "I don't want to know." What's your response when you hear bad news? Your first response is nearly always "Oh, no!" This is the wish not to know in its simplest form. Your not wanting to know can take much more elaborate forms, such as pathological grief. Here you don't want to know that a loved one is dead.

Not knowing has a number of negative consequences. I treated one man who would develop a relationship with a woman and believe everything was going along well. Then, without warning, the woman would break off the relationship and leave him. He said this happened over and over again. The problem was that he would gloss over the everyday problems that came up. They were never dealt with until it was too late.

While most people have isolated areas of not wanting to know, some people use it as a general coping device. I worked with one secretary who refused to admit her mistakes. If anyone questioned her many typing errors, she would see it as the other person's problem ("He's a nitpicker").

As a result, she never learned to correct her mistakes. Her boss asked me what he could do. I suggested he ignore the mistakes and reinforce her for what she did right. He came back a couple of weeks later and told me it wasn't helping. When he told her she did something right, her reply was "Yes, I know: I'm very competent."

He decided to fire her. On her last day she told me, "That guy really has a psychological problem. You ought to talk to him, Gary. Only last week he was telling me how good I am and this week he's firing me."

Disbelief. After saying "Oh, no!" upon hearing the bad news, your next response is usually "I don't believe it!" The message at this stage is "I know it, but I don't want to believe it." In other words, you believe it intellectually, but you don't accept it emotionally.

Dave was at this stage the first time I saw him. He said, "It's incredible that someone with my artistic talent doesn't have a steady source of income. I should have been born back in the days when artists were supported by patrons . . . I'm a true Renaissance man . . . It's incredible that I can't be paid for the art I produce."

The distortions at this stage revolve around how you feel the world should be. Dave felt the world should provide for intellectuals and artists. The gap between how you see the world and how you feel it should be causes you pain.

Anger. After you say "No, I don't believe it," your next thought is "Whose fault was it?" We're raised with the idea that when something bad happens, someone bad must have caused it. And that person has to be punished to set things right and even the score. Often it doesn't matter who is to blame as long as someone is; thus, the long-held tradition of scapegoating.

When you don't want to accept something, you usually can find someone to blame. When a person close to you dies, often the doctors, nurses and hospitals are the target. One man I saw said his ninety-three-year-old father, who had been ailing for five years, was killed by incompetent hospital staff.

Another standard target for anger is the victim. Men who beat their wives and parents who abuse their children often say their victims were to blame. Some people believe women who are raped must have been "asking" for it.

People you're dependent on are the most common targets of your anger ("It was my husband's . . . wife's . . . parents' . . . fault"). One of the ways to pinpoint your dependencies is to see who you blame your unhappiness and misfortunes on. You wouldn't be caught in a traffic jam if your husband made enough money so that you didn't have to work. You wouldn't have overslept and missed your plane if your wife hadn't insisted on having sex the night before. You wouldn't have lost your way if your sister had taken down the directions correctly when she made your appointment. You wouldn't have a low-status job if your parents had encouraged you to go on in school.

How do *you* play the blame game? If you can't think of any person to blame, you can always blame abstractions—God, your religious upbringing or lack of it, the system, the establishment and society.

Once Dave began to see that he would have to work to get money, he became angry. At first he blamed his parents for not seeing to it that he had a professional career, and then he blamed society for not supporting artists like him.

The distortion in anger is the belief that you can change the fourth aspect of reality—the rest of the world—by stamping your foot and willing it.

Depression. After you get through the anger, your next response to bad news is "What about me, what have I lost?" Whenever you focus on loss you get stuck in the sadness or depression stage. You can suffer different types of losses: some are tangible ("I lost my job"); some are intangible ("I've lost my self-respect").

After you focus on your losses long enough, you will come to see yourself as a loser. This conclusion works to keep you losing. Your distortions revolve around exaggerations of the extent, degree and duration of your loss. You often believe that your sorrow over the loss is frozen in time and will go on forever.

In addition to focusing on your losses, you stay in this stage by acting on the idea that you're a loser ("Why try? What's the use?").

The only option for a loser is to give up, and this is what keeps you stuck in this stage.

Anxiety. After you ask about your losses, your next question will be "What will happen to me?" Depression is dwelling in the past; anxiety is dwelling in the future.

Your anxiety is caused by not accepting the possibility that something bad could happen to you in the future. It's a demand for your guaranteed safety in the future. By not accepting that life can't offer such guarantees, you become stuck in this stage.

Lucy couldn't accept that her choices could be wrong. Like other anxious people, she exaggerated the degree of danger and belittled her ability to handle potential problems. Fear is the biggest block to leading a more independent life. You become independent by learning to overcome your fears.

Once you accept the possibility that danger could happen, you move on to *acceptance*. It's at that point you tell yourself, "Okay, I accept it happened. Now, what can I do to get on with my life?"

Self-awareness

Acceptance starts with awareness. Once you become aware of your thoughts, feelings and actions, you can start to make more independent choices. Alan Watts, talking about self-awareness, says, "You have to see and feel what you are experiencing as what *is*, and not as it is named. This very simple 'opening of the eyes' brings about the most extra-ordinary transformation of understanding and living, and shows that many of our most baffling problems are pure illusion." The more independent you are, the more you go through life with your eyes open.

Psychotherapists of all persuasions have been groping with one central question ever since Freud started the whole business. *Why do people repeatedly make the same poor choices?* Even the most successful people have areas of their lives where they act in highly dependent ways. Why is this? What leads to it? I believe people aren't fully aware of what they're doing when they're doing it. They are frequently asleep—self-hypnotized—when it comes to their self-defeating dependency patterns. That's why if you want to become independent, you first have to become more self-aware, or self-awake.

You can increase your level of self-awareness by putting the following guidelines into practice. Note which ones would help you the most and use them on a daily basis.

Own Your Own Actions. Even if you follow someone else's demands, you're the one doing the following. You're the one making the choice to do it. We have a long tradition of not owning our own actions. Adam said, "Eve made me do it." Eve said, "The snake made me do it." Throughout the day, when you catch yourself disowning your actions ("I have to go to the bank" . . . "They're making me work late"), replace this with ownership ("I'm choosing to go to the bank" . . . "I'm choosing to work late"). Gradually you come to see how you are authoring your own life. You come to see that if you don't want to work late, you can choose to quit your job.

Own Your Own Feelings. You're not owning your own feelings when you say, "My husband made me angry by coming home late." As a result, you have trouble seeing how you could choose to feel any other way. Start putting your feelings in the first person ("I feel angry when my husband comes home late"). By putting your feelings statement in the active voice instead of the passive voice, you'll begin to see the role you play in their creation.

Own Your Own Success. Not owning your successes is potentially more damaging than not owning your shortcomings. Here, you attribute your successes to others ("I couldn't have done it without his help") or to chance ("I was awfully lucky"). When you do this, you block out of your awareness the role you played in the success. You may do this out of the belief that you really are at the mercy of others. In any case, stop making these automatic attributions. They blind you to what you do right and you need to know this so you can do it right again. Throughout the day, tell yourself what you're doing right.

Approach What You Fear. When you're dependent, you're afraid to do many activities ("I'll lose my job" . . . "I'll be bored if I go alone" . . . "I'll be rejected"). One of the best ways to learn about yourself is to confront what you're afraid of. Speak up to your boss, go someplace by yourself, take a risk and ask someone out. While you may be uncomfortable, you can gain valuable information. Fear, if nothing else, wakes you up.

Watch Your Visual Images. As you approach what you fear, be on the lookout for vivid images. At the University of Pennsylvania, we found that over 90 percent of anxious people have visual images, often in color, of a catastrophe occurring. By being alert to your fantasies and daydreams, you can become more aware of what you fear.

Think Through Unpleasant Experiences. A painful memory that makes you shudder is a good place to begin to increase your self-awareness. This might be the memory of what you said or did at an office party, the letter you didn't answer, or the loan you didn't repay. Your inclination is to put this memory out of your mind as quickly as you can. Take ten or fifteen minutes and force yourself to think it through. Look at the *who*, *what*, *where*, *when* and *why* of the situation.

However, don't confuse thoughtless rumination ("Why did this have to happen?" . . . "Why didn't I do better?") with thoughtful self-examination ("Exactly why did I choose to do what I did? I'll reconstruct it in my mind and see what happened").

Fully Experience Your Feelings. At times you'll have experiences that allow you to learn something about yourself. If you find yourself with a group of people where you feel discomfort, you have three choices: (1) You can physically leave; (2) You can tense up your muscles and psychologically escape by telling yourself "I don't want to be here" and trying to distract yourself; (3) You can stay and feel the way you do. You can say to yourself, "Let me experience this feeling."

Boredom, for example, is a feeling that you may be trying to block out of your awareness ("I can't stay home tonight"). You may be so concerned with avoiding this that you don't find out why or how you're boring yourself or how painful it really is. A way to greater self-awareness is to fully experience feelings you've been trying to turn off ("No, I'll stay home tonight and work this out").

Increase Your Range of Emotional Experiences. John Wood, a psychology writer, has listed some of the more common feelings. Ask yourself how you feel when you're: accepted, affectionate, afraid, angry, anxious, attracted, bored, competitive, confused, defensive, disappointed, free, frustrated, guilty, hopeful, hurt, inferior, jealous, joyful, lonely, living, rejected, repulsed, respected, sad, satisfied, shy, superior, suspicious and/or trusting.

Take some time out to try to see what these emotions feel like. Those you can't relate to are most likely the ones you aren't aware of. Suppose you say you never feel superior. Go through the day and notice how often you do feel superior. One woman found she felt superior to her friends because she had bigger problems than they did. By tuning into new emotions and fully experiencing them, you'll start learning more about yourself.

Keep Your Mind Open. You may decide you have the facts before they're all in. You bring down the curtain before the show's over. One woman saw me on television talking about depression. She wrote me and said, "What you say about depression is all wrong. I'm not going to read your book because I already know all about it." She wrote this despite the fact that she was chronically depressed and unable to get over it for any length of time.

Many people, having reached a certain point in their lives, choose not to change any of their beliefs. They work new experiences into their old belief systems. They assume that what they tell themselves about their experiences is beyond question. Such firmly held certainties cloud your vision and stunt your growth.

You need to question your vision if you have nearsightedness ("I'll take the nickel now instead of the quarter later"). Learn to tolerate ambiguity and uncertainty before reaching conclusions. With farsightedness ("I think it'll take care of itself in the long run"), check into it now. With tunnel vision ("My job is so important that I don't have time to think about my family"), expand your interests. Learn to tolerate blind spots. Tell yourself, "I'll keep an open mind about this."

Stop Setting up Self-fulfilling Prophecies. Stop setting up situations that reaffirm your beliefs. You may have some notion about yourself ("I'm helpless") that you automatically act out ("Only my husband can help me out of this situation"). When you set it up that only your husband can do it, you don't learn anything new about yourself. This can be so automatic that you almost don't realize what you're doing. Whenever you make a prediction ("They won't like me"), see how you work to make this a reality.

Seek Out and Listen to Feedback from Others. I've noticed when I talk with clients about sensitive material, they often have one of two responses: either their eyes glaze over or they start to yawn. Your mind is for the status quo and it doesn't want to hear anything that goes against your present beliefs. When you're talking to others and find yourself starting to tune out, consciously force yourself to stay awake.

Question All Your Present Beliefs. List all the beliefs you once held firmly and no longer do. When you start to examine your present beliefs, refer back to this list; this will give you pause about what you now believe.

Eric Hoffer said, "The weakness of a soul is proportionate to the number of truths that must be kept from it." Ask yourself, "What don't I want to know that would contradict my present beliefs—and why don't I want to know it?"

Develop New Friends and Associates. One way to see yourself in a true light is to associate with people who don't share your world view. One of the reasons people go into group therapy with strangers is to find out more about themselves. When you develop new friends and associates, you can get the same result—you get a fresh feedback on yourself, and you also get a chance to bounce your old beliefs off new people.

Limiting your associations can be lethal to self-awareness. Not surprisingly, the most unaware people are the most dependent. They often can be found among the religious, spiritual and political cults. Here the glaze-eyed person moves over to become rabbit-eyed. I've noticed that when people in cults talk, their eyes don't focus on you. Instead, they appear to be talking to the cosmos somewhere behind you. Such groups keep members from questioning by limiting social contact to fellow members. They dress and act differently to shut out others.

Seek Out New Experiences. To learn more about yourself, you have to have a variety of experiences. Apathy leads to a dulled sense of your senses. A paradox is that often the only way you can find out why you're dependent is by acting more independently. When Al and I started working together, our joint goal was to get him to enjoy himself more. We started with simple tasks, like going to a movie. Once he began to get out and become aware of the fact that he could have a good time on his own, he learned there was a lot about himself he liked.

Take an Active Instead of a Reactive Approach to Life. Many of your dependency habits are so automatic that you do them without thinking. Like eating, you do them by rote. You just react to what's in front of you. You may, for example, find yourself buying a new type of coffeepot, not because you want it but because a celebrity on TV told you to. To see what you're doing, you have to take an active—instead of a reactive—approach. You can begin to question yourself ("Do I really want this? If so, why?"). As you begin to take an active approach, new insights about yourself begin to develop. You always have the choice of saying yes to life, or no. Once you say yes and stop holding back, you start finding out more about yourself.

Be More Honest with Others. Most people find it difficult to be honest with others and even more difficult to be honest with themselves. For example, some teenagers have sex in the back seat of a car and never admit it to each other or to themselves. People engage in similar forms of dishonesty continuously.

When you're honest with others, they're more likely to be honest with you. This works the opposite way as well. Lies beget more lies. Several years ago I talked to two others about forming a business. We met periodically for about a year. We fell into a pattern of lying to each other at these meetings. One of us would say, "I'll get the details and make the call," and then never do it. At first, I believed myself when I told them I was going to do something. Then I began to realize I was lying to them and to myself—I never intended to do it. Once I became more honest about what I was willing to do ("I don't think it's a good idea to do that"), they became more honest with me. The more honesty that's in the air, the more you know about yourself.

Be Honest with Yourself. You may be involved in inner face-saving efforts. You don't do this out of ignorance, but out of a lack of courage to be honest with yourself. Self-dishonesty can take many forms. One way is to overstate your faults ("I'm a jerk because I'm always late"). Globally, or totally, blaming yourself is a way of blotting out what really happened. When you say, "I'm totally bad," you're not admitting the real problem at hand ("I am fifteen minutes late for this meeting"). This is why people with chronic problems, such as obesity, have trouble admitting their problem. Their guilt stops them from being honest with themselves, and their awareness is blocked.

Question Your Inconsistencies. You can learn a great deal by questioning your dishonesty. For the last few years I've kept an honesty/dishonesty book. Whenever I'm dishonest, or want to be dishonest, I write it down in the book. This particular exercise has taught me a great deal about myself that I didn't previously know.

Another form of ignored dishonesty is inconsistent behavior, such as accepting invitations and then not showing up. By questioning your inconsistencies, you can start to learn more about yourself ("If I don't want to go, why am I afraid to say so when

I'm asked? . . . What consequences am I afraid of?"). Keep in mind that the more independent you are, the more honest you are. When you move toward honesty, you're moving toward increased independence ("I'm sorry, I won't be there because I don't enjoy costume parties").

Deprive Yourself. Being too comfortable can block out your self-awareness. You become more awake and aware when you're a little cold and a little hungry. Sleeping when you're not tired and eating when you're not hungry keeps you unaware.

The opposite is true too. Adam Smith (the contemporary writer, not the classical economist), after a year of practicing a variety of self-awareness programs, wrote, "For a year I had no alcohol and little refined sugar, and all that awareness—reaching, reaching, tasting, tasting—produced a fuller stomach with less food. I didn't think I was fat or even bulky when I began; we never know how we look. . . . I became a scale addict, for effortlessly, without tension, my weight was dropping, one pound, two pounds a week, past my Army weight, past my college weight, and it finally leveled off at the weight last registered when I was a skinny seventeen."

Keep Looking. Self-awareness is a continuing process without end. When you say, "I finally know myself," you can assume you've just lost your awareness. Taking stock of yourself is one of the best habits you can develop. If you're on the path of independence, self-awareness helps you avoid many detours. If you've been suffering from dependent and self-defeating behavior, awareness can give you the power to choose to be more independent.

Correcting Distortions

Have you had times when you could see the world with great clarity? At such times, you can see that your limits are illusionary. You see that you're no better or worse than anyone else—you are just who you are. When this happens, you're seeing the world directly, as it is, without filtering it through your belief system.

Eric Berne quotes one of his patients who had this experience. She said, "It all began six months ago. At that time, I was looking at my coffeepot and for the first time I really saw it. And you know how it is now, how I hear the birds sing, and I look at people and they're really there as people, and best of all, I'm really there."

Your beliefs filter out and distort certain aspects of reality. By learning how to correct your beliefs, you rid yourself of these filters and start to see the world as it is. Once you can do this, you become more spontaneous; you become able to choose freely the kind of life you want to lead.

You can use two general methods to change your distorted thoughts: an *experimental* method and a *written* method. I'll talk about how you can use both methods to become more independent.

Your mind will not want you to question your belief system. After developing it over the years, your mind doesn't want you to tamper with it. As a result, your mind will give you all kinds of reasons why you shouldn't do it ("Not now, this isn't the right time or place" . . . "It won't help" . . . "It's stupid"). If you find you have trouble getting started, write out all the reasons why you don't want to do it.

Over the years, in treating people with severe emotional and behavioral problems, I've found one important difference between those who get better and those who don't. The difference isn't due to the type of person or to the type of problem. The difference is that those who do homework (experimenting and keeping records) get better; those who don't get better are the ones who don't do the homework.

About 60 percent of the people I see do the work and nearly all get better. About 20 percent don't do the work and get better anyway. Another 20 percent don't do the work and they don't get better. In other words, patients who do the work increase their chance of getting better by almost 100 percent. The same applies to you; if you do the work, you'll become more independent.

Run Real World Experiments. The first way to correct your distorted thoughts is to run behavioral experiments. The thoughts that keep you dependent and away from reality are often predictions ("I can't go there on my own" . . . "I won't be able to enjoy myself if I'm alone" . . . "They will make me feel uncomfortable" . . . "I'll mess it up" . . . "If I don't ask their help, I won't know what to do").

By running behavioral experiments, you test your thoughts. In this method you test your thoughts out by doing something ("I'll go to the party on my own and see what happens" . . . "Before I decide I can't live alone, I'll try it out for awhile"). You get more evidence before you jump to conclusions.

You begin to see that your thoughts are merely hypotheses or hunches that need to be tested out; they are not "givens." Start writing down your predictions of dire consequences. Later, you can evaluate them. This way, you begin to see that just because you *think* something, it doesn't make it so. As one prediction after another fails to occur, your rigid beliefs begin to loosen up. The following are some types of real-world experiments you can run.

- *"I can't make a decision."* Tell yourself to decide to pick up a pencil or to decide not to. Look at all the decisions you do make during the day.
- *"I can't make an outline of what steps to take next."* Tell yourself to take a pencil and paper and to sit for five minutes to make up an outline. Your mind doesn't want you to know that you have a choice.
- *"I can't talk to strangers."* Tell yourself to go into a store and make some small talk with a clerk ("Too bad it's icy today"). You can continue to run experiments like this throughout the day.
- *"I can't be alone."* Monitor all the time you spend alone for one week (taking a bath, driving to work, before your husband or wife gets home). You'll be surprised to find out how absolutely wrong your mind really is.

The best way to change your distorted beliefs is to get contrary evidence—you need facts and experiences to show that the belief is wrong. Running real-world experiments is how you get this evidence.

Behavioral experiments are particularly good to run when you're afraid. One woman I treated began having panic attacks in stores, automatic laundries and other public places. Soon she stopped going out altogether. Her prediction was that if she went out she would have a panic attack and this would cause her to go crazy. I showed her ways to control the panic attacks and encouraged her to test her prediction by going to various public places. As her predictions failed to be realized, her confidence increased. The key to her recovery was setting up her trips as experiments.

When you run your experiments you can use the form in *table 2* (p. 33) as a guide. First, clearly spell out what your predictions are ("I couldn't go out to a restaurant for dinner alone. People would stare at me. I'd be too nervous to eat"). Second, devise some way to test them (go alone to a restaurant you've been to before). Third, develop a way to measure the outcome (look around and see what is happening). Finally, build in a way to generalize from the experiment ("I can do more by myself than I realized").

Many times you're unable to devise experiments. At these times you need to use logic and reason to answer your distorted thoughts.

Keep a Written Record. You need first to buy a notebook and carry it with you at all times. In the written method of discerning old beliefs, you use your symptoms of dependency (negative feelings and avoidances) as cues to get your notebook out.

Draw a line down the middle of one of the pages. In the first column, write out your automatic thoughts ("I feel sad" . . . "I'm angry"); keep writing them down until you get to your basic beliefs ("I'm unlovable . . . my mother doesn't love me"). In the second column, write out the answers to the automatic thoughts. In this column you put down more realistic and more balanced ways of viewing the situation ("Love doesn't have anything to do with it. I want a car, so I'll have to pay for it myself").

In *table 3* (p. 33) is an example of how one person did this. When you do this, it's important that you give your full attention to the task. If you do it halfheartedly, the method isn't effective. As you get more practice at it, you'll be able to do this exercise much faster. Remember, doing this exercise is an act of independence in and of itself. You are learning to think for yourself.

Your dependent beliefs and the automatic thoughts they generate are usually the legacy from your childhood. Sometimes it's helpful to give this part of yourself a name from your childhood, such as "Little Jimmy," and the more mature part of yourself an adult name, such as "Jim." The written method, in essence, is a dialogue between these two parts of you. When you get in dependency-producing situations, you can ask yourself what these two parts of yourself are saying.

You can use the following suggestions to correct your distorted ideas and strengthen your mature part.

- *Ask yourself, "What exactly do I find unacceptable?"* By questioning what you don't want to accept, you'll be able to pinpoint which of the beliefs you need to challenge the most. Elizabeth was afraid to speak up at church meetings. What was unacceptable to her was the idea that she might make a fool of herself. This then became the belief she worked the hardest at changing: "I have to appear competent to others."
- *Ask yourself, "What would make what I don't want to accept more acceptable?"* Incorporate any information or ideas that would help you accept the situation. Elizabeth wrote that there really isn't any such thing as a fool. This is an abstraction and not something that exists in reality. And since it didn't exist, she couldn't become one. She also wrote she couldn't control what others thought of her. This was out of her hands.

She also considered how bad the consequences would be if she appeared incompetent. She decided the consequences wouldn't be that severe and that she could live with them. She also decided that even if she did incur the disapproval of others, she could use the experience as a way to practice acceptance: she could accept that it had happened and choose not to feel shame and humiliation. Thus, she could be independent of others' opinions.

Straighten Out Twisted Thinking. When you're dependent, you're twisting your thinking in some way. When your thinking is straightened out, you accept the world as it is. For this reason, you want to spot and correct your thinking errors. Here are five of the most common thinking errors to look for.

- *Personalizing.* Believing that you're the center of everyone's attention—especially if you act badly or incompetently—and that you're the cause of misfortune ("It's my fault no one came to my son's party").

• *Overgeneralizing.* Believing that if it's true in one case, it applies to any case that is even slightly similar ("Everyone else can eat anything they want and they stay thin. I have all the bad luck").

• *Either/or thinking.* Believing everything is either one extreme or another ("I wasn't elected president of my club. Nobody likes me").

• *False comparison.* Believing you are just like someone else; if they do well that means you've done badly ("He and I graduated from school at the same time and he owns his own company. Why aren't I the president of a company?").

• *Jumping to conclusions.* Believing if it's been true in the past, then it's always going to be true, or if it appears true, it must be true ("You have to be young to get good jobs").

In *table 4* (p. 34) I've given some more examples of these five errors and ways you can answer them.

Seek Objectivity. The reason you have so much difficulty viewing the situation objectively is that you're too involved in it. When you're stuck in one of the stages of nonacceptance, your perspective is severely limited. When you look at it from a different, less biased point of view, you can see it more clearly. This is why therapy or counseling can work—it provides an objective viewpoint.

One of the roles of a good manager is to look at problems in a different way than those he or she supervises. The manager often solves problems by redefining them ("This isn't really a problem with this product; you haven't taken all the factors into account").

You can do much the same by looking at your situation as another might look at it. Look at your situation the way an objective friend or a hired consultant might. To do this, you may have to put the problem away for an hour or two and then come back to it with a fresh perspective.

Suppose your girlfriend has decided to break up with you. You may feel that you don't know what to do. What would you tell a friend who called up with the same predicament?

Assess Probability. Realistically, ask yourself what the probabilities are. Many of your dependency-producing thoughts have to do with confusing low-probability events with those of high probability. Are you making a slight possibility into a certainty? You need to look at this exaggeration in a more realistic way.

For example, I once saw a woman with many fears and dependency problems. She could drive but she insisted that her son chauffeur her to the session. I asked her, "Why don't you drive here yourself?"

She said, "I'm afraid I'll have an accident."

"What is it about a car accident that scares you the most?"

She said, "That I'll die. I'm scared to death of dying."

I then asked her, "If you could only die in a car accident—that is, if you couldn't die any other way, not by any illness or any other kind of accident—how long do you think you would live if you could only die in a car accident?"

She said, "I don't know. About a hundred years, I guess."

I told her, "Well, statistically, if you could only die in a car accident you would live to be over thirty-five hundred years old. Your life span would go back to before Caesar's time."

She said, "That's really stupid."

I said, "It may be, but I thought you needed to know what the real probabilities are."

The next week she drove to the session on her own. The first thing she said to me was, "If I could only die in a fire, how long would I live?" I looked it up and told her over thirty-two thousand years.

Dr. John Marquis at the Palo Alto Veterans' Administration Hospital has figured out the probabilities of dying in a catastrophe. If your fear of a catastrophe is keeping you from being more independent, you might consider some of the other life expectancies: scheduled-airline crash, 1,000,000 years; homicide, 27,000 years female, 6,666 years male; and all firearm accidents, 83,000. Being killed in any type of violent accident is a long shot.

Consider the Worst Possibility. One of the best ways to reach acceptance is to think through the worst possible scenario. Once you can face and accept this possibility, you've crossed the final hurdle.

Arnold Lazarus has suggested that whenever you tell yourself, "What if?" ("What if I'm rejected . . . insulted . . . fired") that you add a "so" in front of it ("So what if I'm rejected . . . insulted . . . fired"). This helps take the sting out of it. Willingness to accept the worst outcome frees you from worry and dread over it.

Once you have decided what the worst could be, you need to put this in perspective. You can construct a *catastrophe scale* that goes from 0 (nothing bad happening to you) to 99 (the worst possible event). The worst possible event might be the people you love most dying in an accident or, as Albert Ellis suggests, your being slowly tortured to death (he says it can never be 100 because they could always do it slower). After you have constructed this scale, put your worst possible outcome on that scale. By doing this you place the situation in proper perspective.

Marjorie was an actress who finally got a break and tested for a commercial. She'd been in Los Angeles for nine months and had used up her savings. She couldn't accept losing the part because she believed that without it her try for a career would be over ("I'll be broke and a failure"). She was in a full-blown anxiety attack waiting for the producers to call when she came in to see me. We were able to put losing the job into perspective (60 on the scale) and her anxiety level went down.

You want to push beyond just imagining the feared situation occurs. You have to question the consequences. If you don't get what you want, does this mean your career or life is over? Will your family disown you? How long will you feel badly? Forever?

Spell out in detail what you think the ultimate consequences are so that you can face them. You have to force yourself to think about the fearful outcome because you don't want to think about it. Once you've done this, you resolve the blocks to the problem and free yourself to accept that something might be done to improve the situation. Initially, Marjorie believed she would have to go back to South Dakota if she didn't get the job. Her first thought was "I couldn't accept it. It would be the end of the world."

However, after she reanalyzed the situation, she saw that such was not the case. She would accept the possibility of taking a part-time job and working to get another part. Best of all, she could accept that she didn't have to stay as unhappy as she was now because of her anxiety.

A number of writers, including Bertrand Russell, have recommended that one overcome fear by accepting the worst. Dale Carnegie, for example, suggests that to get over fear you first ask yourself, "What's the worst that can possibly happen?" Second, you prepare yourself to accept it if you have to; and then you calmly proceed to improve on the worst. This procedure may increase your fear temporarily; but after the worst has been faced, you nearly always feel better. It's common to believe that if you face the feared event it will actually come to be. You can disregard this belief—it's not true.

Another belief that can keep you from facing the issue is "If I no longer worry about this, then it will happen." However, after you face the worst your anxiety is lowered and you actually have more resources to prevent the feared event from occurring.

You may use a personalized strategy to prevent yourself from thinking the feared scenario through. One method you may now be using is to tell yourself such catch phrases as "This is silly. Stop thinking about it," or "This is stupid." These global and childish words stop your fears for a short time only. These attempts at *thought stoppage* are not successful because, instead of resolving the problem, you only achieve *premature closure;* this means you block the problem out for a period of time, but it will reappear, usually with much greater intensity.

Rescue Factors. Look for compensating factors. In nearly every case you're fearful or unhappy over, you can find some saving or compensating factors. This may be something you've gained or learned from the situation. A man I met who spent many years on the streets and in jail told me, "No matter how down and out people appear, if you question them, you'll find they have some ace in the hole. For instance, I can always tend bar." Ask yourself, "What is my ace in the hole?"

You may have some of the following rescue factors:

- You or someone you know may have had situations similar to yours in the past.
- You may have some outside help you can call upon.
- Your situation may be time-limited.
- You may have a chance to repeat an activity if you perform poorly.
- You may be able to change some part of your situation.

Ask yourself, "What are my choices?" Many times the rescue factors don't appear until later, so sometimes you have to hang on until the rescue or compensatory factors appear.

See if you can find any benefits in the situation you're in. Most of life is a series of trade-offs. The greater the opportunity, the greater the risk. Ask yourself, "What opportunity is hidden in this situation?"

Marjorie decided that if she didn't get the part, she could accept the fact that she would then be forced to go out and get a job. She found a compensating factor—working would be an asset to her as an actress. She would have an opportunity to learn more about life and have experiences she could draw upon as an actress. She could also use the job as a way to meet new people.

In general, human nature is quite hopeful, so until proven otherwise, you might as well put the best possible construction on what happens. Doing this in conjunction with acceptance frees you to make choices that are in your best interests.

TABLE 1

STAGES OF ACCEPTANCE

Example 1—Relationship Problem

STAGE I: Nonawareness ("I don't want to know")
"We don't have a problem."

STAGE II: Disbelief ("I know it, but I don't want to believe it")
"I don't believe we'll really get a divorce."

STAGE III: Anger ("If the people who are responsible are punished, everything will change")
"Our friends should keep their noses out of it."

STAGE IV: Depression ("I'm a loser")
"The breakup is all my fault."

STAGE V: Anxiety ("I can't accept that the future could be dangerous")
"How will I ever make it alone?"
STAGE VI: Acceptance ("Whatever is, is")
"I can live on my own."

Example 2—Employment Problem

STAGE I: Nonawareness
"I don't need to get a job."
STAGE II: Disbelief
"I can't believe no one is going to come to my aid."
STAGE III: Anger
"It's my parents' fault I don't have a good job."
STAGE IV: Depression
"I'll never find a job."
STAGE V: Anxiety
"How will I stand the rejection of being turned down for a job?"
STAGE VI: Acceptance
"I'll keep at it until I get a job."

Example 3—Perfection Problem

STAGE I: Nonawareness
"I didn't make a mistake."
STAGE II: Disbelief
"Did I really make a mistake?"
STAGE III: Anger
"Others made me do it."
STAGE IV: Depression
"I always mess everything up."
STAGE V: Anxiety
"What if I make the same mistake again?"
STAGE VI: Acceptance
"I'm not perfect and will do the best I can."

You can use these stages as markers to see where you stand on the road to acceptance on any issue. You can also determine in which stage you spend the most time. This will help you focus your energy. If you're anxious most of the time, then you'll need to work on those of your thoughts and beliefs that exaggerate danger.

TABLE 2

BEHAVIORAL EXPERIMENTS

STEP 1: Spell out what your prediction is.
"I will not be able to find an apartment to live in that (a) I can afford (b) is safe."
STEP 2: Devise a way to test your prediction.
Begin an apartment search.
STEP 3: Develop a way to measure the outcome.
"I'll give the search one month."
STEP 4: Evaluate results and devise new experiments if needed.
(a) "I did find an apartment, but it's too expensive."
(b) "I'll see if I can find one with a roommate."

TABLE 3

THOUGHT RECORD

AUTOMATIC THOUGHT: "He made me feel sad when he criticized me at dinner for my housekeeping. I feel helpless to change him."
REALISTIC AND BALANCED ANSWER: "I choose my own feelings. I can't choose what he thinks of me. I'm not helpless in how I respond. I can speak up to him next time."

AUTOMATIC THOUGHT: "She's right. I am a bad father!"
REALISTIC AND BALANCED ANSWER: "It may be true. I'm not the best father and I don't have to feel bad about it. I don't have to agree with the negative label, even if she believes it."

AUTOMATIC THOUGHT: "I have no control over my own life."
REALISTIC AND BALANCED ANSWER: "I don't have control over others. I do have control over my feelings, thoughts and actions. Trying to control others puts me out of control."

AUTOMATIC THOUGHT: "Nothing ever works out for me."
REALISTIC AND BALANCED ANSWER: "That's an overstatement. True, this evening hasn't worked out, but so what? I can live with it."

TABLE 4

FIVE MOST COMMON THINKING ERRORS

1. PERSONALIZING

Example: "If I go to dinner by myself, everyone will stare at me and think there's something wrong with me."

Answer: "People are too concerned with themselves to think about me. It's grandiose to think I'm the center of the world. This is a form of 'self-spectatoring.' I'll focus on others and on eating my dinner instead of on myself."

2. OVERGENERALIZATION

Example: "I always make the wrong decision when it's up to me."

Answer: "Just because I make some wrong decisions doesn't mean all my decisions are wrong all of the time. I make hundreds of decisions throughout the day that aren't wrong. I'll also accept that I do make mistakes."

3. EITHER/OR THINKING

Example: "I'm either loved by Sally or not loved at all."

Answer: "Love is on a continuum. People can love me more at one time than at another. People's affection for others is constantly changing."

4. FALSE COMPARISONS

Example: "My sister has a nice home and career and I don't have anything, so I'm worthless."

Answer: "All social comparisons are false. Everyone of us is exclusive. Building others up to tear myself down is self-defeating."

5. JUMPING TO CONCLUSIONS

Example: "I know that she won't go out with me if I ask."

Answer: "Where's my evidence? I won't draw this conclusion until I have the facts. Ask her and see what happens, and accept the possibility she won't. She's not the only girl in the world."

CHAPTER THREE

Step Two: Choice

LIFE IS A SERIES OF CHOICES. Some choices are good and some are bad. Some save your life and others end it. But you always have two choices: (1) you can choose to be dependent; 2) you can choose to be independent. When the world is falling into place, the second choice is easy. The challenge is to be independent when the world is falling in on you. You can do this when you realize that you have the power to choose how you think, feel and act, even if you can't control the rest of the world. You can't control the cards that are dealt you, but you can choose how you want to play them. In philosophical terms, the cards dealt you are *determined*, how you choose to play them is *free will*.

Choice is the second step in the ACT formula. You might accept that you're afraid to meet new people. What's the next move? You can choose to not be afraid or you can choose to act, even in the face of the fear. You aren't locked into negative feelings, nor do you have to let your feelings be your jailer. After you realize how much control you have over your emotions, you'll wonder why you didn't see this before. You'll find you've been needlessly holding yourself back with your feelings of anxiety, jealousy, anger, fear, guilt, shame, worthlessness or depression.

You can stop holding back, you can make a positive move if you use the ACT formula with such feelings. First, *accept:* "I did have my wife lie for me; I accept this choice." Then *choose:* "I choose not to feel guilty about it." And finally, *take action* that supports your new independence—stop using middle people to do your dirty work for you.

Remember that it's your choice. Choose to be independent. The more independent you are, the greater ability you have to make free choices: you have increased choice-ability.

The Importance of Choice

When you believe you have choice in your life, you suffer less distress. Studies have found that the more freedom you believe you have, the better you're able to meet and master the challenges of living. Scientists also believe that choice serves a survival function. The more choices a person or animal has, the greater the chances for survival. In one of these studies, pigeons and rats were given a choice between two cages. The first cage had one lever that gave food; the second cage had two food levers to choose from. Even though the type and amount of food were the same, the animals always preferred the cage that provided choice.

Similarly, many studies have found children perform much better on tasks that allow them choices. The studies have also found that children overwhelmingly prefer activities that offer choices. It doesn't seem to matter what the outcomes of the choices are—children simply prefer the freedom to choose.

People in general respond much better when they're given a choice. This is found in the age-old way of managing people ("Would you like to clean up the storeroom first or do the outside work first?"). Giving someone choice makes him or her much more cooperative and productive. This has been found in assembly lines where workers are given some choice over the type of jobs they want to do. "Flex time" is also popular with workers who prefer choice: they can schedule their own time.

Becoming Aware of Your Choices

Usually when you say you have "no choice," you really mean you don't like your options. One woman in a bad marriage said, "I have no choice. I have to stay in the marriage." In reality, she could have chosen to leave but she didn't like the alternative of living on her own with a reduced standard of living.

Believing you have no choice brings the worst out in you. You may then act against what's in your own best interests. Most procrastinators, for example, say, "I have no choice, I have to get the work done." Then they go about proving they do have a choice by not doing it. You are using the wrong strategy. Whenever you give yourself commands such as "I have to . . . ," you're limiting you choice-ability. If you have the freedom to do something, you also have the freedom to choose not to do it. You're supporting your dependency by telling yourself "I have no choice."

Choice and Feelings

Similarly, telling yourself "I should feel good" is counterproductive. Self-commands run against one of the most basic laws of human behavior: *you don't want to do what you are told you have to do.* The result is the same whether you're giving the orders to yourself, or someone else is—you don't like it. If Adam and Eve had been told thay *had* to eat the apple, do you think they would have wanted to? Telling kids "Don't put beans in your ears" almost guarantees that they will. When you choose how you're going to feel, you want to see this as a free choice, not as a command.

Responsibility Versus Accountability

As a human being you can always choose how you think, feel and act—you're choice-able for these. You may have a large menu of options to choose from ("I'm capable of traveling by myself anywhere in the world") or you may have a small menu to choose from ("I can go anywhere in my house but I'm afraid to go outside"). The greater your independence, the greater your choice-abilities are. The more choices you're free to make, the more you own your own life.

Your accountability to yourself and others is a separate and often related issue. You can own your own choices and be self-accountable ("I chose not to water the lawn"), or you cannot be self-accountable. ("I would have liked to water the lawn but my friends came over.")

Another way to see the difference between responsibility and accountability is the Adam and Eve case. Each was fully responsible for his or her own choice to eat the apple. The snake was not responsible for either of their acts. Yet according to the Bible, all three were held equally accountable. It seems to me that the snake got a bad deal. He was held accountable for something he wasn't choice-able for.

Similarly, you can choose to be accountable to others ("I said I would water the lawn, so I did") or you can choose not to ("I didn't get around to it"). Many times, people hold you accountable in appropriate ways but, at other times, they're inappropriate and arbitrary. You can always choose not to buy others' accountability of you. Explaining this concept to one client, I told him I was holding him accountable for coming an hour before the session and washing my windows. He said, "I don't do windows." You can always refuse to buy an account that others are trying to sell you ("You're the woman, so you do the laundry"). However, if you refuse to buy into any accounts at all ("I don't want to make any commitments"), you often end up lonely and isolated.

Increasing Your Choice-ability

People vary in the range of choices they are able to make and in the quality of the choices they make. Some people, for example, may make very good economic choices but poor emotional choices.

Not only are some people better choosers than others, but apparently animals have the same characteristics. Psychologist Abraham Maslow writes, "Chickens allowed to choose their own diet vary widely in their ability to choose what is good for them. The good choosers become stronger, larger, more dominant than the poor choosers, which means they get the best of everything. If then the diet chosen by the good choosers is forced upon the poor choosers, it is found *they* now get stronger, bigger, healthier and more dominant, although never reaching the level of the good choosers. That is, good choosers can choose better than bad choosers what is better for bad choosers themselves." We aren't chickens. However, I do believe everyone can learn to become a better chooser.

How do you become a better chooser? Basically, you do it by having a variety of learning experiences, failure experiences, success experiences and neutral experiences. That's why it's nearly always a good idea to err on the side of inclusion ("I'll go and get a facial to see what it feels like") than to err on the side of exclusion ("I couldn't do that"). You also try to learn as much as you can from the experiences you do have. Throughout the book I'll be talking about specific ways you can increase your choice-abilities.

Plan A/Plan B Strategy

Your dependency usually involves a plan for how you're going to act in a specific situation. This plan involves how you're going to think, feel and act when you confront the situation. You're usually only vaguely aware of this plan and have to question yourself to find out what it is.

One of the best ways you can use the reverse principle, which I talked about earlier, is to develop an alternative plan; one that's the opposite. By writing the two plans out in detail, you can start to see more clearly your choices. The Plan A/Plan B strategy gives you greater choice to act in your own best interest. I teach this strategy to all my clients; nearly all of them find it a helpful tool.

To use this strategy, first write out Plan A—what choices you would have to make to keep yourself dependent. The plan should include what you would think, how you would feel, and how you would act. Keep the plan consistent. Next, write out Plan B, the opposite plan, to make yourself independent. (*Table 1* [p. 45] is an example of two plans.)

Maryanne was going to be left alone while her boyfriend went out of town for the weekend. I discussed with her the Plan A/ Plan B strategy.

CLIENT: I don't know what I'll do. Probably just be miserable.

THERAPIST: It sounds like you have a plan. What do you think you'll do over the weekend?

CLIENT: I'll probably mope around and feel lonely.

Therapist: Okay, let's call that Plan A. What would you have to tell yourself to keep yourself miserable? What would your specific thoughts be?

Client: "I'm all alone. No one really cares about me—Tom's probably taking another girl with him—going away without me is a way of rejecting me."

Therapist: Write those down. What kinds of thoughts would keep you dependent?

Client: Well, the same thoughts, but I could tell myself, "I can't be alone . . . I need to see someone to keep me from being bored" . . . something like that.

Therapist: Okay. Write that down in Plan A. How would you feel if you wanted to be consistent with this? What feelings would you focus on?

Client: I guess feeling lonely, vulnerable . . . unhappy.

Therapist: How would you act to keep yourself dependent?

Client: Well, I could call or ask Tom to call me four or five times a day. I could not plan anything . . .

Therapist: What else?

Client: I guess I could go over and spend some time with my sister. That's what I always do. But, I don't enjoy it. She's always complaining about something. I guess it's better than being alone though.

Therapist: Anything else you could put in Plan A?

Client: I'd probably go on a food binge. When Tom's gone I feel like I deserve it. But this only makes me feel worse.

Therapist: Okay. Put that down. Now, to give yourself a choice you need to have another plan, Plan B. The best way to do this is to make one that's the opposite of Plan A. What could you tell yourself that would make you feel more independent?

Client: I guess I could put into practice some of the things we've been talking about. I could tell myself that I don't *need* to have someone with me, that it's just a habit. I could tell myself that he's not rejecting me and not add that surplus meaning onto it.

Therapist: What could you put down about opportunities or potentials?

Client: I guess I could tell myself this is a good opportunity to become more independent.

Therapist: What could you do if you were going to do the opposite?

CLIENT: Well, I wouldn't be calling Tom all the time, and I wouldn't go on a food binge . . . but I don't know what I would do with myself.

THERAPIST: Remember, you want to think reverse. What would you do if you were an independent person? Remember, you don't have to do this or want to; you just write it down.

CLIENT: I wouldn't go over to my sister's. I'd do some of the things that I've been wanting to do.

THERAPIST: Like what?

CLIENT: Well, I've wanted to refinish a table I've been working on.

THERAPIST: Any place you've wanted to go?

CLIENT: Well, I've always wanted to go to the art museum. I could go there Sunday on my own, or call a friend to come with me.

THERAPIST: What kinds of feelings would you focus on in Plan B?

CLIENT: I'd choose to feel in control and good about myself.

THERAPIST: Well, put that down. You now have a choice of Plan A or Plan B. The choice is totally yours. The only thing I suggest is that you stick with whichever plan you choose. This helps to let you see the consequences or the costs of your choice more clearly.

At the next meeting, Maryanne said she was able to follow Plan B. She said she was amazed to find that she really had the choice to determine how her weekend went. If she had chosen the other plan, we could have discussed the costs of this choice.

Plan A/Plan B guidelines. You can use the following suggestions to put this method into practice.

- Use it on small and big projects. Maryanne not only used this technique to plan her weekend, she also used it to plan here telephone conversations with her father. Before the Plan A/Plan B method, she would always end up arguing with him.
- Write Plan A out in the most dependent way. When Maryanne used this method, she always exaggerated Plan A a bit. For instance, when outlining her phone conversation with her father, she said, "In Plan A, I'll ask my dad whether he thinks I should keep going out with Tom. Then I'll let his answer hurt my feelings and make me depressed."

• Think the reverse when you make Plan B. After making Plan A, Maryanne would reverse it. She'd say, "I won't bring Tom up with my dad. If he brings Tom up, I'll change the subject and not get my feelings hurt."

• If you can't think of anything for Plan B, think of how an independent person would act. When Maryanne started the Plan A/Plan B method, she often couldn't come up with much for Plan B. She would tell herself, "An independent person would choose her own boyfriend and realize that she didn't require her father's approval . . . and if he disapproved, she wouldn't let it matter."

• Write your plans out as a script. Detail a role you could play in the script. Maryanne could have prepared such a script for her conversation with her father:

Dad: Well, are you still seeing that bum Tom?
Me: Dad, let's not talk about me. Did you get your garden put in?
Dad: What about Tom?
Me: Dad, I don't want to talk about it.
(Repeat this until he gets off the topic.)

• Stay with one plan or the other. When you stay fixed in one plan without switching, you can more clearly see what choices you're operating from. When Maryanne was making Plan A, she would follow it through, even past the point where she realized that she preferred Plan B. She came to realize that switching to Plan B too soon would not make her into a better chooser.

• Even if you choose the plan that's not in your best interest, use this as a chance to see that a choice does exist. You can then explore your reasoning in making choices not in your best interest.

Critical Choice Strategy

Your wish to avoid independence can range from a mild desire to an overwhelming urge. Thus, you may tell yourself, "I'd like to have someone else do this for me," or "I can't go on living without this help." As I said, your dependency includes a plan for how you can fulfill your wish to stay dependent. The process entails not only a plan but also at some point a choice.

When you want to act in a dependent way, an interesting phenomenon occurs. You'll find that how you choose to act can be pinned down to a particular moment. When you examine this process in detail, you'll find this happens in nearly every case.

You increase your freedom by becoming more aware of choice points. The better you become at recognizing choice points, the more likely you are to make choices in your own best interest. Often, your last chance to change the course of events occurs at this choice point. In *table 2* (p. 45), I've listed some examples. The first step in the strategy is to accept that you're the one who's choosing to be dependent or independent. Once you do this, your freedom will increase.

After you've acted on your dependent wish, you'll have difficulty talking yourself out of what you're doing. When you believe you're helpless, and are about to take some action on this, you aren't likely to question your conclusion that you're helpless. Once you decide to strike, it's often too late to question whether the contract in question is reasonable or not.

I discovered the critical choice strategy when I was teaching a class at Montgomery County Community College in Pennsylvania. One of the students caught me in an error. My inclination was to hide behind the podium and skip on to new material. Instead, I decided to take the opposite tack. I made myself more vulnerable by walking toward the class and discussing the mistake in great detail.

In that moment I saw my two choices clearly. I could either give up and hide behind the podium or make myself vulnerable. As soon as I did the latter, I felt myself become more powerful and more in control. I also put an end to what could have been a painful experience had I tried to ignore it and not accept it. The critical choice includes the three components of the ACT formula: you accept the situation, you choose to be independent and not to let your feelings overwhelm you and you take some concrete and constructive action.

The second part of the critical choice strategy, once you recognize it, is simple: *you choose to do the opposite of what you feel like doing*. When your instincts tell you to flee, you stay. If you want to protect yourself, you make yourself more vulnerable. If you want others to do something for you, you do it for yourself.

While going with your feelings or instincts is a good idea most of the time, when you're in critical choice situations you want to do the exact opposite. For example, if you are talking to someone and you want to back away and hide, it's better to force yourself to move forward; you approach instead of avoid.

Your thoughts at this moment are "This will go on forever . . . I can't stand it . . . I'm going to go crazy or out of control." Keep in mind that at this point you can make a choice—you can tell yourself, "Get back on track, take the opposite tack." Then force yourself to do the opposite. That can determine how you react to the total situation. One client, a runner, compared the critical choice to what's called in running "hitting the wall." He said, "When you 'hit the wall' you believe you can't go on but if you continue to push forward you can get through it." He says many runners quit when they "hit the wall." A woman runner added, "The moment feels like the transition period in childbirth—that point where you're convinced you can't go on, but of course you can."

Look Out the Window of Time. Your concepts of time relate to the critical choice strategy. When you have a strong inclination to escape or to seek help, you believe that the difficulty will go on forever. You think your discomfort won't end and that you'll have to endure it forever. Keep in mind that the discomfort will pass—often quickly. The discomfort associated with becoming independent comes in waves, with a beginning, a middle, and an end. During the critical choice period you're usually at the peak of the wave; the discomfort will usually recede no matter what you choose. You're at a point where you think the worst will happen, so no matter what the outcome is, it's usually better than what you expected.

Critical moments are like windows in time. You can look out and see yourself down the road. You can see yourself holding your ground and being independent, or you can see yourself relapsing. One choice strengthens you, the other weakens you.

The critical choice is a crisis—at times a serious crisis, at other times a mini-crisis. The crisis may require a *radical change in perspective* from you; the critical choice is a turning point. It's a crucial period of increased vulnerability and heightened potential—it can be a point of standing up or falling down.

TABLE 1

PLAN A/PLAN B

Plan A

THINKING: "I'm helpless. I can't be on my own. This is terrible. I'm rejected. I can't stand it."

FEELING: Lonely and vulnerable.

ACTION: Calling Tom, food binge. Stay with sister.

Plan B

THINKING: "I'm resourceful. I can be self-reliant. This is a good opportunity to be independent. I can make an adventure out of it."

FEELING: Complete and in control.

ACTION: Plan activities and follow through. Go to museum on own.

TABLE 2

EXAMPLES OF CRITICAL CHOICES

Situation	*Critical Choice*
You're at a party and uncomfortable and you see some people you think don't like you.	To move toward them or away from them.
You're angry at your husband and he comes into the room.	To forgive him or stay angry.
You're stuck with a broken light switch.	To try to fix it yourself or call for help.
You're home from work before your wife and dinner hasn't been started.	To start setting the table and fixing dinner or watch TV until she gets home.
Your husband always fills your car for you, but he's at work and you want to visit a friend.	To go to a gas station and fill the tank yourself or to wait for another time to visit your friend.

CHAPTER FOUR

Step Three: Taking Action

AT THE UNIVERSITY OF PENNSYLVANIA, I worked on several depression-treatment-outcome studies. I treated two patients, Leo and Sharon, in one of the studies. They were almost exactly opposite in how they responded in the sessions. Sharon responded enthusiastically; she would nod her head and say, "That's right, I can't believe how well you can put your finger right on the problem." Leo, on the other hand, continually gave me a hard time. "Did they really give you a Ph.D. for learning all of these clichés?"

The interesting part was that Leo would grudgingly do all the homework assignments between sessions. Sharon never seemed to be able to get around to doing any of her assignments. Who do you think got better, and who do you think didn't? The Leos of the world—the people who do the work no matter how begrudgingly—are the ones who make the progress. And those who don't do the work are the ones who fall behind.

Taking action is the third and most crucial part of the ACT formula. To become more independent, you have to put your *acceptance* of the situation and your *choice to feel in control* into practice. You have to translate your new ways of thinking into action—make that call, speak up to your boss, learn to balance your checkbook, figure out your own income tax, go and do what you're afraid of doing. In this chapter, I'll talk about the role action plays in becoming more independent.

I Wish I May, I Wish I Might

Your dependency always has a wish component. For example, you might wish someone could come along and do your work for you. Or you might wish something were different. Wishing gets in the way of accepting reality.

Drs. Bulman and Wortman conducted a major study of how people cope with crippling accidents. They write, "The following statements are more or less typical of the poor copers. 'All I wish is that I had gone home with the other girl. I wish I would have had my feet on the floor. I was in the process of doing that and bang. I wish I had sat up in the seat. I would have grabbed the wheel.' " The wish component of your dependency is the key to the action you need to take: *you have to ignore your wish.* The problem isn't in having the wish, the problem is in carrying the wish out. If you wish someone would do the job for you, do it yourself; if you wish you could leave a frightening place, stay; if you wish you could be taken care of, take care of yourself.

Most of the time you have to take action that is the opposite of what you wish would happen. This means when you want to leave ("I wish I could just disappear"), you stay and hold your ground. When you want to protect yourself ("I wish I could stay home"), you have to make yourself more vulnerable. When you want to avoid a situation ("I wish I could call in sick"), you move toward it. When you want some difficult task to go away ("I wish I didn't have to give them the bad news"), you accept and face it. When you want someone else to do the job for you ("I wish my husband would do it for me"), you do it yourself.

Importance of Action

Setting Free Your Power. You strengthen the beliefs you act on. If you believe you're helpless and then act helpless, you believe all the more that you are in fact helpless. You reaffirm to yourself that you *are* a loser by giving up, by talking in a weak and passive way, by apologizing, by withdrawing from others and by not starting or not carrying out projects. Your beliefs have power over you, and your actions keep them in power.

A basic principle of psychology is that if you act on a belief as if it were true, you'll begin to believe it more strongly. Your actions reinforce your beliefs for both physical and psychological reasons. When you've been working very hard, it's difficult to stop ("I'm exhausted from cleaning, but I'll just finish the closet"), and when you haven't been working it can be difficult to start ("I *must* clean this house!"). Your body has a memory, and when you do an action enough times, there's a push to repeat the action ("It's Saturday morning, time for my weekly housecleaning"). You're prone to develop habits. That's why you have to realize that when you start to do some activity this could easily become a habit. Pat's advice to her friends has always been, "Don't do anything the first week you're married unless you want to do it for the rest of your life." You almost automatically repeat what you did before.

Your actions often have an *aftereffect* that causes you to want to repeat them. This is like an afterimage—after you've looked away, you can still see the image. Asking for reassurance causes you to ask for more. The more you do something the more you want to do it. You often can make yourself hungry by eating. The appetite comes with eating. If you stop eating and go on a fast, your appetite will start to go away.

If you act one way long enough it's difficult to act any other way—even if you want to. Some children decide to quit talking. They are called elective mutes. After they have done this for any period of time, it becomes very difficult for them to choose to talk, even if they want to.

The power of action is not good or bad, it's neutral. However, it's in your best interest to use it by acting in independent rather than dependent ways.

Developing Your Independence Skills

Learning to be more independent is similar to learning any skill. The closer you are to the real situation, the more difficulty you have with the skill. When the coach is throwing tennis balls at you during the lesson, they're easy to hit. But when you get into a real game, hitting the ball is a different story. You have much more difficulty putting into practice what you thought you had learned. The same goes for learning to be more independent. You can expect to have some difficulty putting the ideas I've been talking about into practice.

Repetition. To learn, you have to hear the message over and over. Repetition is helpful because you're learning something different at each stage of learning. At earlier stages of learning, you hear messages differently and apply them differently than you do at later stages.

Here are some ways you can use the principle of repetition in learning independence skills.

- *Key phrases.* When learning to be more independent, it's helpful to repeat key phrases that represent important concepts—such as "It's better to do as much as I can for myself" or "I can do it no matter how I feel."

One man was having trouble learning to take care of his house. He believed that no one who felt bad needed to, or could be expected to, do any work. I had him ask other people if they did work when they didn't feel well. One person told him, "Most of the work of the world is done by people who don't feel well." He started repeating this to himself when he didn't want to do some task. As you begin to repeat such ideas to yourself, you start to incorporate them into your repertoire of choice-abilities.

- *Different situations.* You start to really own new skills when you're able to practice them in different situations. This means you have to practice your new skills continually. You will find that you learn something new in each situation in which you practice your independence skills. Suppose you want to learn to cook for yourself. You need to practice this skill when you're comfortable and when you're uncomfortable; when you're in secure and insecure places; when you want to and when you don't want to; when you know what to do and when you don't.
- *Look for cognitive clicks.* When you put into practice what you're learning you'll have cognitive clicks or moments of insight when

the ideas make sense and you can see it's not that difficult. You need repetition to reach these moments.

• *Make the repetition interesting.* Each time you try the skill, try to learn something different. Focus on one part. You can ask others for advice. For example, if you have trouble using the phone, ask others how they get over phone phobias, such as fear of taking directions down, and then practice their methods.

Areas of Meaning. You learn more and faster when what you're learning is relevant to your specific concerns. You're more likely to decide to be independent if the area is important to you. This increases your motivation and level of involvement. That's why learning to identify the areas where you need to be more independent is so important. The following are some suggestions that could help you along this line.

• If there are activities that you started in the past and gave up, you might want to develop independence skills in this area. For example, Bill, a government official, had wanted to work with his hands. He had started working in stained glass and had given it up. As part of his goal to be more physically independent, he went back to working with stained glass.

• Go back to areas you have worked on repeatedly but haven't mastered. The fact that you continually return to them indicates your interest. For years Jo had wanted to learn to sew. She had taken lessons but had never followed through on them. She decided to go back and really master the skill this time.

• Choose skills that fit in with your overall goals. If you want to be a writer, you might learn how to type or run a word processor. One student wanted to go on to graduate school. She forced herself to learn how to work with computers.

• Learn skills that have tangible payoffs to you. One woman learned how to do basic electrical and plumbing repairs because she didn't want to pay the high service costs.

• Learn skills that you've always dreamed about or talked of having. For example, you may have dreamed about traveling. Traveling is a skill that you can learn. If you have a limited budget, learning to travel on a tight budget is a special skill.

• Learn skills that relate to your other interests. One friend, Allen Church, enjoys fine wines, so he learned how to make his own wine.

The idea is to develop independence in areas that have some meaning to you.

First Rung First. Learning to be independent is a gradual process. You master simple skills and then move on to more complex ones. Ed decided to start his retirement by becoming more useful around the house. He began by offering to vacuum for his wife daily. Soon he was sharing other cleaning duties with her, as well as fixing breakfast each morning.

The best learning strategy is to work on one skill at a time. After you've learned one, you move on to the next. Eventually, you'll have a variety of skills that you can use in a wide range of situations.

Step-by-Step. Because you usually don't want to take the independent action, you have to approach it on a gradual basis. Attempting to do it all at once can backfire.

For example, Rhonda was timid and had trouble going places alone. She started by going shopping on her own. She did so well this time, she took a big step: she went to a large party alone. However, this was too big a step. She had a panic attack and left the party early.

The sink-or-swim method rarely works. You may have tried independent behavior before, but because you attempted it all at once, you may have failed. The all-or-nothing approach usually doesn't work, because you're unable to stay in the uncomfortable situation long enough. For this reason smaller steps have a great deal more chance of success.

Each step you take is determined by your degree of comfort and the degree of difficulty. By taking one step at a time you can sidestep much of your resistance.

Below are some ways that you can use to put this learning principle into practice.

- *Make specific, reasonable goals that you can control.* Goals give direction to life. They allow you to move forward in a relatively orderly way. Goals vary in usefulness, however. Vague, open-ended goals ("I'm going to be more independent") provide no direction. Unrealistically high goals and goals outside your control ("I'm never going to ask for help again") often backfire. When they're not met, you become discouraged and give up.

The art of independence involves setting realistic goals that are under your control ("I'm going to learn to do my own taxes this year"). When you make goals, be honest with yourself. Take stock of what you've done in the past and decide what you can realistically do in the future.

• *Develop the steps in a hierarchy from most difficult to least difficult.* Merely establishing a hierarchy of steps toward a goal can lead to your thinking differently about it. You begin to see that your global problem can be broken down into manageable steps that you can take. Completion of each step allows you to see that your goal can be reached as a result of your own effort and skill. For example, suppose you want to learn how to service your own car. You could break this down into the following steps: (1) pump gas; (2) check oil; (3) check water; (4) check air pressure in tires; (5) check brake fluid; (6) check transmission fluid; (7) add oil, brake and transmission fluids as needed; (8) change air filter; (9) change oil filter; (10) change oil.

• *Advance step-by-step.* The general rule is not to go on to the next step until you have finished the one before. If you do leave or stop before you've finished the step you're on, you should return to it again as soon as possible and stay until it's finished. Frequently, in performing the graded tasks, you experience a cognitive click and are able to take big strides toward your goal. You may, for example, see that mechanical problems aren't beyond you. You realize that your thoughts are wrong and that you're overestimating the degree of danger or difficulty.

• *Use fantasies as means—not ends.* Fantasies can entertain, inspire and help solve problems. They can provide the energy to tackle projects you normally wouldn't. But they can also stop you from taking action. If you fantasize too much about something, you lose interest in it because you feel like you've already done it. (The same process occurs when you share your fantasy with too many people: you become tired of it.)

Don't become so engrossed in how it's going to be that you let the present slip away. Focus on steps, not goals. If you find you're spending too much time on a fantasy, put a time limit on it.

Fantasize more about the means (how you can become more independent) than about the ends ("People will think I'm really self-confident"). For example, if you want to learn to repair televisions, fantasize about how you find the right class to take rather than about rebuilding one for your next-door neighbor.

Don't tell others your fantasies. Don't say, "I'm going to learn to fix gourmet meals!" Don't create a situation where you'll feel uncomfortable if you can't prepare an elaborate meal. When you do reach your goal, you can surprise your dinner guests.

• *Use catch phrases.* Catch phrases or proverbs are really condensed philosophies. You can use these to your advantage. One person found the catch phrase "Little steps for little feet" helpful. He was able to have more success experiences; this helped him to motivate himself. Some other proverbs or catch phrases people have used are "Small strokes fall great oaks," "A journey of a thousand miles begins with one step," "I'll plan my work and work my plan," "I'll take one day at a time" and "First things first."

Remember, positive motivation follows successes. After you have finished a few steps you'll be more motivated to move on.

In situations where you have to decide whether to act, you'll have a variety of involuntary thoughts: "I can't stand it" . . . "I want out" . . . "I hate this" . . . "I can't go on." Your mind won't want you to take the action.

You'll also have physiological defenses against the experience —tight muscles throughout your body and a variety of other physical reactions. The inhibition is a result of your wish or desire to protect yourself. This goes into effect because your mind wants you to avoid the situation. As a result, your action is often stopped.

For these reasons, you have to provide yourself with psychological aids to counteract your strong inclinations to avoid doing anything. Following are some techniques you can use to help take constructive action.

Initiation Technique. You can strengthen your motivation by initiating the first step. You usually feel like doing the activity when you're away from it, but the closer the time comes to doing it, the less you want to do it. However, if you make some move toward the activity, any movement, this can motivate you. For example, you can tell others specific steps you're going to take. Thus, you can use your stated intention as one way to get yourself moving.

You do have to be careful that this procedure doesn't work against you. One patient, for example, broke her stated intention to make a cross-country trip. The trip was too frightening for her. This led her to think "I let everyone down" and brought on feelings of depression. As in similar procedures, you want to structure this as a no-lose situation: no matter what happens, make it work for you. She was eventually able to use this situation as a way to find out how she scared herself out of going.

Here are some other ways you can use the initiation strategy.

- *Make a date with yourself.* Plan to do the activity when you have a specific time and place to do it ("I'll go to the Y for a workout Wednesday at noon"). You're more likely to meet specific commitments to yourself.
- *Write out a promise to yourself.* Your promise can have a powerful effect on carrying out your intentions ("I promise myself I'll call Mary and ask for a date tonight"). Don't do this unless you, as a general rule, keep your promises.
- *Reward yourself for taking the first step.* You can buy yourself a small present or do something nice for yourself for completing the first step.
- *Make failure to follow through costly.* You can make an agreement with yourself that if you don't do the activity you have to do something unpleasant—like getting up an hour earlier for a week or staying late at work.
- *Use your imagination.* Put aside five minutes to imagine yourself doing the activity. See yourself struggling to do the action and then finally completing it. An alternate strategy is to imagine a very dangerous or unpleasant situation and then to imagine yourself escaping into the situation you're now avoiding. One woman, afraid to dine alone, imagined she was being chased by a gang of thugs and escaped into a restaurant to eat a meal by herself.
- *Plan at least one action a day toward the goal.* There is something about doing *anything* toward reaching your goal that keeps you motivated.
- *Keep a record or graph of what you do.* Any visual reminders will help keep you in the mood to do it.

• *Write out a physical script of what you need to do for the action.* "Legs, walk into the restaurant; arms, pick up the menu; tongue, give order."

• *Act as if you were another person.* At times you can get yourself to do something that is out of character by acting *as if* you were a person that could easily do it—a TV or movie actor, for example. This way you have less of *you* at stake. You can take risks you normally wouldn't when you imagine you're Burt Reynolds.

• *Reminders.* Write out the five most important reasons you want to do the activity. Often when you're in a situation where you can act, you forget why you wanted to. You can periodically review these points.

• *Exaggerate or make a production of the action.* One of the ways you can overcome resistance is by blowing it up. Overdo the activity. One person pretended he was a carnival pitchman to get himself to do something he didn't want to do. He would tell himself "All right, step right up. Let me tell you what I'm going to do. I'm going right in there and be cool and calm. All right, step right up."

• *Just do the activity.* For no reason, just decide to jump in and do the activity. This often is one of the best ways to get started.

• *Ignore your wants.* When you get right down to starting the project, you'll tell yourself, "I just don't want to do it!" This is expected—that way it's an avoidance, not an approach activity. You have to tell yourself that "wanting" or "not wanting" to do it is irrelevant. You can choose to do it anyway.

Be Your Own Teacher. One important aid you can use to overcome your resistance is *self-instruction*. Here, you actively talk to yourself. You give yourself such instructions as "Stay with the job" . . . "Stay task-relevant and the discomfort will lessen" . . . "My purpose is?" . . . "Don't self-evaluate or be judgmental." Your brain can actually tell your body to stay and move in different areas. When you speak out loud to yourself, the power of your self-instruction increases.

Challenging your impulses to avoid action takes some work; however, you'll find by actively talking to yourself you can start to follow through on just about any action. Following are ways you can use this method.

• Write your self-instructions on 3" x 5" cards and use them as part of a general coping plan.

• Remember you have control over your body—at least the gross motor movements, if not the finer movements.

• Practice self-instruction with yourself first to combat action-inhibiting thoughts that you'll have later. When you're in the real situation, you can use this practice as a mental map to follow.

• Work out a series of self-instructions you can use. Following are examples of self-instruction statements a woman used to control her anxiety with authority figures, such as a store manager, when she went to return some merchandise.

Don't give in.
Go the extra distance.
Don't be a sap.
Be persistent.
Be strong.
Chin up. Feel tension in the neck.
Ask questions as much as possible.
Be like steel, an immovable object.
Be firm and decisive.

She was able to use these self-instructions effectively to cope with a variety of potentially conflicting encounters.

Relating to Other People. You don't live in a vacuum. How you act affects how others think and act toward you. Their behavior toward you in turn reinforces your beliefs about yourself. When you're learning new skills, you have to take others into account. If you believe you're helpless, you'll act helpless around others. They in turn will treat you as if you are, helping to confirm your belief that you are indeed helpless.

In the early stages of becoming more independent, you can use aids or safeguards to enter a feared situation. Such an aid could be the presence of another person—your husband, wife or friend—or it could be some psychological aid such as the diversion technique (focusing on something outside yourself). However, as you progress, you'll need to enter the situation without the aids.

Researchers have found a number of reasons why it's beneficial to give up the props as soon as possible. Efforts to protect yourself from pseudo-threats make you more frightened and dependent. I talked to one client about this.

CLIENT: But I feel better when my daughter goes out with me.

THERAPIST: I know. In fact, that's the major reason aids are so hard to give up—they do make you feel better. But do they make you more independent?

CLIENT: You mean in the long run?

THERAPIST: Yes, in the long run do you think it's better to *feel* better or become more independent?

CLIENT: Well, I know that I would rather be independent.

THERAPIST: Why do you think that it would be better to go out on your own now instead of with your daughter?

CLIENT: I guess I would believe I'm more capable if I go out by myself. I can't always be with her.

THERAPIST: That's right. If you go out with your daughter you're likely to say you were successful *because of* your daughter, not because of your own abilities.

You want to see your success as the result of *self-mastery*. She was eventually able to give up this aid and go out alone.

The Full Experience. Another reason to go without aids is so you fully experience your feelings and actions. Researchers have found that if you turn off mentally when you're experiencing discomfort, you don't get the full benefit of the exposure to the discomfort.

You have to experience your discomfort fully to get the most from it. The more you can stay in the fearful and uncomfortable situation physically and mentally, the better your chance of overcoming the fear.

The quality of your action is important. There's no doubt that your action helps to increase your independence. However, you won't get the most out of this experience. Any effort to shut off your experience (tightening your muscles, telling yourself you don't want to be there) will rob you of the benefits of your action.

When you take action, you can use the following guidelines to get the most out of it.

- Tell yourself to experience what's happening ("Stay with this experience, don't run from it").
- Focus on what's real and in front of you ("What is he saying?").

- Don't turn off or block your feelings ("I'll remain open").
- Don't be concerned with the time ("I hope this gets over with").
- Limit your comparisons. When you go through learning experiences, don't compare your performance to others' or to how you think you should be performing. Ask yourself, "Do I have to compare myself at all? Is this type of thinking helping me, or robbing me of my experience right now?" Don't ruminate about who's better or worse, but rather focus on the experience.
- Keep your expectations down. Your expectations (good and bad) of what should be happening stop you from accepting what is happening. With expectations you're claiming ownership before the experience is really yours. Maximize your surprises by minimizing your expectations.
- Appreciate your experiences. Any fantasies, goals or expectations take you away from what you have: the present. Appreciate what you're doing right now—good or bad.
- Do one activity at a time. When you find yourself going off the present, tell yourself to stop and focus on where you are—the sights, sounds, smells and feelings of where you are right now. You have to fully experience your actions, physically and mentally, to get the most from any learning experience.

In the final analysis, before you can become independent you have to experience what you believe to be bad and discover where you're wrong. If you're afraid of strangers, you have to face strangers. If you're anxious about driving, you have to drive. If you're afraid of confronting someone, you have to do it. If you're afraid of being alone you eventually have to stay alone and learn to endure this discomfort and finally how to enjoy your own company. If you wait for others to take care of you, you need to do it for yourself.

While there's no easy way out of it, keep in mind that *fantasies are consistently worse than reality*. The action is rarely as difficult as you imagine.

CHAPTER FIVE

Physical Independence

YOU MAY BELIEVE IT'S EASIER to have your mother, father, husband or wife take care of your dirty work. When I first saw Ron, he was thirty and still hadn't developed his physical independence. He had a good job, but he depended on his mother to cook his food, pay his rent and mend and wash his clothes. He disliked being so dependent—but not enough to be independent. He felt the effort was too difficult.

I suggested that Ron work on becoming more independent. Every living part in nature grows by becoming independent from its source. Remaining dependent on others stunts your growth. You have to find your own way if you want to become more than you are. Your dependency in turn stunts the growth of those you remain dependent on. Anything that stops independence stops growth.

When you don't separate and individualize, you recede, atrophy and become less. In human development, you don't stand still—you're either moving ahead or you're falling behind. Because of our extended period of childhood and adolescence, there is a great risk for something going wrong in the individualization process.

Ron's first step toward physical independence was taken when he moved out of his mother's house and started doing more for himself. He began to cook his own meals; he started with TV dinners and gradually became an adequate cook. At first, he took his dirty clothes back to his mother to wash; then he chose to start doing them himself at the corner machine laundry. Even though he didn't enjoy many of these basic tasks and didn't do them well, he persisted. As he became more physically independent, his self-respect began to grow.

Your first job in growing up is learning how to take care of your basic needs—how to feed yourself, put your clothes on, keep yourself clean and keep yourself safe. This gradually comes to include getting yourself from place to place on time, preparing your food, cleaning your clothes, taking care of your health and eventually supporting yourself.

However, like Ron, you may want or have someone to take care of the basics for you; someone to clean up after you, someone to see that you aren't bothered with the everyday hassles of making coffee, doing the laundry, fixing flat tires, making plane reservations and paying bills.

Physical independence is basic housekeeping. The most common reason people don't do their own housekeeping is because they think it's easier for someone else to do it. This seldom is the case. Robert was a sales representative for electronic parts. His life was in disarray. His girlfriend was fed up with him because he rarely kept the promises he made to her. He would say, "I'll pick you up at five," and then not be there. He had an excuse for everything. He would tell her, "I was tied up in a business deal and couldn't get away," when in reality he was talking with a friend in a coffee shop. He had always counted on others to get him where he was supposed to be on time.

His business was in serious trouble, so he first worked on getting it in shape. His suppliers were angry at him for not following up on sales leads or putting enough orders in. His customers were angry at him for not seeing that they got their parts on time. His basic problem was that the flow of his business was hopelessly cluttered. He would lose purchase orders and follow-up letters in the piles on his desk.

His mother, ex-wife and girlfriend had always cleaned up after him in the past. When his business was doing better, he could afford a secretary to sort out his paperwork for him. After he had to let her go, his business went down hill even faster. He had trouble keeping track of any of his transactions. His rationale was

"I'm an idea person; I shouldn't have to be bothered with obsessive details."

I suggested that he could start to pull his life together by cleaning off his desk at the end of each day. A month went by before he was willing to give this a try. But once he began to do this daily, he found that taking care of it put him in charge of his work. He said that this was more efficient than having it done by a secretary, because he could now put his hands on whatever he needed.

Robert's reluctance to take the time to be more physically independent is a common reason people give for not taking care of themselves. Many people don't realize that time is like money—you have to spend it to make it. Once Robert started to take more care of himself, doing housework and making simple repairs, he found more time for the activities he enjoyed. He didn't have to waste time supervising and policing others while they took care of him.

You may try to get others to do jobs for you to see how much they like you. Taking care of your physical needs becomes a measurement of love. Many people mistakenly believe love has to be tested daily. This testing usually has the opposite effect. People will start to resent having to take care of you. Your mother or father will do it for a while, but even they may soon tire of it.

One woman never checked the oil in her car. She thought, "If my husband loves me, he will keep the car maintained." He, on the other hand, thought that because it was her car, she should take care of it herself. After she burned out the second engine, she decided to start checking the oil herself.

Do you want people to dislike you and avoid you like the plague? Act helpless around them. Every time you see them, ask them for help. Try an experiment. Ask someone to tie your shoe for you and see what the response will be. People have enough trouble taking care of themselves. They don't want to spend their limited time and energy taking care of you.

You may get others to take care of your basic housekeeping to show how important you are. I once worked with a woman who made a show of asking her secretary to do tasks that she could more appropriately do for herself. If she needed new panty hose, she'd send her secretary out for them. She would also criticize her in front of others. She had an attitude of "It's sure hard to get good help these days." Like most attempts to impress people, this failed miserably. The others in the office had a low opinion of her, and in addition she had a tough time keeping secretaries.

Others may encourage you to be helpless. One woman called my office and asked if she could bring her son in to see me. She said he was drinking and hanging out with the wrong kids. I was expecting a teenager. Jack turned out to be six foot four, two hundred pounds and twenty-two years old. During the session, we made a list of everything his mother did for him. It was a long list that ran from urging him to brush his teeth each morning to paying his health insurance.

I suggested that the first step Jack needed to take was to get to the sessions on his own. Since he didn't have a car, he would have to take the bus. He agreed to do this. At the next session, he showed up with his mother again. She said she drove him to make it easier for him. Her false notions about helping Jack bolstered her ego and deflated his: we discussed the advantages and disadvantages of helping him in this way. After that, Jack started getting to the sessions on his own.

Not all cases turn out this well. Dr. Richard Bedrosian, a colleague, has talked about a similar case.

> The patient experienced apathy, fatigue and hoplessness, and had not shown up for his job for several weeks. The intern began treatment by asking the patient to record his daily activities, a standard assignment in cognitive therapy. Unfortunately, the man's wife did the recording for him. When the task was reassigned, the wife again completed the activity schedule for her husband. If the patient wanted to reschedule or cancel an appointment, his wife would call the clinic for him. At one point, she became quite indignant when the therapist telephoned their house and asked to speak directly to the patient, rather than relay a message to him through her. Although she said she wanted to see her husband improve as rapidly as possible, she repeatedly counseled him to be cautious in attempting new behaviors. Perhaps not surprisingly, the patient failed to show up for his fourth appoint-

ment. Thereafter, he could not be coaxed into returning to the clinic.

When you're able to take care of yourself physically, you're more likely to have the underlying conviction that you can survive —no matter what happens. This becomes the basis for feeling secure across a variety of situations.

World Travelers and Physical Independence

Pat and I spent almost four years traveling around the world. During this time we became part of a subculture of other world travelers. This subculture is made up of men and women whose goal is to see as much of the world as they can. They travel on the cheap and work along the way to pay expenses. The fraternity is loosely held together by shared information ("You can get a cheap boat from Mombassa to the Seychelles" . . . "The best place to stay in Hong Kong is . . .") and shared traveling paths and resting spots. You're likely to meet a traveler in the Nairobi Youth Hostel, then run into him or her again a year later at a traveler's hotel in Singapore.

To be in this "fraternity," you have to be physically independent. The life-style demands it. For example, Pat and I arrived in Tokyo in the winter of 1969 with twenty-five dollars; we didn't know a word of Japanese. We had to take care of ourselves because no one else would. After traveling for a while, you develop the sense that you can survive anywhere.

World travelers have provided me with some of the best models for how to be physically independent. Keith and Wendy Shipman are good examples. We met them in Otavala, Equador, in 1972. Keith had been traveling for eight years. He left his home in England to travel in the Middle East, Asia and Africa; he met Wendy, also from England, in New Guinea. We traveled with them through Equador and Peru and were on a native steamer on the Amazon together. When we saw them again two years later in Philadelphia, they were on their way to travel through the heart of Africa.

They were always self-sufficient. Like all travelers, they traveled light and lived out of the packs on their backs. Whether they washed their clothes in the sink of a dollar-a-night room or in a river, they were always clean. No matter where in the world they were, they could always find some local produce to cook up a good meal. They always showed initiative and creativity.

While we were traveling on the Amazon together, Keith noticed I wore an uncomfortable moneybelt and said, "That won't do." He bought some cloth and ribbon from an Indian merchant in a river village and sewed me a customized money pouch that was easy to wear and inconspicuous under my arm.

Keith and Wendy are always giving of themselves and never holding back. They pay their own way. They spent a week with Pat's parents. Pat's mother, Lavona, said that when she came home from work, she found the house completely cleaned and Keith and Wendy fixing dinner.

Above all else, they keep their word. They do what they say they are going to do. When we were in Equador together, I asked if they would ever stop traveling. They said they were going to see South America and travel through the middle of Africa. Then they would settle down on a farm and have a bunch of kids.

Several years ago, while I was teaching in England, Pat and I went to see them on their farm in Wales—so far they have three children.

Another good model of physical independence is Charlie McBride. We met Charlie in Banos, Equador, a few weeks after we met Keith and Wendy. He has an equally varied travel background that had brought him to South America. We ran into him again six months later in Buenos Aires. We were boarding the same ship—one that was going to Cape Town, South Africa. We traveled with Charlie for a while in Africa and we have periodically seen him over the years.

Travelers at first glance don't seem to have much self-discipline or self-control. It may seem they don't want to settle down or take on responsibilities. However, they often are highly disciplined and take on jobs others only talk about. Charlie, for example, learns the language and history of every country he lives in. What he sets out to do, he does extremely well. He's a skilled vegetarian cook and when he comes to visit us, he does all the cooking.

He's one of the best writers I know and has kept a detailed travel journal for the last fifteen years. As far as I know, he doesn't have plans to publish it, but he works continually at improving his writing.

I've never met anyone who is better at keeping up personal correspondence. He's met dozens of people over his years of traveling and working in different countries, people with whom he has formed close personal relationships. Unlike most of us, he hasn't let these relationships founder and become lost. They are not disposable friendships. He keeps up a continual personal correspondence with over fifty people he's met over the last few years, such as a lumberjack in the Northwest Territories he helped build a house with, a missionary he met in Botswana, an artist in Norway. He doesn't write "Hi, how are you?" but rather highly interesting and personal letters. To keep track of his correspondence he keeps a code book that details the letters he's written and received.

Traveling is one way that you can increase your physical independence and self-confidence. Charlie and Keith and Wendy are examples of travelers we've met and respected because they have faith in their ability to take care of themselves and are physically independent.

Everyday Physical Independence

You may not be able to take off and travel around the world. That form of independence is special and time-limited. However, being physically independent is an everyday job. You show your degree of independence by how you handle yourself throughout the day. Countless times, when you run into the small jobs of making your own coffee and cleaning up your own messes, you have a choice to be independent or dependent. You can choose to take care of yourself or you can wait for others to do it for you.

People will often take care of your small jobs for you; however, everything has its price. Small forms of dependency are the stuff of which resentments, estrangements and divorces are made.

The following is a list of some everyday dependent behaviors. You may have overlooked or ignored such jobs for so long that they may be almost invisible to you. You may find that, after answering the questions, you're helping to keep someone else physically dependent, or that you are physically dependent on someone else. Answer the questions in the space provided. Then ask those you live and work with to answer them for you so that you can see if you're being honest with yourself.

Physical Dependency Checklist

1. Who refills the ice tray after I use the ice? ______
2. Who picks up my clothes from the floor? ______
3. Who sweeps up the pile of trash I notice? ______
4. Who puts the lid back on the catsup after I use it? ______
5. Who puts the lid back on the toothpaste after I use it? ______
6. Who refills the water jug if I drink the last of the water? ______
7. Who replaces the toilet paper roll if I use the last of it? ______
8. Who puts the fresh roll of toilet paper onto the holder after I bring it into the bathroom? ______
9. Who cleans the bathtub after I use it? ______
10. Who rinses the sink after I use it? ______
11. Who makes my bed? ______
12. Who makes sure my clean underwear is where it should be? ______
13. Is the newspaper folded back in place for the next person after I've read it? ______
14. Who closes the bread wrapper after I make a sandwich? ______
15. Is there dust under my rug? ______
16. Who changes my light bulbs when they burn out? ______
17. Who fills the gas tank of the car after I drive it? ______
18. Where are tools after I use them? ______
19. What happens to books I borrow? ______
20. How do I get a telephone number if the phone book is out of reach? ______
21. Why don't I know how to start the washing machine? ______
22. What happens to pens I borrow? ______
23. Who cleans up when I make a mess? ______
24. What happens when I can't find something—who looks for it? ______
25. Who erases the chalkboard after I use it? ______
26. What happens to the paintbrush after I use it? ______

27. What happens to the coffee cup after I use it? _______
28. Who turns off the lights or TV after I leave a room? _______
29. How do I get my spending cash? _______
30. Who takes care of my needs when I visit my family or friends? _______
31. Who picks up my child from school in case of sickness? _______
32. Who cleans up after my pets? _______
33. Who waters my plants? _______
34. What do I do with food wrappers when I'm driving or walking down the street? _______
35. How do I act when I come into the middle of a TV show—do I expect others to tell me what has happened? _______
36. What happens when I smoke—do I expect others to tolerate it and clean up the ashes? _______
37. Where are files after I use them? _______
38. Who fills the stapler if I use the last staple? _______
39. Who gets my coffee for me at break time? _______
40. Who dials my calls at work? _______
41. How do I get lunch if I don't feel like going out on a rainy day? _______
42. Whose work and time are most important in my family? _______

After completing the checklist, you may have identified areas where you're physically dependent. In case you had to answer most of the questions with someone else's name, you can resolve to do something about it. Next time you confront one of the jobs mentioned in the quiz, ACT on it. Accept that the unmade bed is in front of you, choose to be independent and confront it, and then take constructive action by making it yourself.

If you haven't taken on these jobs for a long time, you can expect difficulty in doing them. But in nearly every task, you will find that after you've done it, the job wasn't nearly as difficult as you had imagined it to be. In fact, once you resolve to do it, the difficulty often goes away. Your mood usually improves; you like yourself better and your self-respect goes up. Doing these everyday acts of physical independence can start you moving toward greater independence in the other areas of your life.

In addition to your ideas about the difficulty of a certain job, your ideas about time stop you from taking action. You may think you don't have enough time to get the iron out or fill the water bottle; you have more important things to do. However, you have to spend time to make time. Ignoring a certain task saves you time at the moment, but you lose much more time over the long run. Suppose you've been pulling the screen door closed by hand because the spring is broken. Maybe it does only take half a minute to close, and fixing it might take an hour. However, when you go in and out of the door enough times you use up the hour's worth of minutes—you pause, grab behind you for the handle and pull the door closed—and it's *still* going to take an hour to fix it.

Also, every time you pull it closed you'll be reminded of the fact that you haven't fixed it yet. This wears you down and makes you lose respect for yourself.

Most people can readily see the usefulness of becoming more independent and taking care of themselves physically; and they can usually see their excuses for what they are. However, they often come back with one sentence: "I don't want to do it." End of conversation.

I hear this from just about everyone I see somewhere along the line. The man who's trying to lose weight doesn't want to give up the foods he loves. The woman who's trying to break off a destructive affair with a married man doesn't want to stop seeing the man she loves. The man who has avoided taking care of his basic tasks doesn't want to start doing the work he hates. As a therapist, I try to help people do what they don't want to do. These same people don't need help in doing what they *want* to do. My job is to help people do what's in their best interest, and that should be your job too—you should help yourself do what's in your own best interest. In the next chapter, I'll talk specifically about ways you can let go of old habits that have been hanging around for too long a time.

Damn Short Order. Increased physical independence is both a cause and a result of growth. You're born dependent on others. As you become independent of them, you mature and move forward. If you want to continue to grow, you have to keep this process going throughout your life. When you stop increasing your independence, you stop growing.

In each stage of maturity you have to break free from dependency to move ahead. When you were in the womb you were tied to your mother for survival. The severing of this tie was your first step into independence. You can see this process in nature. As animals mature physically they start to separate from their parents. If they don't do it themselves, they are pushed out of the nest to fly on their own. The major task of all offspring is to become independent as fast as they can.

Becoming physically independent when you're young lays the groundwork for being successful later in life. Unlike the other kids, Paul never grumbled when the teacher gave out assignments or tasks. Rather, he'd say to himself, "I'll get this done in damn short order."

He would pitch right in and do the job. He was the first one to get a paper route and the first to buy his own bike. When the rest of his friends got bikes, he showed them how to fix them. Years later no one was surprised when they heard that he had become a successful businessman. They suspected he got there by solving his problems in "damn short order."

The reason Paul was able to master his environment was because he moved toward it. He didn't ignore his jobs and hope they would solve themselves. He didn't curse God, fate or others for not doing his work for him. The essence of independence ("Spend yourself, don't hold back") involves moving *toward* what is, rather than away from it. When you try to save yourself from the real world because you don't like its looks, your problems grow.

Getting Started

You usually have an aversion to doing something you've let others do for you. If you didn't feel this way, you would have been more physically independent by now. The following are some ideas you can use with the "I-don't-want-to" problem.

"Wants" Are Irrelevant. What you want to do is usually irrelevant to your goal. So what if you don't want to? Most of the work of the world is done by people who don't want to do it. Do you think the telephone operator wants to spend her time placing your calls? No; chances are she wants to go shopping and lie on the beach. Most people seem to wake up Monday morning and say, "Boy, I sure don't want to go to work today." *But they go;* their "wants" are irrelevant.

Don't Like It, Do It. What's important is that you choose new options and become more physically independent. It's probably asking too much for you to like it. When you're asking anyone, even yourself, to give up an old habit, what's important is that they give it up. It's not important that they like doing it. For instance, if you ask your husband to quit flirting with other women at parties, be satisfied that he stops. It's asking too much to expect him to like it. As a parent, you may make this mistake: do you punish your child for reacting with anger, even if he or she does as told? It's enough that your child follows the limits you set; he doesn't have to like them, just follow them. The same goes for being physically independent. What's important is that you do something for yourself; you don't have to enjoy doing it.

A Thing Worth Doing Is Worth Doing Poorly. If doing something is worth doing at all, any portion of it is usually better than no part. If setting up your home filing system is worth doing, it's worth doing less than perfectly.

The house of a friend of mine is in shambles. The plumbing is bad in a number of places. Electrical outlets don't work. He's a good mechanic and could easily fix any of the problems. But he doesn't do any of them because he believes "Anything worth doing is worth doing right!" He can't get himself to fix a leaky faucet because, thinking as he does, he'd have to put new pipes throughout the house. The same goes for the electrical outlets. He doesn't fix one because he believes it would mean an expensive two-week electrical project. You are always more effective when you don't demand perfection.

ACT

Here is how you can use the ACT formula to become more physically independent. I'm going to use one person's goal as an example. You should substitute your own task and adapt the ACT formula to the task.

Task: "I want to learn to launder my own clothes."

ACCEPTANCE:

1. Accept that you're responsible for yourself.
2. Accept that the dirty clothes are in front of you—it's not a mirage.
3. Accept that you have to wash them yourself in order to become more independent.
4. Accept that the task is as hard or as difficult as it is—no less, no more. You'll learn how to do it when you do.
5. Accept that it will take as long as it takes to complete—no longer, no shorter.

CHOOSE INDEPENDENCE:

1. Choose to be physically independent—to move toward the dirty clothes and washing machine.
2. Choose to do the task, no matter how imperfectly it turns out.
3. Choose not to let your mind trick you out of doing it.
4. Choose to own the task as yours ("I'm the one who wants to do them").
5. Choose to do it, no matter how you feel about it ("So what if I don't feel like learning right now").
6. Choose to be in control ("No use getting upset about it").

TAKE ACTION:

1. Don't *think* about the task, do it. Grab the clothes and go to the washing machine.
2. Take the first step. Ask someone how to run the machine.
3. Keep doing your new skill over and over—you are now more physically independent ("I'll keep doing my own dirty clothes until I've mastered it").
4. Build on this by trying to do one new physically independent thing each day ("Next I'll work on becoming a better cook").

Physical Independence Inventory

A bonus in becoming more physically independent is that when you can take care of yourself, others will move toward you.

Because people don't feel put upon, they want to be around you more. One study asked single women what they looked for most in men. The number one answer wasn't appearance or money, but a man's confidence in handling everyday problems. This type of confidence starts with becoming physically independent.

You can take the following inventory to see where you now stand in terms of taking care of your basics:

> Physical independence refers to your ability to take care of your basic needs. This has to do with how you manage your food, clothing, shelter, transportation and care and maintenance of your body.
>
> Read each group of statements carefully. Then circle the number beside the statement that best describes you. After you have completed the questionnaire, add up all the numbers circled. Check your total with the totals given at the end of the chapter.

1. 0 I'm able to do basic housekeeping tasks (making beds, doing dishes).
   1 I have some trouble with basic housekeeping tasks.
   2 I have a great deal of trouble with basic housekeeping tasks.
   3 My house is a mess.
2. 0 I'm able to do my own cooking.
   1 I have some trouble doing my own cooking.
   2 I have a lot of trouble doing my own cooking.
   3 I don't do any of my own cooking.
3. 0 I take care of my personal hygiene.
   1 I have some trouble taking care of my personal hygiene.
   2 I have a lot of trouble taking care of my personal hygiene.
   3 I don't take care of my personal hygiene.
4. 0 I am able to keep track of my personal belongings.
   1 I have some trouble keeping track of my personal belongings.
   2 I have a lot of trouble keeping track of my personal belongings.
   3 I have to ask others where my things are.
5. 0 I can look up and dial numbers regularly.
   1 I dial a few well-known numbers, but seldom use the phone book.

2 I answer the phone but rarely dial.
3 I never use the telephone.

6. 0 I can take care of all my own shopping.
1 I can shop for small items but want assistance with large items.
2 I want to be accompanied on shopping trips.
3 I'm unable to shop for myself.

7. 0 I can plan and make meals for myself.
1 I can make adequate meals if given the food.
2 I can heat prepared meals but don't eat adequately.
3 I'm unable to make my meals.

8. 0 I can maintain my house alone.
1 I need help for everything except tasks like dishwashing and bedmaking.
2 I need help with all housekeeping tasks.
3 I can't do any housekeeping tasks.

9. 0 I can do all of my own laundry.
1 I can launder the small items but not large items like sheets and towels.
2 I can launder a few small items.
3 All of my laundry is done by someone else.

10. 0 I can travel by myself in my car or by public transportation.
1 I use public transportation when assisted or accompanied by another.
2 I travel by car with assistance of another.
3 I almost never travel.

11. 0 I take care of my own medication—the dosages and timing.
1 I take my own medication but occasionally forget.
2 I can take my own medication if someone reminds me.
3 I don't take care of my own medication.

12. 0 I'm able to do most household repairs.
1 With some help I can do moderately difficult household repairs.
2 I do simple repairs such as hanging a picture or changing a light bulb.
3 I'm unable to do simple household chores or repairs.

13. 0 I can drive alone.
1 I can drive alone but sometimes get lost.

2 I drive when someone else is with me.
3 I can't drive.

14. 0 I always take care to look clean, neat and well dressed.
1 I take care to bathe and be neat, and sometimes dress well.
2 I bathe and dress myself, but don't care how I look.
3 I don't bathe and dress myself and I don't care how I look.

15. 0 I enjoy preparing and eating regular meals and my favorite foods.
1 I regularly prepare simple meals.
2 I occasionally prepare simple meals, but don't enjoy eating.
3 I don't eat regular meals and eat only when I become very hungry.

16. 0 I keep my daily agreements (what I say to myself and others that I'll do).
1 I keep my daily agreements, with some help.
2 I keep my daily agreements about half the time.
3 I cannot keep my daily agreements.

17. 0 I do not feel ashamed of how I keep my daily agreements.
1 I occasionally feel a little ashamed of how I keep my daily agreements.
2 About half the time I feel ashamed of how I keep my daily agreements.
3 I feel ashamed of how I keep my daily agreements.

18. 0 I get along well with salespeople and tradespeople.
1 I usually get along well with salespeople and tradespeople, but have minor arguments.
2 I often argue with salespeople and tradespeople.
3 I have many arguments with salespeople and tradespeople.

19. 0 I'm in good physical condition.
1 I'm in fair physical condition.
2 I'm in poor physical condition.
3 I'm in very poor physical condition.

20. 0 I exercise regularly.
1 I exercise occasionally.
2 I rarely exercise.
3 I never exercise.

21. 0 I don't smoke.
1 I occasionally smoke.

2 I'm dependent on a pack of cigarettes a day.
3 I'm dependent on more than a pack of cigarettes a day.

22. 0 I have no trouble with drinking alcohol.
1 I occasionally drink too much alcohol.
2 I often drink too much alcohol.
3 I'm completely dependent on alcohol.

23. 0 I'm not dependent on any drugs or medication.
1 I habitually take some drugs or medication.
2 I'm partly dependent on some drugs or medication.
3 I'm completely dependent on some drugs or medication.

24. 0 I wake myself up in the morning when I have to be some place on time.
1 I usually wake myself up in the morning when I have to be some place on time.
2 I rarely wake myself up in the morning when I have to be some place on time.
3 Someone always wakes me up in the morning when I have to be some place on time.

25. 0 I can use a map to find my way around.
1 I can usually find my way around.
2 I sometimes have to ask for help to find my way around.
3 I have to count on someone else to help me find my way to places I've never been before.

26. 0 I always make my own reservations (dinner, flights, and so forth).
1 I usually make my own reservations.
2 I rarely make my own reservations.
3 I never make my own reservations.

27. 0 I always return unwanted merchandise myself.
1 I usually return unwanted merchandise myself.
2 I sometimes return unwanted merchandise myself.
3 I rarely return unwanted merchandise myself.
4 I have someone else return unwanted merchandise—or I keep it.

RESULTS:

Score of 0–6 = high level of physical independence.
Score of 7–17 = moderate level of physical independence.
Score of 18–25 = low level of physical independence.
Score of 25 or above = severe problem with physical independence.

CHAPTER SIX

Letting Go of Physical Dependencies

The Why Question

Recently I gave a talk on weight reduction to a group of psychiatric residents at a medical school. The professor teaching the seminar asked me, "Dr. Emery, why are these people fat and what can we as psychiatrists do about it?"

The question "Why are these people fat?" immediately brought to my mind the picture of Dr. Albert Stunkard. I did my doctoral dissertation on weight reduction. Before you can complete your doctoral research, you have to get a committee of three professors to agree that the research is sound and worthwhile. I decided to ask Dr. Stunkard to be on my dissertation committee. He is the world's foremost authority on obesity and has been the chairman of the psychiatry departments at both the University of Pennsylvania and Stanford University. He has spent a lifetime studying the question "Why are people fat and what can we do about it?" This has been his magnificent obsession.

The other two members of my committee gave tentative approval for my research. When I went to see Dr. Stunkard, he asked me, "Gary, why do you think these people are fat?" I told him it's basically an energy imbalance—people are taking in excess amounts of energy in the form of calories relative to the amount of energy they are expending in activity. He told me I should do more reading on obesity—"It's a bit more complicated than that."

Mildly discouraged, I went back to the medical school library.

I developed a better grasp of the problem, so I returned to Dr. Stunkard with my new proposal. Again came the question "Why are people fat?" I told him, in effect, "People are overweight because of a combination of biological, social, cultural, developmental and environmental determinants. The exact cause differs from person to person. However, because of these different determinants, certain people are at a greater risk to gain weight than others." I went into each of these determinants in some detail. He said, "You have a better grasp of it, but I think you need to do more reading in the area."

At this point I became quite discouraged. Several months had passed while I saw classmates completing their research and getting their degrees. Pat and I decided to drive down to Florida to get away from the snow in Philadelphia as well as my thoughts of the dissertation and graduate school. Somewhere along the way I decided, "If I have to become an expert on obesity to get this Ph.D., I will!" I came back determined to find out everything I could about obesity.

I threw myself into the project. I spent my evenings and weekends reading about obesity. I began finding all kinds of interesting questions. Why do Arabs esteem plump women while Americans don't? Why are Santa Claus and other "good guys" fat, while witches and other "mean" characters are always thin? Why do Japanese-Americans, after two generations, become as fat as most other Americans? Why do Americans love milk and Chinese hate it? Why are upwardly mobile women less fat than downwardly mobile women? What's taste? Why are black women generally fatter than white women? Why do troubled families have more problems with weight than stable families? Why are so many fat people depressed? Is depression a result or a cause of obesity? Do fat people have heightened sensitivity to food cues? Does the timing and type of fat cell a person develops relate to being fat? Do fat people eat differently than normal people? What are the physiological mechanisms of eating? What role does genetics play? Why do certain fat parts of the body—such as fat thighs—run in families?

I found hundreds of interesting questions. For each question there were numerous and conflicting answers. The psychoanalysts had some answers, the sociologists and anthropologists had others, the experimental psychologists and clinical psychologists had sharply differing opinions, and the physiologists and geneticists had their opinions.

A year went by. At first, I had periods of feeling dispirited and angry; I would daydream about hiring a hit man to get Dr. Stunkard. These gave way to periods of ecstasy as I fell in love with the question "Why are people fat?" It became at times a mystical experience as I dug into this question. I kept going back to the library to chase down new questions.

Pat asked one day if I ever thought about getting out of graduate school. I decided that I had better call an end to it. I then wrote a summary of what I had found (my dissertation turned out to be four hundred pages long). I then dropped the proposal off at Dr. Stunkard's office and asked for an appointment. His secretary called and said he didn't have time to see me, but he would respond to my proposal through a cassette tape recording. On the tape he said, in effect, that I needed to do a little more reading in the area.

I was despondent—yet I wasn't satisfied myself with my answers to the question of why fat people are fat. I still wanted to follow up some other avenues of research myself. So I began to dig even deeper into the bottomless literature on why people are fat. A month later I was looking into what the hunger mechanism is and ran into this quote by Dr. Garrow, an expert in hunger research: "Feeding behavior in man is a very complex subject and the situation is steadily becoming less clear." I stopped right there.

I went directly to Dr. Stunkard's office and insisted on an appointment. I asked him if he wanted to be on my committee or not. I said, "I'll be damned if I know why people are fat. They just are." He said, "I think you're ready now."

I believe the question of why people are fat was for me like a Zen Koan: "What is the sound of one hand clapping?" The answer to that one it turns out is the same as to "What is the sound of rain?" The sound of rain is the sound of rain and the sound of one hand clapping is the sound of one hand clapping. The answer to why fat people are fat is because they are fat. I wasn't surprised to learn later that Dr. Stunkard's other passion in life is Zen Buddhism.

What's the moral of this story? Don't become hung up on why you have certain habits. Don't continually ask yourself, "Why do I drink too much . . . smoke . . . not exercise . . . binge eat?" Accept that you do. The crucial questions are "What can I do about it and what do I want to do about it?"

Most procrastinators would prefer to read a book on time management or on why they procrastinate rather than to stop procrastinating. Most people spend much more time talking about why they are in a bad relationship than in what they can do to get out of it.

Physical Dependencies

Habits such as smoking, overeating, inactivity, and sexual inhibitions are dependent relationships you have with yourself. You may not like these relationships, but that doesn't alter the fact that you have them. If no matter what you say, feel or do, you continue to drink too much coffee, avoid leaving the safety of your home, let your body deteriorate or whatever, you have a problem relationship on your hands.

Before you decide to end this relationship, think about other past relationships that didn't work out. This may have been with an employer, friend or lover. At first, you may have had high hopes for the relationship—it looked like a good thing. Then it began to turn sour. The same process happens with physical dependencies. Think back to when you first started to smoke, to stop for a drink after work, to eat a danish every afternoon or to retreat to the safety of your home. You probably found the experience relaxing, refreshing and pleasurable. Slowly, however, like other failed relationships, the experience began to have drawbacks. The costs began to outweigh the pleasures.

Bad relationships feed on themselves. People don't stay in bad marriages because they like them, but because they don't see any alternative ("There's no way out"). Now, you smoke not because you enjoy it, but because you're uncomfortable without it. You drink to cure last night's hangover and eat to ward off the hunger pains that are now demanding more food. You stay in your house not because you feel safe but because you're terrified to leave. You're hooked.

Choosing to End the Relationship

You run into the same predictable problems in dropping a habit as you do in dropping any long-standing relationship. You travel through the same territory with the same risks of getting stuck along the way. Before you end a relationship, you go through four stages: the *magical* stage ("This relationship isn't that bad"); the *illusion*, or hope, stage ("The problems with our relationship may work themselves out"); the *trying* stage ("Let's have a trial separation"); and the *last straw* stage ("I've had it"). This is followed by your choice or the other person's choice to end the relationship.

You go through the same stages to drop a habit. You first go through the magical phase ("Eating doesn't make me fat" . . . "Smoking doesn't really cause cancer" . . . "Being late all the time doesn't bother anyone"). This is followed by the illusion stage ("I can quit whenever I want" . . . "My drinking problem will take care of itself"). Next comes the trying stage. Here you try a variety of solutions and often trial separations from the habit ("I won't smoke for two weeks" . . . "I'll go on the wagon for a month"). This is followed by the last straw stage. Here, either you become disgusted with the habit, or the costs outweigh the benefits in a clear way ("I spend ten dollars a week on cigarettes" . . . "I'm too fat" . . . "This habit is disgusting").

At this point, you choose to get rid of the habit. You must continue to reaffirm and act on your choice or you'll slip back into the old habit. Your mind will continually not want you to own up to this choice and will use dozens of little tricks to try to get you to disown your choice.

Getting rid of a habit is similar to running an obstacle course. Just as you've finished wading through a mudhole, you find yourself facing a barbed wire fence. Before I describe a specific twenty-one-day program for letting your old habits go, I'd like to talk about some of these obstacles you can expect to meet along the way.

The Hopelessness Obstacle. "I can't control my eating (or drinking, smoking, laziness, nailbiting)." This belief, like its cousins "I don't have the will power" and "Nothing will work for me," is a self-fulfilling prophecy. By predicting the results, you bring them about. When you believe nothing works, you don't act and then of course nothing happens. This belief stops you before you start.

Similarly, when Burt said, "I'm naturally lazy," he was in effect saying "I choose not to put forth the effort." If this is your choice, accept it as such and don't put yourself down or get angry, insisting it isn't fair. Neither attitude will help. Accept yourself as you are and own up to the consequences of your choice.

For those willing to invest the effort in letting go of old habits, a mandatory first step is getting rid of the "I'm naturally and hopelessly this way" notion.

Your habits *are natural* in that they are overlearned and normal *for you*. Choosing new ways of acting and thinking and feeling is unnatural. However, if you stick with the new habits, they'll eventually become natural to you. It takes a while for new habits to become second nature, so you have to stay with them for a while if you want to learn to love them as you did your old habits.

Question your hopelessness. Ask yourself:

1. Have I chosen to let habits go in the past?
2. Am I confusing a difficulty with an impossibility?
3. Where is the evidence that I can't choose to be different?
4. Am I a certified fortuneteller who can predict the future?
5. Am I now finally ready to choose to let my habit go?
6. Can I think of any reason that would compel me to choose to let my habit go—such as if my life or the life of a loved one depended on it? If the answer is yes, I can do it for myself.
7. Am I *completely* lacking in inner resources and strengths?

Another version of hopelessness is telling yourself "I don't care." This thought comes in a variety of disguises: "I don't care if I'm getting cancer, everyone has to die" . . . "It's not worth the effort" . . . "What difference does it make?" Other people may provide you with this last thought. One client's daughter told her, "It doesn't matter if you get fat—you're already married."

The "I don't care" thought usually pops into your head just

before you have to choose whether to engage in the habit or not. This lie is easy to knock down—of course you care, or you wouldn't feel bad about doing it.

It's helpful to answer your mind's thoughts on a sheet of paper. The absurdities of your thinking become readily apparent once they are written down. When it's in black and white, you're more likely to choose in your own best interest.

The following are samples of answers others have used successfully to let go of their depending-producing thoughts.

THOUGHT	ANSWER
I don't care if I learn to play a sport.	That's not true. You do care. You are just lying to yourself because it's a little difficult.
What difference will it make if I stop smoking?	It makes a lot of difference if you want to live longer. Good health is one of your highest priorities. Don't forget it!
I don't care about losing weight if it means I can't eat what I want to.	Listen to yourself for a moment. Of course losing weight means you *can't* eat everything you want to. Just because you want something doesn't mean you *have* to have it.
The hell with it. I'm going to do what I want.	Oh, that's mature! If you are going to use excuses you'll have to be more creative than "the hell with it." Any three-year-old could come up with better excuses.
It's not worth the effort.	Who ever said it would be easy? Anything you have ever done that you are proud of has taken hard work.

The Morality Obstacle. Most people who want to get over a habit snarl at themselves, "You're a loser" . . . "I hate you" . . . "You're no good." Their motto is: "I'm a loser because of this habit."

Upon closer inspection you'll see your derogatory remarks are nearly always self-defeating. By putting yourself down, you're giving yourself permission to continue with the habit. If a person is "no damn good," what difference does it make if he or she drinks too much, smokes and never exercises? It's to be expected.

Newspaper columnist Sidney Harris says:

> People who blame others are immature, but people who constantly blame themselves are also avoiding genuine responsibility for their acts. Blaming oneself is indulging in a kind of neurotic pleasure—you feel remorse, you castigate yourself, you feel purged, and then go out and repeat the same wrong actions over again. . . . Children are not grown up until they accept reality by beginning to relinquish the pleasure of blaming others; grownups are not truly adult until they give up the more treacherous pleasure of blaming themselves as a substitute for facing themselves and changing what they do not like.

One vice-principal always made a point of showing others how he used paddling to keep kids in line. To irk my friend, a visiting psychologist, he said, "This is the way we handle troublemakers here." The psychologist, to get back at him, replied, "Isn't this the same kid I saw you paddling the last time I was here?" You can continue to paddle yourself, but don't confuse this with rehabilitation. You'll find yourself back in the vice-principal's office again and again.

The Motivation Obstacle. Motivation works backward. You first have to have some success; then you feel motivated. It's as simple as that. If you follow the twenty-one-day program I outline, you'll be motivated after you've completed it, even if you have absolutely no motivation now.

The Environment Obstacle. Your surroundings do play a part in your choosing to let a habit go or choosing to keep it. It's more difficult to break up with someone when you see them often—they may live in the same building, neighborhood, go to the same school or work in the same office. Often people end these types of relationships by moving or quitting their jobs.

The same process occurs when you try to break off the relationship you have with a long-standing habit. You want to put some distance between you and the enviornmental cues that lead to the habit.

You are much better off at first to avoid times and places that are associated with the old habit. For example, if you are choosing to let smoking go, you can do some of the following.

- For a while, avoid friends and associates who smoke a lot. Sit with a different group of coworkers.
- If your partner smokes, ask him or her to smoke as little as possible in your presence.
- If you normally smoke when you drink, cut back on drinking until you have put some distance between you and your smoking.
- For a while, avoid activities that are coupled with your smoking—such as playing cards or having an afternoon cup of coffee.

This is just a sample list. You can make up your own list for whatever habit you choose to dump.

In addition to engineering the environment to avoid problem areas, you can engineer it in favor of new behaviors you want to have. If you want to learn a sport, invest in equipment—such as a tennis racket—and leave this equipment around where you can see it every day. Join a group or club that specializes in the activity you want to do and associate more with this type of person.

When I want to get myself to write, I make the environment as conducive to writing as possible. For example, when I prepared to write today, I looked out my window and saw blue, sunny skies and palm trees in the distance. My mind whispered to me, "The Santa Monica Beach is only twenty minutes away." I immediately closed all the blinds and made the room as dark as possible. I left one small light to write by. I then put on an environmental cassette tape called "The Ultimate Thunderstorm." Now I began to feel happy to be home, all cozy, warm and dry while I wrote with the sound of rain in the background.

What do I do when it's really raining outside? I put on a tape called "Crickets in Summertime." I then feel more like I'm choosing to stay home to write.

The Goals Obstacle. Goals can cause you a great many problems in letting go of old habits. They create resistance (you don't like to *have to do* something), disappointment (when your goals aren't met) and relapse ("I've reached my goal, what next?"). A better policy is to make choices, not goals ("I'm going to be a person who will not be housebound" . . . "I'm going to be a person who . . .").

The Lack-Specific-Plan Obstacle. Unlike general goals, specific plans or goals can be helpful. You'll have to develop your own specific plans to end the habit. You will have to make your own specific plan. (Remember, this is a book on becoming more self-reliant.)

I'll go into one sample plan in detail. Let's take overeating. Books or programs on how to lose weight usually urge you to follow either a well-rounded diet with counting and recording calories or carbohydrates or an extremely strict diet, such as the grapefruit-and-eggs diet. Both approaches have advantages and disadvantages. The well-balanced diet makes sure you have good nutrition and gives you enough food choices so that you don't feel too deprived. However, this approach creates too many choice points, which increase the probability that wrong choices will be made. Also, for most people, it's too tedious and complicated to count calories. Most people want a simple way to lose weight.

The second model, the strict diet, overcomes the problem of choice points by eliminating most of them. Your daily menu doesn't change much. You eat the same foods for nearly every breakfast, lunch and dinner. This style of diet is also much simpler because it doesn't require recording foods or looking up calories before each meal. The drawback is that few people can or should follow such a rigid (and unhealthy) routine for very long.

The major problem with both approaches is that they fail to let you *individualize* your diet. It's the Scarsdale . . . Weight Watchers . . . Mayo Clinic . . . Beverly Hills diet, not *your* diet. The authors falsely assume that everyone is the same—that everyone can change his or her daily routines enough to meet the requirements of whatever diet is urged. This may work for a short time. You may pack a dietetic lunch and carry it to work for a few days or weeks, but if you regularly eat out, eventually you'll be back to the Big Mac—and the end of the diet.

I've found that the best diet combines both approaches: you develop your own diet plan and then follow it within an independent framework.

To construct a diet (or any new strategy) that is right for you, ask yourself a series of questions that will help you determine the choices that are right for you. Some typical questions are:

- Have you been successful before? If so, what tools seemed to be most helpful (protein, low carbohydrates, fish, health foods, and so forth)?
- What is your life-style? (Do you snack continuously or eat excessively big meals—or both?)
- What is your environment? (Do you eat out a lot or do you mainly eat at home?)
- Who are the other people in your life? (Do you eat with your family or a friend, or alone?)
- What are your problem areas? (Certain foods like pizza or ice cream? drinking beer?)

The answers allow you to personalize your own plan.

In the case of a diet, draw your plan up from a wide range of foods in your particular environment. This will allow for a nutritional balance, yet it will provide restricted choices. Because you'll have to look up the calories for a few items only once, this will eliminate constant checking. Thus, the individualized program will have the benefit of both the more restricted diets and the well-balanced diet.

After the foods have been chosen, it is important to put them in psychological context. The following plan was developed by Ruth, a client I saw. Ruth led a busy life. She worked full-time and always ate lunch out. She also took classes three nights a week. Her diet choices were:

PHASE ONE: Days 1–10. During this period Ruth ate 1,000 to 1,200 calories per day. She made three meal choices each for breakfast, first snack, lunch, second snack and dinner. The choices were based on foods that fit into her life-style and calorie allowance.

Breakfast: Choose between (1) cereal and juice; (2) one egg, one slice of toast and juice; (3) fruit and one slice of toast with one teaspoon peanut butter.

Snack: Choose between (1) one small fruit; (2) ½ package peanut butter and cheese crackers; (3) one glass low-fat milk.

Lunch: Choose between (1) a quarter pound sliced roast beef and half a pound coleslaw from nearby deli; (2) tuna salad platter from employees' cafeteria; (3) Quarter- Pounder without top half of bun from McDonald's.

Dinner: Choose between (1) bowl of chili and three crackers from nearby restaurant; (2) bowl of soup, roll and dinner salad from nearby restaurant; (3) baked chicken and salad at home.

Snack: Choose between (1) one small fruit; (2) diet milkshake; (3) 1 teaspoon peanut butter on one rice cracker.

PHASE TWO: Day 11–21. Ruth now adjusted the number of calories allowed each day to 1,200. This adjustment reflected how easy she found the first phase. She increased her meal choices from three to four.

PHASE THREE: Day 21 and beyond. Ruth maintained her calorie limit of 1,200. She added one more meal choice. She chose to stay on this program six months and then reevaluate her program. After six months she decided to keep under the 1,200 calories for the rest of the year.

Ruth developed her own diet using the calorie-counting principle. She took the specific bits and pieces from diets that had helped her in the past and worked them into her life-style. Ruth decided that if she gained more than three pounds, she would begin again and go through all three phases.

This was Ruth's plan; she chose what was in it and how she wanted to follow it. *She owned it completely.* The one you work out may be different, but make it *yours.*

Plans

The type of plan you develop for yourself will depend on what kind of person you are and the type of habit you're leaving. Following are some general guidelines.

- Make the plan for twenty-one days and be specific about what you're going to choose to do during this period.
- If the habit is one of strong avoidance, start with little steps. If you've developed the habit of not leaving the house, you might develop a plan consisting of these steps: (1) walk halfway around the block with a friend; (2) walk all the way around the block with a friend; (3) walk halfway around the block and meet your friend halfway; (4) walk around the block on your own; and so on.
- Use creativity in your plan. One woman had a fear of being touched by men. She started by touching herself until she felt comfortable with that. She then went to an elderly woman for massages. After she was comfortable with that, she went to a blind male for massages and eventually to a massage class at a local university.
- If it's a problem of alcohol or drugs, as a first step you may have to go to a hospital or outpatient center to become detoxified.
- With alcohol and smoking, you're usually better off to plan for complete abstinence. With alcohol this is particularly important if you drink for psychological reasons or if you have marked personality changes when you drink.

Twenty-one-Day Choice Program

You want to work your plan in a systematic way that will allow you to drop your "old friend." The underlying program rationale is that your mind doesn't want you to choose new behaviors and will try to trick you into keeping the relationship. The best way to overcome this is to inoculate yourself with some of the same medicine your mind will try to use on you. This may not be clear to you right now, but as you get into the program, you'll see its mechanism.

Following are the general rules for applying the twenty-one-day program.

• Don't start the program unless you're willing to give it the full treatment and follow through for twenty-one days. If you believe you have too many other projects going, come back to it another time when you can give it your full attention. If you start the program and then stop in the middle, you can make the habit all the stronger. It's better by far not to do it than to quit in the middle.

• Do the twenty-one days of the program in straight succession. Don't let weekends, holidays, sickness, guests or unexpected events such as hurricanes and earthquakes get you off the program.

• If you do break the program, wait at least a month and then start over again with Day 1.

• Don't tell others that you are going through the program. Make this a bargain you keep with yourself.

• Work on letting one habit go at a time.

• Buy a weekly schedule that you can carry with you at all times. You can get one at any stationery store. At the top of each page, write the name of the program day (for example, "Excuse Day"). The weekly schedule is an important part of the program, so buy a good one that you like the feel of. The days of the program follow.

Day 1: Wakeup Day. Your job for today is to become super-aware of the choices you are now making. Awareness is the first step toward fully accepting that you are now choosing to have the habit. As you go through the day, look *nonjudgmentally* at how you're keeping your old friend around. For ten minutes in the morning, run through your mind how you're planning to keep the habit going. Make this review explicit. (Smoking was Marsha's old friend. On Wakeup Day, she sat down and planned all the times she would be able to light up and where she would stop on her way home from work to buy her evening pack of cigarettes.)

You may want to make notes in your weekly schedule of the whens, whats and whos involved in feeding your habit. Remember, be completely nonjudgmental. Take the role of a friendly investigator or observer watching you keep the habit going. It helps to tell yourself, "I choose to do this" as you engage in the habit ("I'm choosing to bite my fingernails right now").

At the end of the day, take ten minutes out and review everything that you did that relates to your habit. The major purpose of Day 1 is to wake yourself up to how you're keeping this habit around. Throughout the program you'll be using ten minutes in the morning and ten minutes in the evening for review.

Day 2: Pay Day. Your old friend is not without redeeming qualities. You wouldn't have struck up the friendship in the first place—nor would you have kept it going so long—if there weren't. Again, take ten minutes in the morning to think about the payoffs you get from the habit and ten minutes at night for a review of everything that your old friend gave you today and other days. As you go about Day 2 nonjudgmentally, look at all the positive benefits you're getting from your old friend. (George was chronically late. He was late for work, late for meetings, late in turning in projects, late in returning calls and answering letters. He never paid his bills until he got five-day shut-off notices. As we went through Pay Day, he saw the following benefits: his procrastination reduced his anxiety about having to do a good job; he liked the attention he got as he entered meetings late; he found being late made him feel in control of situations where he believed he had no control; and he found that being late was a way he could safely rebel against authority.) Like George, you can write your observed payoffs in your weekly schedule.

Day 3: Liability Day. The aim of today is to assess the damages. Again, use the two ten-minute review periods. What does your old friend cost you? Many, if not most, of the costs can be covered up and suffered in silence (you can wear clothes that hide your figure and lie to your friends about your reason for not leaving the house). Many of the liabilities of your habit you simply avoid—the warnings on cigarette packages; the articles that tell how alcohol destroys brain cells; the staircase that leaves you winded at the top. Your friends will join in the conspiracy of silence—they will let you know you have a weight problem only after you've lost some weight. After you regain it, they won't say anything. They know it and think it, but they won't say anything.

Today, as you go about totaling the costs, don't bring blame or guilt into the picture. This will only cloud it.

Day 4: D-Day. Today you focus on the decision to be made. In your ten-minute review periods, ask yourself, "Can I decide to give all of this up—the good and the bad of my habit? Can I decide to give up the comfort, support and security of this habit?" Go through each of the benefits and costs of the habit. Throughout the day, as you engage in the habit, ask yourself, "Can I choose to let this go?"

The focus isn't on the answer but on the question. You don't even have to answer the question. You only need to ask it as often as you can throughout the day.

Day 5: Feed-Up Day. The purpose of today is to help you see more clearly what your relationship is with your habit—what it brings you. Today, you need to saturate yourself. If your habit is watching TV excessively instead of being active, you should watch TV straight through from 6:30 A.M. to 1 A.M.—from "Captain Kangaroo" to the "Late Late Show." If you have two sets, bring both into the same room and watch two shows at the same time. Eat all of your meals in front of the TV; leave only to go to the bathroom during commercials. Do the same, no matter what your habit is. Spend your ten-minute review periods thinking about the habit in as much detail as possible.

Often the best way to break up a relationship is to spend inseparable time together. Many couples in unsatisfying relationships break up after going away on a vacation together.

By satiating yourself, you bring into clearer focus the choice you have over the habit. You reaffirm your ownership of it and you more clearly see the consequences of it.

Day 6: Letting-Go Day. Today is the day you choose to put into action your personalized plan (to stop smoking, to get more exercise, to diet, to overcome fear of elevators or other fears or habits). Starting today and throughout the rest of the program you'll put the plan you've already worked out into action. In your review periods and throughout the day, focus on choosing to give up the old habit—tell yourself you've quit trying to force the habit to bend to your desires.

As you work your plan, tell yourself, "I'm choosing to let go of this habit—I refuse to give in to urges to overeat (oversleep, drink, and so forth)."

Day 7: Grief Day. The goal of today is to mourn the loss of your old friend and to continue to choose to stay with your new plan. During your review periods and throughout the day, focus on the loss ("I miss the comfort of my old friend"). At the end of the review periods and during the day, tell yourself, "I miss the habit; however, I'm choosing to let it go."

To end any relationship, particularly a bad one, you have to allow yourself some sadness over the loss. This leads to eventual acceptance of the loss.

Day 8: Blame Day. You probably have a long list of people you believe are to blame for your habit—your parents ("They didn't teach me any better . . ."), your friends ("They got me started . . ."), outsiders ("Those damn radio and TV commercials . . ."), doctors ("They should have warned me . . ."), and so on.

Today you want to make all of this blame explicit in your review periods and during the day. You use the same process as on Day 7: you experience the anger and resentment and choose to let the habit go. For example, you might say, "My husband's drinking and my doctor's incompetence got me hooked on tranquilizers; however, *I'm* choosing to let it go."

These exercises today will help you get the ball back into your own court.

Day 9: Special Day. Each of your days is special or unusual. Today, your husband or wife might be sick, your car might be broken down, you might have a fever blister. Your mind will try to use the uniqueness or specialness of a week, day, hour or moment to get you to make up and get back together with your old friend. Today, you want to stress to yourself in the reviews and during the day why today is "different" and why this should mean you should give up the plan and go back to the old habit. For example, you might say, "Today is a weekday (or a weekend day), a slow day (or a busy day); however, *I'm* choosing to give up the old habit." In this practice, try to think of as many ways as you can why today is special or different ("It's Buddha's birthday . . . My paper at school is due . . . It's snowing").

Day 10: No-Hope Day. Today you want to tell yourself as often and as creatively as possible all the reasons why it's impossible for you to let your habit go. During your reviews and throughout the day, bring out the big guns: *morality* ("I'm too weak"), *history* ("I've failed every other time"), *mathematics* ("The chances or odds of my succeeding are nil"), *biology* ("I'm naturally this way, it's in my system"), and *psychiatry* ("Unconsciously I want to punish myself"). After each of the arguments of why you can't let the habit go, tell yourself, "However, *I'm* choosing to let go of this habit."

Day 11: Pain Day. You will run into some physical discomfort in letting go of your habit. Today, focus on all the discomfort and pain this breakup is causing you and then add, "However, *I'm* choosing to let the habit go."

Day 12: Boredom Day. It can be boring without your old friend around. If nothing else, your old friend was entertaining. Today, in your review and practice periods, tell yourself how boring everything is now—no drama, no surprises, just monotony and empty hours. Tell yourself how the sameness is almost killing you. And at the end, tell yourself, "However, *I'm* choosing to let the habit go."

Day 13: Cheat Day. All is fair in love and war. Your mind will go to any lengths to get the love relationship between you and your habit going again. Your mind will try to get you to cheat on the bargain you made with yourself. In your review periods, think of all the ways you can cheat on your plan and get away with it. Focus on how good that can feel. During the day, when you see a chance, tell yourself, "I could cheat right now (by having one cigarette, missing one practice, whatever). Then add, "And *I'm* choosing to give this habit up."

Day 14: Amnesia Day. Today, during your review periods and in the actual situation, focus on how you could easily forget your plan. Tell yourself how easy it would be to black out. And add, "However, *I'm* choosing to give this habit up."

Day 15: V-Day. When your mind sees that it's losing, it uses a very clever strategy: it joins the resistance and declares the victory is yours. This is the "if you can't beat them, join them" school. The mind switches over and tells you you've finally done it, you've really beat the habit. The strategy of your mind is to lull you into overconfidence. As a result, you soon find yourself sleeping with your old friend again.

Today, in your review periods and in life experiences, tell yourself how wonderful you are for having won the battle—and follow this with "However, *I'm* choosing to give up the habit."

Day 16: Slip Day. Today will be different from the others. You will purposely make a slip in your plan—you will have one cigarette for example. After the slip, tell yourself you've completely blown it and there is no use going on. Then tell yourself, "However, *I'm* choosing to give the habit up." In your review periods, stress to yourself all of the sayings and beliefs that could cause you to go back to the habit: "Once you've killed one man, what difference does one more make" . . . "I'm either a success or I'm a failure" . . . "I'm either a winner or a loser" and add, "However, *I'm* choosing to give this habit up."

Throughout the day, look at all of the points you could slip and use all-or-nothing thinking—and add, "However, *I'm* choosing to give up this habit." Pick one incident purposely to slip on.

What you learn today you'll be able to use in your future chance meetings with your old friend. You'll be able to tip your hat and keep moving.

Day 17: Alibi Day. Today you want to focus on all of the excuses you could use to get back together with your old friend ("Someone offered me a cigarette" . . . "I ate the candy bar because I had low blood sugar" . . . "The test made me nervous so I chewed my nails"). Use the same general process—two ten-minute review periods and remind yourself throughout the day.

Day 18: Not-Fair Day. Today you want to inoculate yourself with all of the reasons why it's unfair you have to give up the habit ("Other people can eat without gaining weight" . . . "There's worse things to do than smoking"). Use the same general procedures.

Day 19: No-Big-Deal Day. The purpose of today is to discount the importance of the habit in your life and discount what you have chosen to do about it. Use the same general principles to inoculate yourself.

Day 20: Your Day. Today, listen to the strategy your mind is trying to use to get you and your habit back together again. This may be one of the strategies you have already inoculated yourself with (you may need another dose), or it may be a new one. You can use the same general procedures to take the sting out of this trick.

Day 21: ACT Day. Today in your review periods, go over: what you have to *accept* to stay separated from your old friend (for example, "I have to accept some discomfort"); what your *choices* are ("To smoke or not to smoke"); and the *actions* you'll have to *take* to continue to give up the habit. Use this ACT formula throughout the day as your mind throws out urges, cravings and temptations.

To make this twenty-one-day choice program work you'll have to continue to use the ACT formula daily. For most habits such as overeating, your mind will keep trying to get you back together for at least one year. If you continue to use the ACT formula and choose to be independent of the habit, your mind will lose interest in it.

If you find that you have chosen somewhere along the line to get back together with the habit before a year is up, you'll have to go through the program again from the start. To prevent yourself from choosing to go back to the habit, periodically inoculate yourself with your mind's strategy that has the most power over you.

You can use this program with any of your physical dependencies. I would like to talk in more detail about three other common forms of physical dependency—fear of and overconcern with physical and health problems, chronic pain, and sexual dependencies.

Fear of Disease and Physical Disability

The most common form of physical dependency is fear of or overconcern with illness. This is caused by buying into parents' attitudes about how vulnerable you are to physical illness. This problem is often passed on from generation to generation—it becomes part of the family's heritage. Hugh Missildine, a psychiatrist, talks about how this problem was passed on in Charles Darwin's family. Darwin had seven children who were highly successful in life. Missildine says, "Yet of the seven, only two escaped hypochondriasis and nearly all of them, adopting the household symbol of ill health, took to wearing shawls in adult life years before they died."

Dr. Missildine goes on to talk more about how you become obsessed with your health.

> Hypochondriasis originates, in most cases, in the fearful attitudes toward disease expressed by parents and heard by a child. The child, helplessly dependent on his all-knowing parents, absorbs and adopts as his own the anxious attitude of his parents, imitating them. It helps him to feel close to them and secure—literally like them, the only adults he knows and his protectors. On becoming a parent to himself as an adult, he continues these old parental attitudes because this is the way he has learned to take care of himself and to feel secure.

Because it is transmitted, like other attitudes, from parent to child, hypochondriasis often expresses fears that were current many years ago when little was known about disease in a scientific sense and when such fears were more common than today. This attitude is secondarily supported by the gains in sympathy and indulgence which the "ailing person" obtains from those around him.

Again, the most important question becomes what can you do about it if you have bought and now own these attitudes? The most important principle to keep in mind is that the more you try to protect yourself, the more vulnerable you feel. The following are some general guidelines for choosing to let this physical dependency go.

- *Stop the doctor search.* Going from doctor to doctor only makes you feel insecure. You may get momentary relief when he or she says there's nothing wrong, but this is always followed by "But what if he missed something?" *Accept what doctors have told you.* Constantly doubting leads to increased fear.
- *Stop the cure search.* The same applies to overengaging in searching out cures—there can be no cures for something that doesn't exist.
- *Stop excessive efforts to protect yourself,* such as strange diets, elaborate health rituals and protective clothing. You may feel more secure in the beginning, but you end up more frightened.
- *Stop trying to stop the frightful thoughts that are scaring you.* This only serves to make them more powerful. When you try to fight them, they come back all the stronger. Treat them as teasing children. If you don't respond to them, their teasing eventually stops. Let these thoughts pass as they come to you.
- *Accept and be kind to that part of you that is trying to scare you.* This is part of you, you needn't reject it—just don't let it rule your life. Being mature is accepting your immaturities.
- *Accept and tolerate the discomfort of not knowing 100 percent for sure that you're healthy.* Running to the doctor for reassurance is like the junky running for a fix—you feel better for a while, but the addiction becomes stronger.
- *Don't talk to others about their health.* If you're not careful, you'll develop a circle of friends whose only common link is health fears.
- *Don't talk to others about your ailments.* This serves to increase your overconcern with your health. Hold your tongue when you want to talk "health."

• *Assume the best.* Life and nature are optimistic. If they weren't, our ancestors would have become extinct centuries ago and we wouldn't be here today. To prove this to yourself, list all of the health fears and concerns you've had in the past that haven't come true. Periodically, review your list and add new imagined ailments as they appear to you.

• *Accept that this is a problem that may reappear from time to time.* However, you can still choose to let it go.

Living with Pain

Many times you will have real pain. The choice here is whether to handle your pain in an independent or a dependent way. One form of physical dependency is to allow pain to run or ruin your life. This pain may be intermittent or chronic. Here are some ways you can use the ACT formula to become independent from your pain.

Acceptance. The first step is to become aware of your pain. You may say, "That's the problem—I'm *too* aware of it." However, in reality you're probably trying to block it out of your awareness. I've found that becoming more aware of your own pain is helpful. You can see your errors in thinking more clearly ("I hurt all the time" . . . "The pain never stops" . . . "It's awful" . . . "I can't stand it"). For one week, keep an hourly schedule of how much pain you're experiencing from 0 (none) to 10 (the maximum). Color in those hours the pain doesn't go over 3 with a green marker, color 4–7 in with a yellow marker, and above 7 in a red marker. This will give you a visual picture of your pain and allow you to see how many of your ideas about your pain are mistaken and thus exacerbate the problem ("I don't hurt all the time" . . . "The pain does vary" . . . "I can tolerate it").

Awareness also leads to increased acceptance. The role acceptance plays in pain is enormous. First, many times the pain is caused by something in your life that you're not accepting ("The job's a back breaker" . . . "My son is a pain in the neck" . . . "Trying to oversee this house is a real headache" . . . "I get sick to my stomach when I think about it"). Time after time I have seen patients' pain go away when they accept something (the death of a child, the loss of a job) they don't want to accept.

Acceptance of real physical handicaps and real pain puts you back in the driver's seat. Drs. Bulman and Wortman, in their study of how people cope with crippling accidents, found that those who accept the inevitability of an accident cope best. They write, "The following are representative of remarks by individuals who coped best: 'I really couldn't have avoided it; if I didn't drive maybe—but I like to drive.' 'It just happened; we were engaged in a contact sport. We both were doing something we wanted to do. Really, I don't think I could have avoided it.' "

Acceptance of the pain will also diminish and often alleviate pain. One form of this has been called by the pseudononymous Adam Smith "The Great Central Philippine Headache Cure." Many cultures use a version of this technique to alleviate pain. The basic technique is to accept, not reject, the pain. Smith writes:

> Close your eyes and look at your headache. Tell me about it. What color is your headache? Where do you see the color? Where is the headache in your head? Do you still feel it's there, or is it moving? How big is your headache? If it were liquid, would it fill a quart jar? A gallon jar? A bathtub? Can you pour the headache into one of those containers? When I say pour, start pouring, and see if it overflows. Pour.
>
> What does your headache make you think of? Look at that. Now look at the color of your headache. Is it the same? Tell me about the color. A dark shade or a light shade? Is the headache still the same size as when we started? Would you say it's as bad as when we started? No? Keep your eyes closed, breathe evenly, and tell me how big you headache is now. Describe the experience of your headache exactly. All of life is experience and this is experience, what is the experience? What color is the headache now? What does it feel like? How big is it?
>
> And so on. I have seen, in one startling demonstration after another, the Great Central Philippine Headache Cure work.

Choose to Be Independent. While you may not always be able to do something about your pain, you do have the great leeway in how you choose to lead your life in the face of pain. You can choose to constrict your life ("I have a backache, I can't go to the picnic"). People vary enormously in the degree they let physical pain and other physical handicaps rule their lives.

Take an experimental approach. See what you can do in spite of the pain. See what you can do when you have mild pain (the yellow zone I talked about earlier) compared to the red-zone pain. It may be that at the milder levels you can do much more than you realize.

This is particularly important if you have chronic pain. Bed rest for a couple of days might be the best remedy for someone with an acute backache; however, if you have a chronic backache, staying in bed can make you into a cripple. A colleague, Dr. Dolores Gallagher, has worked with many arthritic patients. She has found that how people perceive their ability to perform is much more important than the actual degree or extent of pain or handicap.

Shame. You may feel shame about your physical handicap or problem; this can increase your dependency on it. You can choose not to feel shame (see the antishame procedures I've outlined in chapter 12).

Own Your Own Pain and Handicap. In their study, Bulman and Wortman found that those who blamed others for the injury coped poorly with the problem. "Individuals who blamed another for their accident also showed great difficulty in coping." Non-blamers coped very well. They got on with their lives. Resentful people stayed stuck.

If someone else is at fault for your pain or injury, it's to *your* advantage to choose to forgive them. *If you're not forgiving, then you're for keeping.* You end up being the one who has to carry around and keep the excess baggage of hatred and resentment. When you forgive (this includes yourself for perhaps making an unwise choice) this lightens your load.

I know of one bitter man who holds the Japanese to blame for his accident. He says, "The Japanese have maimed and killed more young American boys with their motorcycles than they did in all of World War II." He doesn't own up to any of his choices in bringing the accident about.

Take Action. I'm constantly surprised at the number of people in pain who don't take action that is within their control to reduce the pain. Excessive weight, for example, exacerbates many painful conditions, yet many people don't work on reducing this weight. To be more independent from your pain, take the action that will help alleviate it. Follow the right diet and exercise plan and take the other medical steps that will reduce or relieve the pain.

If you can't do anything at all about the pain, your best bet is to try to lose interest in it. I used to live where there was a Jacuzzi. Ed was always sitting in it talking about his bad back. He had trained others who came to the Jacuzzi to ask how his back was feeling. So even if he was talking about another subject, someone else would bring it back to his bad back and he'd be off again talking about it. I'm sure his constant focusing on the pain made it worse. If you have chronic pain, don't talk to others about it or center your life around it. Instead, you can choose to lose interest in the pain and become more interested in other areas of your life.

Sex and the Independent Person

Problems with sex are usually a sympton of dependency. The most common reason for sexual problems such as impotence or frigidity is fear. You may, for example, fear that the other person won't like your performance. This causes anxiety, which interferes with the sex act. The solution to this problem is to concern yourself with your choices, not the other person's.

What your partner likes and enjoys about your performance is his or her choice, not yours. Once you start trying to do the impossible (control what the other person is going to choose), you start getting into trouble. So your solution in anxiety-related sexual problems is to focus on and own your own pleasure and let the other person do the same. Remember, whether the other person enjoys the sex or not is the other person's choice.

Lack of Sexual Desire. Dependency often can cause problems in your sexual desire. Usually what you're looking for when you're dependent is a substitute parent. For this reason, it can be difficult for both conscious and unconscious reasons to have sex with your partner. If this is your problem, accept the reality that your partner isn't your father or your mother and let go of the wish for a parentlike figure.

Dr. Helen Singer Kaplan, one of the foremost authorities of sexual treatment, has written about how you turn yourself off by creating negative emotions. You do this by focusing on negative aspects of the partner ("She's too fat"), or the relationship ("All he cares about is sex"), or by remembering past injustices.

Dr. Kaplan suggests confronting the patient with this fact: "The therapist now points out that the patient has a *choice* and that he has chosen not to feel sexual."

If you have low sexual desire toward your partner, you can increase this by selling yourself on the advantages of a good sexual relationship. Think of the pleasure you're losing and the harm to the relationship you're causing. And then take action that supports this. By starting to act more sexual, you'll soon start to feel more sexual.

Allow the other person to initiate sex. Don't make sex so serious. Put some humor and creativity into choosing the how, when and where of having sex. In other words, work at increasing your sexual choice-ability.

Mechanical Sex. Another type of sexual dependency is to engage in sex as a purely mechanical function. Here, you use sex as if it were a tension reducer or a way to treat your other dependency problems. Dr. Aaron Stern has this to say: "In terms of sexual functioning, the more dependent are less able to express themselves in intimate, spontaneous interactions. They are driven to the mechanics of performance in order to gain reassurance during lovemaking."

You can use the following points to stop being a sexual mechanic.

- Don't initiate sex simply as a way to release tensions caused by other areas of your life that are making you uptight, such as a fight with your boss. Instead of just trying to feel better, get better by focusing on the problem that is causing you the trouble.

• Don't use sex as an avoidance. You should engage in sex because you want to, not as a way to escape tasks you don't want to do, such as writing reports.

• Don't use sex as a way to seek validation of yourself or of the relationship ("Was it as good for you as it was for me?"). Enjoy sex for its own sake. See it as an enjoyable pastime, not as a self-test or a contest.

• Focus on the process, not the product. Don't become overconcerned about the number of orgasms; this is product- rather than process-oriented.

• Don't focus on *body counts*—how many people you have sex with or how often has nothing to do with the quality of the sex.

• Get your feelings, thoughts and actions going in one direction. If you're making love, be there in your feelings, thoughts and actions. Don't talk sexy and then do nothing about it. Don't act sexy and think about what's for dinner. Don't act sexy and feel turned off. If any of these three are going in opposite directions, you'll have problems.

While sex is the most common topic of conversation, in the next chapter I'll talk about the second most common topic—money.

CHAPTER SEVEN

Economic Independence

RECENTLY, AN AEROSPACE ENGINEER from Southern California, William Bell, was arrested for selling secrets to the Russians. Being economically dependent on a certain life-style can have serious consequences. Bell said his problems began when he got himself in over his head economically. He'd bought a condominium and a Cadillac and tried in general to keep up a standard of living he couldn't afford. He said he was pressured into selling the secrets because he needed the money to get out of debt. When you lack economic independence, like William Bell, you are at greater risk of making poor choices that can lead to worse places than the poorhouse.

Closely related to physical independence is the ability to take care of yourself economically. In simple terms, this means you make more than you spend, and the services and goods you use equal those you can afford. Economic independence also means you're able to manage the nuts and bolts of your finances; you understand and handle your taxes, banking, credit arrangements, insurance and financial goals.

Economic independence is important to your self-respect. In American culture, most people don't want to be economically dependent on others; they realize that when someone gives you money, spoken and unspoken conditions are often attached. Most people find the price of these conditions too high.

The relationship between economic independence and self-respect was clearly shown by Janice. Her self-respect was rock bottom when I first saw her for therapy. Her husband had died in a car accident and she was left alone with three kids. She had accepted the loss of her husband, but what bothered her was raising her children on welfare. She hadn't worked in years. She set out to become economically independent. Over several years she went from temporary office work to business school and eventually became an office manager. To get there, she had to overcome shame, lack of assertiveness, and negative predictions from friends and strangers alike. As she moved toward economic independence, her self-respect rose dramatically.

Many women today are in positions similar to Janice's before her husband's death. They have let themselves become economically dependent on their husbands, typically deferring in their economic development to them. The loss of a husband through death or divorce leaves an economically dependent woman in a precarious position.

In a divorce, for example, the wife usually keeps the house and kids, while the husband keeps the business. The woman often can't afford even the upkeep of the house, let alone the other expenses she becomes responsible for. If she hasn't worked in years, she usually has to take a job at an entry-level salary. Many women have seen this happen to others and are now developing marketable skills and economic independence.

This isn't to say that men don't have problems with economic dependency. Many men, for example, use status items as a way to compete with other men. Men's magazines are full of advertisements for status items, such as expensive music systems and monogrammed satin sheets, that are touted as ways to help men feel more virile, secure and competent. The purchase of such items usually has the opposite effect; the man ends up feeling trapped in a job he doesn't like so that he can pay for a playboy life-style he doesn't enjoy.

Holding Back

Your dependency often leads to being unemployed or underemployed. Joe was a twenty-seven-year-old man I saw for depression several years ago. He had a college degree yet worked at a low-level factory job. He wanted to be a supervisor; however, his poor evaluations blocked advancement. One evaluation said he had "low work norms." In other words, he was lazy.

Joe said his bosses were always picking on him because he had a college degree and they didn't. However, as we investigated this and dug deeper, the truth began to emerge. He thought the job was beneath him so he didn't have to give it his all. He saved himself throughout the day and wouldn't go full out on anything he did. He said, "I could do that job with one hand tied behind my back—if my supervisor had any sense he'd see that and give me something more important to do." He was resisting the way the world is.

One of the ways Joe would show his disdain for his job was to be chronically late in the morning. I quoted Emerson's advice on self-reliance to him: "Spend yourself on the work before you, well assured that the right performance of this hour's duties will be the best preparation for the hours or ages that follow it."

Joe's supervisor and fellow workers thought poorly of him because he committed himself only halfway. He felt badly about himself each day as he went about his job in slow motion. I told him that it's full engagement with the real world that makes you feel and act alive. If you put out only 10 percent, all you'll get back is 10 percent. This ancient wisdom is as true today as it ever was: you get what you give.

Withholding yourself deadens you; spending yourself enlivens you. Only when you lose yourself in what you're doing do you begin to live up to your potential. Spending yourself is the currency that buys you advancement in your job and career.

Joe's first step was to get to work on time each day. His next step was to see his job as worth doing for the sake of doing; he came to realize that unless he did today's job well, he would never be given a better job tomorrow.

Working at your right level of employment increases your self-esteem, enlarges your social contacts and provides you with meaningful challenges. Independence allows you to work to your potential.

Lack of economic independence is at the heart of many people's troubles. Bob, for example, couldn't hold a job for any length of time. He said, "I feel hemmed in and confined when I work any place too long," which meant he had to rely on his parents for food and a place to live. His lack of money was his chief source of dissatisfaction. He wanted to travel and to learn to fly, but he was stuck in his parents' house without car or carfare. Because of his lack of economic independence, the freedom he cherished so much was out of his reach.

Bob thought he should have been born into a rich family. A sure sign someone has a problem with economic dependency is when he or she tells you, "I should have been born rich. I have all the characteristics and tastes of a rich person." The irony is that dependent people who are rich are often the saddest cases. They lack the needed push to develop their potential.

If you're not rich and believe you should be, you can easily fall into the downward spiral of further economic dependency. First, believing you need to *impress others* causes you to live beyond your means. You're more likely to buy expensive status items, such as videorecorders, giant TVs and antennas that can get two hundred stations, primarily to impress others. And second, because you are also *impressed by others*, you're more likely to buy the stuff they tell you you need. You impulsively buy what you don't need, don't really want, and can't afford.

Money Madness

Status seeking and impulsive buying are traps that lead you deeper into economic dependency. You clutter up your life with stuff that doesn't impress the people you want to impress; in the end you're stuck with bills you can't pay. Further, because you're stuck with the stuff and the bills, you often have to stay at a job you don't like.

When I was nineteen, I was in love with a girl who was only slightly interested in me. I was going to college full time and working part time. I figured the way to win her was to impress her. I started off by moving into an expensive apartment, even though I had to drop two classes so that I could work more hours to pay for it.

This didn't impress her, so I bought an expensive stereo and better furniture, on credit. She was blonde and I figured blonde furniture would impress her. I had to work five more hours a week to make the payments. She remained lukewarm. I figured it must be my car, so I arranged a loan and bought a Triumph. At this point, I had to drop all my classes and work full time to keep up my new image. But I figured it was worth it and she would soon see my worth. She did in fact say "I admire your qualities." I think now what she meant was my car and apartment.

However, contrary to my expectations, she became even less interested in me. I decided I would have to really impress her with a big date. I got tickets for an expensive play and borrowed money from a friend to buy a new bright gold sport jacket (give me a break, this was 1961). When I went to pick her up, her mother said she must have forgotten about our date because she'd gone out with someone else.

Driving home from her house that night, it finally dawned on me that I was doing something wrong. A postscript: it took over a year to pay all the bills and get back to school again.

How you manage your money is another sign of your economic independence. Many people have noted that two people may earn the same amount of money, yet one leads a comfortable life while the other leads an impoverished one. The difference is due to economic independence. One buys what is needed, shops around first and then takes care of what is bought. When the person makes a purchase, it's something that's wanted and will be used effectively. The other does the opposite. The person impulsively buys what's not needed, and it ends up not being used.

When you're economically independent, you don't look for others to take care of your finances for you. You know how much money is coming in and how much is going out; and you know exactly *where it's going* and *where it's coming from*. You don't hide from the details of managing your money. As a result, you have confidence in where you stand financially.

Economic Independence and Other People

The following questions may help you discover something about how you handle money in relation to other people. Have someone else check your answers and see if you both agree about how you evaluate yourself.

1. When there's a coffee fund in your office, do you pay for the coffee or tea you drink? YES __ NO __

2. When you go out with friends and each of them buys a round of drinks, do you pay for the next round? YES __ NO __

3. When you go out with friends and you split the bill, after you put some money in for your dinner, do you pay your share of the tax and tip? YES __ NO __

4. If you go out with friends, and one of them doesn't add in the tax and tip when paying his or her share, do you speak up and ask for it? YES __ NO __

5. When you go out with friends, do you order the most expensive item on the menu and then suggest the tab be equally divided among everyone? YES __ NO __

6. Do you borrow money continually? YES __ NO __

7. Do you borrow money and then not pay it back? YES __ NO __

8. Do you ask someone to pay back a loan? YES __ NO __

9. Do you pay back a loan before it's asked for? YES __ NO __

10. Do you wait to pay bills until reminded? YES __ NO __

11. Do you refuse to lend money if the person is a bad risk? YES __ NO __

12. Do you overtip, regardless of the quality of service? YES __ NO __

13. Do you always insist on picking up the tab? YES __ NO __

14. Do you often buy something because the merchant is overpowering? YES __ NO __

15. Do you pay for the gas or parking when you're being driven someplace? YES __ NO __

16. If you break something, do you take responsibility and offer to pay for it? YES __ NO __

17. When someone takes you out to dinner, do you order the most expensive thing on the menu? YES __ NO __

18. When someone takes you out to dinner, do you order the least expensive thing on the menu? YES __ NO __

19. When you're a houseguest, do you pay for the food you eat? YES __ NO __

20. When you borrow someone's car, do you fill the tank? YES __ NO __

21. If you live with someone and borrow his (or her) clothes, do you pay for their cleaning? YES __ NO __

22. Do you speak up when you're not given the correct change? YES __ NO __

23. If you know a doctor or lawyer socially, are you likely to seek free advice from him (or her)? YES __ NO __

24. Do you know who's paying for dinner when you go out with friends? YES __ NO __

25. Do you buy stolen goods? YES __ NO __

26. Do you go out with friends and never offer to share expenses? YES __ NO __

27. Do you manipulate friends and acquaintances to do free work, like babysitting or running errands? YES __ NO __

28. Do you pay for long-distance calls you place from someone else's phone? YES __ NO __

Poor Versus Being Broke

Economic independence isn't all related to how much money you have, although this can be a factor. The crucial question is whether money serves you or you serve money. When you let money control you, you aren't independent of it. The late producer Michael Todd used to say, "I've been broke many times, but I've never been poor."

A good example of someone who has money but isn't economically independent is the rich person who's afraid he or she won't survive economically. It's a sure sign that you're economically dependent if you have repeated images of yourself on skid row or as a destitute bag person. This is a symptom that money has power over you; no matter how rich you are, you're still economically dependent. Only when you become truly economically independent will your fearful images disappear.

Misers have a pathological fear of being poor; they are scared out of their wits about living without money. I know a woman who is consumed by this fear. She inherited $5,000,000 and has a guaranteed income of over $300,000 a year, yet she is sick with the fear that she might become poor. She sees everything in terms of money. To her, money is the oxygen that she needs to live. Her fear is that she'll be cut off from it and die.

Daily she pores over the newspapers to see how the financial indicators are doing. She becomes depressed and anxious when she reads about inflation or recession. She rarely concerns herself with money coming in, only with money going out. To her, spending money is the only sin. Once she had to hire a painter to paint her house. After she wrote the check to the painter, she said, "Now go out and *spend* it."

She can't leave her house without being reminded that she could soon be a bag lady. When she drives her car, her eyes are riveted on the gas gauge. As it moves toward empty, she sees money disappearing. The sound of the tires on the pavement is the sound of money being spent on new tires. She imagines leaving a trail of empty oxygen containers behind her. She has constant and repeated images of herself ending up poor and helpless.

She repeatedly tells herself "what things should cost," rather than what they do cost ("Gas should be twenty-seven cents a gallon" . . . "Parking should be twenty-five cents, not two dollars an hour"). No matter how much money she accumulates, she will always remain poor and dependent. She can't see any of her assets, only her lack of financial freedom and the oxygen fading away.

When I worked in a grocery store, I saw a number of people who had problems spending their money. One fellow almost cried every time he had to buy groceries. He was continually afraid he was being cheated. Once he returned a package of toilet tissue and said he counted the number of squares and it was five short. Another time he brought a bunch of bananas up to the checkout stand without their skins. He said he didn't want to buy the skins, only the bananas inside.

Admittedly, these people are extreme cases, but many people have psychological problems with money.

Your Money Isn't You

Separate your money matters from your *self*. As long as you confuse your worth as a person with your financial worth, you'll never be economically independent. By mistakenly believing you're worth as much as you have in the bank, you'll always be insecure. Recession, inflation or a lost job can wipe out your worth as a person overnight. Don't count on money to bring you security. When you're really up against it, you have to find the security within yourself; money won't do it.

Love and Money

You're generally better off if you can separate your personal relationships and your business relationships. I've seen business and personal affairs become intertwined many times—with disastrous results. Make your business deals stand on their own, whether you make them with strangers or family. Money matters are among the most common reasons for families to fly apart and for relationships to break down.

Relying on others to support you after you've become an adult is related to this fusion of love and money. To be economically independent requires that you support yourself. Living at home after you are an adult is a common example of not being independent or master of your own fate. Getting money regularly from your parents, even if you don't live at home, is another common example of economic dependency. This helps to retard your development of independence. Your parents or other relatives may actually keep this dependency going by offering you money. It's much better for your confidence if you can say no to such offers and make it on your own.

Money and Maturity

People considered Dave to be mature. On the other hand, they considered his brother, Steve, to be immature. What do people mean when they talk about maturity? They are usually referring to a person's independence. Dave, for example, worked as a computer programmer. His boss could count on him to initiate projects and finish what he started. No matter what his job pressures were, he could always find time for his wife and kids. His mother was in her eighties and he sent her money each month.

The reason why he had to send money to his mother was because Steve had gone through her savings with one failed scheme after another. Steve worked occasionally as a food caterer, but he was a daydreamer. He dreamed mainly about how others could help him get what he wanted.

Dave was more mature because he had developed his independence. Steve was stuck at a lower level of development, waiting for others to take care of him. Dave was able to adapt to the changing demands on him. Steve wouldn't adapt or compromise. Dave gave more than he was asked to give; Steve less. People were drawn to Dave; they left him feeling warm. Steve used up people's time and energy; people felt drained after seeing him. Dave thought for himself but would bend when he saw he was wrong. With Steve someone else was always to blame for his failures.

Dave was able to earn a living. His brother Steve, however, continually asked his mother for money—usually for one of his schemes. Steve told Dave, "Mom believes in me, that's why she gives me the money." Dave thought about it for a minute and said, "No, Steve, she gives you the money because she *doesn't* believe in you. She doesn't believe you can make it without her money. If she believed in you, she wouldn't give you the money you ask for."

There is an important lesson here for parents who are continually rescuing their adult children from financial disaster. You may just be reaffirming their own helplessness. Many parents do their adult children a disservice by giving them money. They could do more for a grown child and show they believe in him or her by not sharing in the myth "Someday I'll make it big." This isn't to say that there aren't times when parents can help their children. This should, however, be an unusual event—not a predictable ritual.

Here are some guidelines for separating personal relationships from economic relationships.

• If you must borrow money from relatives or friends, pay them back with interest. Treat this as you would any other loan.

• If you lend money to friends or relatives, you should treat it as a regular loan and *ask for it back when it's due.*

• Your only reason to lend or invest money should be because you think it's good business or a solid loan.

• If you continually lend money to someone who never pays it back, quit calling it a loan and call it a gift. This will clear matters considerably.

• Family and money matters often become confused. Try to keep them separate.

• Write out formal contracts with any family business dealings, with responsibilities and accountabilities clearly spelled out.

Analogy: Coins and Calories

I find it helpful to use analogies to look at problems. An analogy —using something that is similar to something else to illustrate a point—helps you see the issues more clearly, as well as the possible solutions. Also, an analogy can help you remember what you will have to do in order to solve your problem.

Next to sex and money, people in America worry most about their weight. Money and overweight have much in common. In both cases there is a balance. When this balance shifts one way or the other, you have a problem. I'll use calories as an analogy to money. Being economically independent essentially means that you have to budget your income in order not to go over what you can spend and still be okay financially. The same applies to controlling your weight: you have to budget your calories to not go over what you can burn and still have your weight be okay.

You can have the same problems with money that you have with food.

GREED: Wanting too much without the calories or money budgeted to support it.

IMPULSIVENESS: Wanting what you want immediately ("That looks good, I think I'll get it").

COMPULSIVENESS: Mindlessly spending your calories or money.

EXCESSIVENESS: Going on binges and losing complete control and spending calories or money wildly or, in the opposite vein, being anorexic or a miser ("I can never be too rich or too thin").

POOR CHOICES: Eating empty calories or buying empty status items.

EMPTY FEELINGS: Trying to fill an empty feeling by spending calories or money (trying to feel better rather than getting better).

Treatment

The solutions to money problems or weight problems are very similar. You can start to become more economically independent by putting the following guidelines into practice.

- *Get your financial matters in order*. The first order of business is to get your financial house in order. This takes some time, but you have to do it if you want to become economically independent. In the next chapter, I'll spell out specifically how you can get out of debt.
- *Aim for steady progress*. Get-rich-quick schemes, like get-thin-quick schemes, rarely work. Even if they do work, it's hard to maintain what you achieve. Countless people in California have made a lot of money quickly on real estate. Some of them got used to a high standard of living. When real estate stopped turning over so quickly, they got stuck living in a style they couldn't maintain without real estate profits. Usually, by the time you hear how others have made a lot of money, it's too late for you to make money this way.
- *Keep track of your expenditures*. I believe it's almost impossible to lose weight if you don't keep track of how you spend your calories. The same applies to how you spend your money. You have to know exactly what's what. You need to know on a daily, weekly, monthly, and yearly basis. I recommend that you start by writing in the activity schedule how much money you spend each day. Do this for a month to give yourself an idea of where your money is going. Just the process of writing down what you spend will help you to control it.
- *Determine what your spending boundaries are*. Keep your spending within this limit. Each pay period, pay yourself first. Set aside some amount for savings—10 percent is a good figure. Then work to keep what you spend within a flexible budget. This program will pay off in many ways. One of the most important payoffs is

that you'll start to feel freer and more in control of your life. Humphrey Bogart, to keep himself independent from the big movie studios, reportedly always set some money aside for what he called the "screw you" account. This gave him greater freedom.

- *Work on both sides of the problem.* Pay attention to what you spend as well as what you earn. You need to take a two-pronged approach toward the problem, just as you do toward your weight, by both exercising and watching what you eat.

In the next chapter, I'll expand on these points.

Economic Independence Inventory

Economic dependency refers to the ability (or lack of it) to provide for your economic needs. This includes the ability to earn, manage, spend and enjoy your money. You can take the following inventory to see where you now stand in terms of economic independence.

Read each group of statements carefully. Then circle the number beside the statement that best describes you. After you have completed the questionnaire, add up all the circled numbers. Check your total with the totals given at the end of the chapter.

1. 0 I didn't miss any days from school or work in the last two weeks.
   1 I missed one day from school or work in the last two weeks.
   2 I missed several days from school or work in the last two weeks.
   3 I didn't work or go to school in the last two weeks.
2. 0 I do my work well.
   1 I do my work well but have minor problems.
   2 I need help with work.
   3 I do my work poorly most of the time.
3. 0 I don't have arguments at work or school.
   1 I usually get along well at work or school.
   2 I have had more than one argument in the last two weeks.
   3 I have many arguments at work and school.
4. 0 I never feel upset at work.
   1 Once or twice I feel upset at work.

2 I feel upset most of the time at work.
3 I feel upset all of the time.

5\. 0 My work is always interesting.
1 Occasionally my work is not interesting.
2 My work is usually boring.
3 My work is always boring.

6\. 0 I'm not afraid to take risks in my work.
1 I'm usually not afraid to take risks in my work.
2 I'm sometimes afraid to take risks in my work.
3 I'm very afraid to take risks in my work.

7\. 0 I don't explain myself or my points too much at work.
1 I sometimes explain myself or my points too much at work.
2 I often explain myself or my points too much at work.
3 I overexplain myself and my points at work.

8\. 0 I'm not excessively worried about money.
1 I worry about money occasionally.
2 I worry about money frequently.
3 I worry excessively about money.

9\. 0 I pay my bills as soon as I can.
1 I sometimes pay my bills late.
2 I often pay my bills late.
3 I always pay my bills late.

10\. 0 I keep track of my financial records.
1 My financial records are pretty much up to date.
2 I'm behind in my financial records.
3 My financial records are hopelessly incomplete.

11\. 0 I eventually pay all my bills.
1 I usually pay all my bills.
2 I occasionally don't pay a bill.
3 I don't pay my bills.

12\. 0 I don't buy things for status.
1 I sometimes buy things for status.
2 I usually buy things for status.
3 I always buy things for status.

13\. 0 I'm employed at my level of training and education.
1 I'm employed slightly below my level of training and education.
2 I'm employed below my level of training and education.
3 I'm employed very much below my level of training and education.

14. 0 I don't rely on others for my money.
    1 I sometimes rely on others for my money.
    2 I often rely on others for my money.
    3 I always rely on others for my money.
15. 0 I don't spend more than I make.
    1 I sometimes spend more than I make.
    2 I often spend more than I make.
    3 I spend more than I make.
16. 0 I've made financial plans for the future.
    1 I've made most of my financial plans for the future.
    2 I've made some financial plans for the future.
    3 I'm unable to make financial plans for the future.
17. 0 I'm not a compulsive spender.
    1 I occasionally spend compulsively.
    2 I often spend compulsively.
    3 I always spend compulsively.
18. 0 I'm not in debt.
    1 I'm slightly in debt.
    2 I'm somewhat in debt.
    3 I'm heavily in debt.
19. 0 I don't rely on others to know how to invest my money.
    1 I sometimes rely on others to know how to invest my money.
    2 I usually rely on others.
    3 I always rely on others to know how to invest my money.
20. 0 I have employable skills and services.
    1 I have some employable skills and services.
    2 I have few employable skills and services.
    3 I have no employable skills and services.
21. 0 I'm always upgrading my employable skills.
    1 I frequently upgrade my employable skills.
    2 I seldom upgrade my employable skills.
    3 I never upgrade my employable skills.
22. 0 I pay my bills on time.
    1 I have some trouble paying my bills on time.
    2 I have a great deal of trouble paying my bills on time.
    3 I can't seem to pay my bills on time.
23. 0 I'm able to balance the money coming in with the money going out.
    1 I have some trouble balancing the money coming in with the money going out.

2 I have a great deal of trouble balancing the money coming in with the money going out.
3 I can't seem to balance the money coming in with the money going out.

24. 0 I have my own source of money.
1 I provide most of my own money.
2 I provide some of my own money.
3 I count on others for all my money.

25. 0 I can manage my money independently.
1 I can manage my money but have occasionally forgotten to pay the bills or have been overdrawn at the bank.
2 I can manage day-to-day purchases but need someone to help me with banking and major purchases.
3 I can't handle my money.

26. 0 My future financial picture is in order.
1 My future financial picture is untidy.
2 My future financial picture is a mess.
3 My future financial picture is a disaster.

27. 0 I'm not in debt.
1 I'm mildly in debt.
2 I'm heavily in debt.
3 I'm bankrupt or nearly bankrupt.

RESULTS:
Score of 0–6 = high level of economic independence.
Score of 7–17 = moderate level of economic independence.
Score of 18–25 = low level of economic independence.
Score of 25 or above = severe problem with economic independence.

CHAPTER EIGHT

Economic Freedom

SOME ANTHROPOLOGISTS SAY happiness is when your work is your play. True economic freedom comes from working at a job you like, one that provides the income you can comfortably live with. Getting the right job is a process or group of skills that you can learn.

An example of how to use this process was Pat's attempt to get a job at the Philadelphia Zoo. She had worked at the Omaha Zoo, so when we moved to Philadelphia, she called the zoo and asked if there were any openings for a zookeeper. The person on the other end said that there were almost never openings and, besides, there was a waiting list of other zoo people for any openings. She learned from other sources that women were rarely hired there as zookeepers.

She decided not to pursue the matter and went to work at the University of Pennsylvania as a secretary. After two years, she had become quite bored. In the meantime, I had had some experience running a job-finding program at a local community college. We decided to put the principles I'd learned in practice to see if Pat could get a job at the Philadelphia Zoo.

She called the zoo and was told again that there were no openings and a long waiting list. This time she insisted that she wanted to come in anyway and fill out an application. Before she went into the zoo she did some research. She called and asked the name of the person who was supervisor of the zookeepers. She also made up a resumé that highlighted her work at the Omaha Zoo. She moved the "Personal Interests" section of her resumé—hobbies, interests and travels—up to the top, rather than leaving it at the bottom.

The personnel manager perfunctorily took her application and said it would be kept on file. Pat was prepared for this and asked if she could talk to the zookeepers' supervisor, calling him by name. The personnel man said, "Well, if you want to come back this afternoon, you can see him."

The supervisor didn't seem thrilled to talk to her, but she gave him her resumé. He quickly glanced at it and saw that she had traveled a great deal in Africa. He was interested in the game reserves and animals there. Pat started talking about the different animals she had seen and how exciting it had been to observe them from a small plane flying over Victoria Falls. This led the interview into the realm of a personal relationship and away from the coldness of a job interview.

Realizing that he cared deeply about animals, she directed the interview toward her experience in animal care. She brought up some of the reasons why she believes women make good zookeepers. The theme of her interview was the importance of taking good care of the animals. He seemed impressed but said that there weren't any openings. He said he would keep her in mind.

A couple of days after the interview, she sent him a follow-up note. She included a photo of herself holding a baby gorilla she'd helped raise while working in the Omaha Zoo nursery.

Two weeks later, she gave him a call. No news. She had to force herself to call him a month later. This time he said, in effect, "Don't call me, I'll call you." She was very discouraged. Then, a couple of days later, he called and said there was an opening. Pat was hired and worked at the Philadelphia Zoo for the next two years.

Getting a Job

Again, to be economically independent means that you live *below* your standard of living. This is what gives you a feeling of economic freedom. In addition to controlling your spending, you can work to increase your earnings or the potential for earnings.

This might be getting a new job, being promoted on your present job, working for yourself, learning new skills, going back to school or getting involved in volunteer work that may later lead to a salaried position.

Most of your options can be boiled down to *getting a job.* The "job" may be volunteering, being accepted at a graduate school or getting a different position at the same place you're working now. Most people have little experience in getting jobs, even though they may have had several. Your lack of job-finding experience can make you feel helpless and vulnerable when you look for work.

Using the skills I've learned, I've taught a number of people how to get jobs. The process isn't that difficult. Once you've learned a few basic principles and put them into practice, you'll find the job of getting a job is manageable.

If you are looking for a job—again, a job might be a school or program you want to join—here are some suggestions you can follow. Most of them were developed by Dr. Nathan Azrin, a clinical psychologist.

- *Make finding a job a priority.* Often when you don't have a job others will see you as someone to take care of busywork ("Ralph's not working, he can wait for the Sears man and do the errand"). When you're on a job search, you have to see this as your present commitment or job. You have to tell everyone around you that this is what you're going to be doing, and nothing else. Then put time each day into this search.
- *Be systematic in your job search.* Get a notebook so that you can keep a record of your contacts. Write down the names of people you've contacted, when you plan to get in touch with them for a follow-up and anyone else that they refer you to. List in one section people you plan to get in touch with and possible leads. Keeping this record will give you a sense that you're accomplishing something.
- *Personalize your approach.* Dr. Azrin has found that getting a job is a personal affair. People hire people. You want to establish a personal relationship with the potential employer; you do this by revealing your personal traits. To help you do this, move the interests and hobbies that are usually at the end of the resumé to

the top. The potential employer is likely to relate to you because he plays the guitar too or because you both like to play tennis. You want the prospective employer to see you as a person.

• *Use references to the fullest.* When Pat gave her resumé to the supervisor, she included two open letters of recommendation. One was from an employer who talked about her as a person; the other was from her supervisor at the Omaha Zoo. Usually references are asked for after the person has decided to hire you; at that point they don't affect the interview. You'll find it's much more helpful to offer open letters of recommendation during the interview.

When you leave a job, ask for an open letter of recommendation ("To whom it may concern"). This way you'll be sure your old boss is giving you a good recommendation. If he or she won't do this, it's a good idea not to use him as a reference. The "To whom it may concern" letters can be from past employers, or people who know you from other areas—maybe you know a member of the city council, or a minister. If the person is well known, it's better. You may have trouble getting yourself to ask for an open letter of recommendation, but most people will be glad to write one for you.

Ask him or her to make the letter as personal as possible, including items that make you more interesting ("Linda played on the tennis team and loves to write poetry"). Also, ask for a description of you as a person as well as what you've done ("Linda is conscientious and can work independently").

• *Generate as many interviews as possible.* The key to getting a job is in generating a large number of interviews. You do this by making at least ten phone calls a day and obtaining leads from friends, relatives, past employers, advertisements and employment agencies. If you get enough interviews, you'll eventually get a job.

• *Decide how you're going to take aim.* In Pat's job campaign she used the rifle approach. She took aim at one specific job and worked all-out at getting it. At other times a scatter gun approach is better. Here you try for many different jobs—even ones that you normally wouldn't look for. You usually find that the drawbacks that had previously kept you from considering a job can be overcome—you can learn the skill you don't know; you can join a car pool to get to the job that's now too far away; the position may have benefits that balance out a lower salary.

• *Learn to have an effective interview.* You want to present yourself at the interview in the best possible light. To prepare for the interview, do some research about the position. If possible, try to get a resumé of the person interviewing you. You often can get this from the public relations or personnel division of the employer.

You want to show interest and enthusiasm. Be prompt and greet the interviewer by name. Don't criticize your past employers. Pay attention to how you walk into the room and sit down, how you're dressed, and how you fill out the application. The employer is asking himself "Does this person really want this job?" You want to present an image that says yes. During the interview, magnify your achievements; this is no time for humility. Don't lie, but don't bring up your deficits. I often role-play with people looking for a job and I'm amazed at how often they bring up their ulcers or how they had a drinking problem in the past, or a police record.

Getting a job is a sophisticated form of bragging; an interview is one time when you want to magnify your accomplishments.

• *Map out the territory of the interview.* The best overall strategy is to ask the interviewer early in the interview exactly what the company is looking for. After you have this information you can tailor your answers to it.

• *Always conduct yourself as if you are determined to get the job you are discussing.* Never close the door to opportunity, even if it sounds as if you don't want the job offered. It's better to be in a position where you can choose from a number of jobs rather than only one.

• *Ask for the position if you are interested.* Ask for the next interview if the situation demands. If the position is offered to you and you want it, accept on the spot. If you need some time to think it over, be courteous and tactful in asking for that time. Set a definite time when you can provide an answer.

• *Have some questions ready.* Usually an interviewer will ask, "Do you have any questions?" during an interview. Some questions you might ask are about plans for company growth and room for creativity. Don't ask about salary or benefits at the first interview. If you are offered the job, you can then ask. When you answer questions, don't just answer yes or no. Explain and tell what about you relates to the job. Remember to thank the person for the interview.

• *Work on building up your self-image.* Success leads to success because a boss wants to hire people who have been successful before. So you have to present a successful image. Tell people what you did in your last job ("I set up a tourist project in my hometown"), tell people what you learned from it (". . . how to organize the community business people and volunteers and how to administer an annual budget of . . ."), and what others thought of it (". . . my system was used as a model for the neighboring city").

• *Don't try to be responsible for an interviewer's choice to hire you or not*. The sole purpose of an interview is to sell yourself. However, psychologically it's better to reverse the strategy. Rather than worrying whether the interviewer likes you, concentrate more on liking the person doing the interview. If you can like the person, he or she probably will like you.

• *Know yourself*. One of the reasons for making a resumé is so that you can be more exact about who you are and what you enjoy doing. Ask yourself, "What do I do best?" One way to help you find this out is to write yourself a letter of recommendation in which you list all of your strengths and interests.

• *Follow up*. Follow up each interview. A good way is to send a note. In it you can enclose other ideas or material you want the interviewer to see. Stress in the follow-up note or phone call that you want and can do the job. If you learn you've been turned down, you can call back and see what the reason was; you also might ask for a referral to another place. Many people fail to do the follow-up.

Finding Leads. Your key to getting interviews is referrals; you want to work as hard for referrals as you do for jobs. People who seem to be lucky are the ones who have developed a network of connections. You need this spider's web approach to get good job leads. Contact anyone who might be a source of information—relatives, friends, business acquaintances, members of clubs and other organizations you belong to. Get out your school yearbook and address book. Remember, people tend to hire friends and relatives more frequently than strangers, so don't discount them as a source for contacts.

One of the best ways to get an interview is to get in touch with the possible employer personally. When you do, consider the following:

- Use the phone rather than the mail.
- Ask for an interview rather than for a job.
- Explain why you should have an interview.
- Follow through on your contacts.
- If the person you talk to says there's no opening, ask if you can fill out an application anyway and if he or she knows of any other opening. If yes, ask if you can say you heard about it from him.
- Get a group of friends together, if possible, and form an informal job-hunting club.
- Set up a game plan: you're either calling to try to set up interviews or you're going for interviews. You're doing either one or the other.

You definitely do need to concern yourself with the preceding ideas as you look for a job. Here are some concerns you can forget about.

- *Shame.* You may feel ashamed because you don't have a job. Keep in mind that shame is a self-created feeling. Because you choose to feel shame, you can choose not to feel shame. What's inherently shameful about being out of work? This is just a fact—your shame is a needless evaluation you place on the fact. You'll be much better off by giving up this shame. To overcome it you can use the ACT formula: accept that you don't have a job; choose to be independent by looking for a job; take action by advertising, not hiding, the fact that you're looking for a job.
- *Hopelessness.* Keep in mind that you don't have enough evidence about the future to be hopeless. You can't know how your job search will turn out. Your best strategy is not to expect that any one contact will lead to a job but to assume that if you keep at it, you'll eventually get a job. Keep your expectations low and your motivation high.
- *Rejection.* Feeling that you're being rejected when you don't get a job is a common problem. You have to turn this notion of rejection around. Rather than seeing this as a personal affront, turn it into a game. See job hunting as a game of collecting no's. The more you collect, the more likely you are to get the job you want.
- *False positives.* When you're looking for a job, you often make two mistakes. First, when an interview goes well, you assume that

you'll be hired and stop looking (it was a false positive). If it doesn't come through, you then have trouble gearing up for the job hunt again.

• *True negatives.* The second mistake is to become discouraged and stop looking when an interview goes badly and it turns out that you didn't get the job. The solution for both of these mistakes is to normalize your response to an interview no matter how it goes. Focus on the process rather than on the outcome of any one interview, and keep looking.

Volunteer Work

Doing volunteer work can be a rewarding and useful first step to getting into the job market. If you do volunteer work and expect something in return, you should be explicit in what you want in return for your labor. Two problems often arise when you volunteer your labor. First, you can try to exploit the employer and this often causes resentment. I personally would never have anyone work for me for "nothing." I've found that when people tell me this, they usually try to take more from me than if I paid them. Because of this widespread problem, many people have a policy of never taking on someone who would work for "free."

The second problem is that when you volunteer the labor the other person will exploit you and not give you what was implied by the agreement (the training, supervision, meaningful experience). To overcome both problems, draw up a contract or letter of agreement. In the agreement, explicitly spell out what the exchange is ("I will be volunteering four hours daily in exchange for training on the word processor"). This helps to clear the air and set matters straight from the beginning.

Being Your Own Boss

If instead of looking for a job, you're going into business for yourself, be sure to guard your economic independence. The most common failure of small businesses is dependency. Don't become overly dependent on a few workers, partners, distributors, a few customers or product lines. Dependency on a few means that if they fail, you fail.

Whatever your skill or talent, keep in mind that *having* talent isn't enough. You must also have the skill to market your talent. In Los Angeles, there are countless numbers of talented people trying to make it in the music, movie and TV businesses. I always recommend to them that they spend as much time learning how to market their talent as they do on how to improve their talent.

Moving Up

Suppose you're now working for someone else and want to advance. The secret is to work at becoming more independent. Don't ask "What can you do for me?" but "What can I do for you?" After you start working on this principle, you can expect to be rewarded. This will get you ahead faster than anything else.

The key to advancing on your job is to increase your response- or choice-ability. The greater the range of responses you're able to make, the more valuable you become. You increase your choice-ability by getting more experience. This is why changing jobs after you've learned one, either within the same company or to a different company, is the best way to increase your choice-ability. After you've mastered a job, move up to the next level. You probably won't have to work any harder but you'll make more money and have greater choice-ability.

Balancing Spending and Earning

One of the ways you can learn to live within your means is to spend less. Overspending often is a form of economic dependency. The following are some ways you can start to live within your means.

Enrichment Through Simplicity. You can cut down on your expenses by choosing to live a more simple life. A simpler life can offer you a much freer existence. Many people are choosing to do this. Duane Elgin writes about voluntary simplicity. It's "a manner of living that is outwardly more simple and inwardly more rich; an integrative way of living that balances both inner and outer aspects of our lives; a deliberate choice to live with less in the belief that more of life will be returned to us in the process; a path toward consciously learning the skills that enable us to touch the work ever more lightly and gently." This is not a prescription for poverty but a choice to live life with less clutter and fewer complications.

Here are some ways you can start to make your life simpler and easier to manage.

• *Don't buy purely for status.* I know a man who has worked in the wholesale clothing business for over fifty years. He says, "Designer clothes are really a fraud. They're ordinary clothes that manufacturers sew their labels into and then up the price 100 percent. People who wear them are trying to become nobility. The joke is that there is no real difference in the clothes." If you want to lead a simple and free life, don't buy clothes, furniture or other merchandise to impress others. Rather, buy items that are durable, practical and comfortable.

• *Don't buy for the sake of change.* You may buy something because you think a new, more advanced model is better. Often, however, you end up with features that don't work, that are more likely to break down, or that are too sophisticated for your skills or wants.

I once had a camera I loved. I traded it in on a more advanced model of the same brand. The new camera had many fancy features. But somehow it never took as good a picture as the more simple one, and it often had to be repaired.

• *Remember that less is more.* Often when you try to buy more, you end up with less. You may think because one boat is fun, two would be better. You usually can get more satisfaction out of less. Once you get too much stuff you don't have time to use it all. You can get more satisfaction out of one product you really like than out of many products.

• *Make "use" the reason for purchase.* If you can't use products, they have little value. As Ari Kiev has noted, "The accumulation of wealth or possessions which cannot be used is not worth the sacrifices required. Whatever you can use has value. If you can't use something, find out whether someone else might use it. This will prove far more satisfying than you ever imagined."

Don't buy what you can't use. You can live a freer and easier life by selling or giving away the possessions you don't use. For example, go through your closet and get rid of all of the clothes you never wear. You can do the same with your tools, books, furniture, and so forth. This can be a liberating experience.

You may be like a pendulum: you believe that you can't live without something (a hot tub, dune buggy, snowmobile), then, after you buy the item, the pendulum swings and you quickly become bored with your new toy. This is replaced by another item you believe you must have to be happy and fulfilled. What items stuck away in your closet or garage fits this description? You can save yourself a great deal of distress by not giving into your urge to buy this type of product.

• *Celebrate holidays and anniversaries in less materialistic ways.* One of the ways you can lead a simpler and less stressful life is to put more emphasis on human giving and less on materialistic giving. You can give some of your own possessions to someone rather than buying new gifts for them. You can also give of your time. One mother at Christmas time gives personal gift certificates ("One favorite dinner" . . . "One day's outing with mother to wherever you choose"). Giving of your time and self is usually much more satisfying than giving of material goods.

• *Rent or buy used what you don't often need.* A good policy is to buy the best product for heavy and regular use. If you live on a farm and cut wood for your heating, you might want to buy the best chain saw you can afford. However, for items you don't use a lot, you might want to rent or buy them used. If you only occasionally saw lumber, you'd be better off renting a saw or buying it used.

• *Question what your motivations are for wanting an item.* For example, you may not want the item primarily for use. The major reason why people buy kitchen gadgets is to learn how they work. We have a kitchen full of electrical gadgets—a peanut butter machine, crepe pan, electric knife, doughnut maker, electric wok. We buy them at yard sales for a few dollars. Usually, we use them only once or twice to see how they work and then put them away. Occasionally, one even turns out to be useful.

• *Simplify transportation.* One of the ways that you learn to live within your means is to simplify your transportation. Join a car pool, learn to use buses and subways, move closer to your job, walk more. See if you can do more of your work at home.

• *Eat more simply.* Almost half of all meals in America are eaten out. You can simplify your life and save money if you eat at home. You may think it's easier to eat out, but in spent time and money, it usually isn't.

Pat and I used to eat out every night after work. We would come home and try to decide where to eat ("What do you feel like" . . . "I'm tired of Italian" . . . "I like the food there, but remember the bad service"). Then we would go to a restaurant, wait to be served and then wait to pay. Most evenings it was 7 P.M. before the dinner ritual was over.

We now almost always eat at home. We prepare quick and simple dinners of salad, steamed vegetables and meat or fish. Often we have something waiting for us in the crockpot. We are not only saving money, we now have at least an extra hour each evening. Another bonus is the increased closeness found in working together as a family preparing the meal, sitting around the table chatting, and quickly doing up the dishes together. Our two-year-old son is much happier eating at home, and he likes to help set the table and do the dishes.

• *Become an informed consumer.* The market today, as much as ever, is one of "Let the buyer beware." You need to investigate and find out the truth about products you're interested in. You can do this by reading consumer magazines, and above all by asking a lot of questions. If you can't get yourself to do this, the next best strategy is to ask someone who does like to do research. For example, if you're going to buy a refrigerator and you don't want to take the time to shop around and investigate the products, ask someone who likes to do this sort of investigation and ask for his or her opinion.

Merchandise That Doesn't Work. To be economically independent you have to avoid being ripped off, and not buy merchandise that doesn't work. Some categories of products traditionally don't work. Each category appeals to a certain desire of yours.

• *Wishful spending.* You may waste your money on wishful spending. Some examples are pouring cans of antileak agent into a radiator with a leak the size of a dime; pouring cans of drain openers down a completely stopped-up drain; trying to control a heavy infestation of bugs with a spray can of insecticide; trying to remove a bad stain from a suede coat with stain remover. Such efforts are nearly always futile and a waste of money. At times, wishful spending can have an effect opposite to the one you desire. The makeup you wear to hide your age may actually accent it; most people overestimate the age of a woman wearing a lot of makeup.

• *False hope.* While there's slim chance that your wishful spending may bring about what you want, there's almost no chance when you buy false hope products. Many of these products have to do with your body. These products promise to cure baldness, enlarge breasts, remove wrinkles or cure incurable diseases and ailments.

• *Magical aids.* Another way to waste your money is to spend it on magic. Products that, as advertised, seem too good to be true, usually are. One of my rules is never to buy a gadget shown on television with the word "magic": magic glue, magic salad makers, magic pots and pans, magic hand-held sewing machines. Such gimmicks are truly magical. They always work on television but never at home. For example, I once bought a magic tape measure on a stick. You're supposed to run the stick across the floor to get the measurement. The probiem is that it's impossible to walk across a room in a completely straight line. One exception is my cousin Mary Lou Long, who sells a facial called "Magic Mud" that really does work.

• *Instant success.* Products and services that offer you instant success rarely pay off. The degree of success offered is inversely related to what you get. The more offered, the less you get. This includes courses in speed reading, acting, writing, modeling, broadcast announcing and financial investing that promise automatic successful careers. There usually are no shortcuts to success, but many people are more than happy to feed you the illusion that there are. They leave you chained to installment payments and deeper in a credit hole.

• *Shortcuts to self-control.* Another group of products and services that rarely work and that can keep you broke are the ones that offer you simple, painless solutions to self-control problems. The classic examples are weight-loss aids. New ones hit the market every day—wrapping yourself in a rubber suit, pills, diets, exercise machines, gym contracts and weight-loss contracts. Such types of products and services can also be found for smoking and drinking problems. In nearly all of the cases the money you spend won't buy you what you need—to do for yourself.

Psychological Spending. You can learn to manage your money much better by learning to overcome the psychological problems associated with the spending. You can apply principles and methods used to become emotionally independent to your problems with money. The following are some of the areas in which, by managing your psychological problems better, you can better manage your money.

• *Assertiveness.* Much of your problem in managing your money is probably related to not being able to say no and not being able to ask for what is yours. Nonassertiveness, masquerading as nonchalance, may cause you not to ask for what you want. For example, you can negotiate for most services you buy and many of the products you use. You just have to give the person a reason why he or she should charge you less (professional courtesy, special circumstances, long-time patronage). By being afraid to speak up, you cost yourself money. You'll find that by speaking up and by saying no, your financial situation can turn around. You may have to endure some discomfort, but in the long run this more than pays for itself.

• *Impulsivity.* Your problem may be that you impulsively buy products you don't need and may not want. This may be a specific and limited problem (you buy pets impulsively) or it may be a pervasive problem. To overcome this, you'll need to learn ways to postpone gratification.

Repeatedly question your thinking that you have to have something right away ("Where's the evidence that I need it? Will I die without it? Am I simply being immature?").

Write down on a 3" x 5" card all of those items that you bought impulsively in the past and didn't really want. Then put this card in your wallet. Look at it before you buy.

Find someone else with this problem or someone who will help you with it, and agree to talk to this person before you buy.

Don't give salespeople who phone or come to your house a chance to get into their sales pitch.

Give yourself a waiting period before you buy something you think you want.

Return merchandise you realize you don't want. You usually have forty-eight hours after you've signed a contract to change your mind.

Avoid places like shopping malls, where you might impulsively spend money.

Practice saying no. Go to places where you would normally spend money impulsively—and don't.

• *Compulsiveness.* Alice compulsively bought shoes. She had hundreds of pairs. Most of them she never wore and kept in boxes. You may have some item that you feel compelled to buy. This may range from cars and boats to land. This excess spending can cause you a great deal of distress (and divorce); compulsive spenders usually deal with this distress by going out and spending more money.

The treatment for any form of compulsion is *response prevention.* You have to set up a situation where you're prevented from giving in to the compulsion. Alice, the woman who had the compulsion to buy shoes, had to leave her money and charge cards at home when she went out. Not spending the money will cause you great discomfort, but if you don't give in to this urge, the discomfort will go away. And if you continue to not give into the urge, the urge will eventually go away.

• *Self-treatment.* You may overspend money as a way to make yourself feel better. Robert is a good illustration of this problem. He couldn't tolerate feeling any negative or boring feelings. He always had to have some excitement to make himself feel better. His marriage ended because he continually got himself into debt. He would go on vacations and run up his credit cards whenever he started getting depressed. This gave him momentary relief but it always worsened his situation.

You can learn to control your moods with ways other than spending money. To prove to yourself that spending doesn't make you feel any better, you can run an experiment. Rate your mood 0–100 before you go out to spend money; then rate it again right after spending money; and take a third rating after some time has elapsed. You'll probably find the initial good mood will give way to even worse feelings. Then repeat the experiment without spending the money. You'll find you feel better in the long run. Attempts to make yourself feel better through outside sources usually backfire. A much better strategy is to work from the inside. Your attempts to make yourself feel secure or worthwhile by spending money on yourself often end up making you feel worse.

Underindulgence. The problems with dependence come in opposites. The opposite of the person who overspends is the person who underspends on himself or herself. Irene almost never bought herself any new clothes. She felt extremely guilty whenever she spent anything on herself. Luxury items such as massages or vacations were completely out of the question. The problem wasn't lack of money. She would spend money freely on others and give herself permission to buy what she "needed," such as a new car. She, however, wouldn't buy a new car just because she wanted one. She also freely gave gifts to her friends, husband, parents and children; but she would rarely buy anything for herself. If you have this form of economic dependency, the following are some steps you can take.

- Accept that taking care of yourself in a loving way is good mental health.
- Accept that if you discount yourself economically, you'll end up discounting yourself in other areas.
- Accept that if you discount yourself, others are more likely to discount you.
- Accept that, to you, you're the most important person who ever lived (see chapter 16 for further discussion).
- Accept uncomfortable feelings about spending money on yourself.
- Own your own money. Continually remind yourself, "It's my money, I can do what I want with it." Irene told herself, "I'm now a grown person and I can freely choose to spend money on myself."
- Choose to be independent of your old beliefs about what is "right" about spending money on yourself.
- For ten days in a row buy yourself a small present. Irene would buy a lipstick, beauty soap or earrings.
- Start a savings fund to blow on yourself and then buy yourself something extra nice. Irene saved ten dollars each payday for six months—then bought herself an expensive nightgown she would never have bought before.
- Expect to fall back into the old rut of putting yourself last. When you find yourself back in this position, repeat the ten-day program of self-giving.

Multiply Your Independence

By becoming more economically independent you can learn to live on less money. This, in turn, will allow you to become even more independent. Here are some ways that you can decrease your spending by increasing your independence.

- *Pay your bills promptly*. Procrastination on anything is a sign of dependency. Accept that the bill is there. Choose to be independent by taking action to pay it. I've found that most financially successful people pay their bills on time. Cause or effect? They tell me that they did this even before they had a lot of money. By paying your bills promptly, you avoid ending up with bills that have become so high you can't afford to pay them and you also avoid paying the late charges.
- *Be self-reliant with money itself*. Find out about banking—the language and the ins and outs. Don't depend on others to tell you what's the best way to use money. See money as a commodity that you buy and sell.
- *Learn personal skills that lead to greater financial independence*. You can learn to do many of the jobs that you now pay high-priced experts to do. If you have to hire an expert, do it in an independent way. If you have to see an accountant, write out what your goals are and do a rough draft of what you want done. By knowing what is going on, you'll save yourself money in the long run.
- *Repair and maintain your possessions*. One of the ways to become more independent is to keep your possessions well maintained. When something breaks down, repair it right away. Every day you put off repairing something it becomes more difficult to do so.
- *Be honest*. Most people are dishonest because they don't believe in themselves. By being more honest, you'll be more independent and usually ahead of the game financially. Most people who are taken by con artists are engaged in some form of quiet dishonesty.
- *Keep your financial goals and plans to yourself*. Talking too much about your financial goals to others takes the energy and steam out of them.

Financial Housekeeping

If you want to stay economically independent, you have to stay organized. Not knowing where you stand with your money is both a symptom and a cause of economic dependency. If you have no true idea of how your money comes and goes, you're not alone. This is a common problem for many people. You don't keep books, and end up in a bad patch because you don't know where you stand.

To get organized financially, you'll need two items: a notebook and a file box. You can buy a cardboard file box that includes folders and tabs at a drugstore or stationery store.

Notebook. You'll use the notebook to record all of your financial information in one place. Pretend that you will be living out of the country for a year and you need to give all this information to the person who'll be taking care of your financial interests. This will take you a while—but persist in getting all of this information down on paper. Your efforts will more than pay you back in saved time and energy in the future. Also, preparing this notebook will give you a great sense of control over your finances.

Important People. Label the first section of your notebook "Important people in my financial life." Write down their names, addresses and telephone numbers (work and home), their roles in your financial affairs and, if known, their social security numbers. This list might include the following: yourself, family members with whom you have financial dealings, persons to notify in case of emergency, guardians of your children in case of death, executor of will, employer, employees, accountant, business manager, tax consultant, lawyer, broker, banker, creditors, landlord, mortgage holder, insurance agent and anyone else that you can think of.

This section of your notebook will allow you to find at a moment's notice people you may need to contact for your financial matters. This will also show you how many people you have in your financial world.

Location of Important Papers. In the second section of your notebook, list your important papers and where they're located. This is a first step toward organizing most of your important papers in your file box. You may want to keep some of the papers in other places, such as in a bank safety deposit box. Write down specifically where the papers are located. List the following important papers along with their location: will, deeds, mortgage papers, marriage or divorce papers, military service discharge papers, passport, rental agreements, insurance policies, loan papers, birth and death certificates, warrantees or guarantees, car registrations, loan papers, stocks, bonds, contracts, tax returns and anything else you can think of.

This list will help you centralize your important papers and make handling business transactions much smoother.

Important Information. In the third section of your notebook you should list information that you need in order to make financial decisions. Include all charge card numbers and the hot line to call if they are lost or stolen. Also list driver's license numbers, social security numbers, names and addresses of insurance companies and policy numbers, serial numbers of valuable items, car license number, list of debts owed you, details of pension plan, credit union accounts, list of assets, bank and trust accounts, health insurance name and number, business licenses names and numbers and anything else you can think of.

Getting all this information together may take you several days, but it can be the first step in becoming economically independent for once and for all. One warning: unless you're committed to following through on it, don't start. Starting and not finishing will make you feel less in control of your finances.

By getting all of this information and recording it in your notebook, you will be taking concrete steps toward becoming more economically independent. Make sure that you periodically update this information.

File Box. I've often suggested to people that they buy a file box in which to keep their financial records. Those who have done this have said that they feel a much greater sense of being in control. When you have your bills and papers stuck around in various drawers and boxes, you feel disconnected. By spending the time to organize yourself, you'll find your financial situation will start to come together.

You can file your papers in a variety of ways. I'll suggest just one of the ways you can do it. First, label folders by category: house, car, work, utilities, insurance, and so forth. Then put all the important papers that relate to each category in its folder.

Have one folder labeled "Bills to pay." As the bills come in place them in the folder, or sit right down and send a check. After you pay a bill, put the statement stub into the appropriate folder. You'll find it helpful to make a note on the bottom of the stub showing the amount of the payment, the number of your check, and the date you mailed it. The day your canceled check comes in, you can put it in the folder or keep it with the other canceled checks in numerical order. Label another folder "Income taxes" and put all receipts and records related to filing taxes in this folder.

Credit Rating. You also need to know where you stand in terms of your credit rating. To find this out you could call your local reporting bureaus. For a small fee they will send you a credit report. After you get the report, check it for accuracy and make sure that joint credit accounts are reported in both your names. A credit bureau has ninety days to respond to any inaccuracies you write them about.

In case you have little or no credit, it is a good idea to establish some. If your husband has credit and you don't, put the utilities or phone in your name. You can also take out a small loan, which you promptly repay, and thus establish credit.

In the Poor House

You may find yourself deeply in debt. Being in debt is a relative matter—one patient owed $800 to a couple of creditors and worried constantly about being heavily in debt. Another patient owed several hundred thousand dollars, with no means to pay it back, and he considered it a temporary cash-flow problem. While many people go through occasional periods of debt, others have serious problems. They are in a sense "debt-aholics" and are constantly in debt. You can take this quiz to see if this applies to you.

1. Have you had a problem on a job because of debts (garnisheed wages, too many advances on salary)? YES __ NO __
2. Have your debt problems led to a divorce or separation? YES __ NO __
3. Do your debt problems interfere with your daily life (you don't answer the phone because of the bill collectors)? YES __ NO __
4. Do your family members talk to you about your debt problems? YES __ NO __
5. Do your friends talk to you about your debt problems? YES __ NO __
6. Have you ever declared bankruptcy? YES __ NO __
7. Do you often feel you've lost control of your debts? YES __ NO __
8. Have you ever sought counseling for your debt problems? YES __ NO __

If you answer yes to two or more of these questions, you could well be a "debt-aholic" and psychologically addicted to being in debt.

Getting Out of Debt. The first question you must ask yourself is "What are the reasons for my being in debt right now?" Unless you can discover the reasons and take steps to alleviate the cause, you're very likely to be in debt again. The following are some of the more common reasons why people choose to get into debt.

• *A way to avoid choice-ability.* You may use debt as a form of self-control. Paul, for example, was deeply in debt. He said he hated his job but had to stay there and wasn't able to open his own business because of his debt. The problem was that he always managed to take on another big debt just as he was starting to see himself clear to start his own business. As long as he was in debt he didn't have the money to put where his mouth was.

If this is your situation, you have to be honest with yourself and make the choice to get out of debt to do the thing you're avoiding (traveling, going back to school, moving, leaving home).

• *Buying friends.* When I was in the second grade, I moved to a new school. I was very lonely. I couldn't seem to fit in or make any friends. I started using my lunch money to buy candy to give to the other kids so they would like me. I quickly saw that they didn't like me, but the candy I was giving away.

Many people with debt problems have learned this lesson. They push money into others or gravitate toward people (friends and relatives) who will exploit them by continually borrowing money. This may come in the form of investing in their projects or helping them out in various ways.

To overcome this problem, accept that you're trying to buy love and choose to be independent from this behavior. If you have taught others to come to you for money and gifts, you can expect them not to believe you when you say no. However, if you choose to, you can stick to your position and tolerate the discomfort of saying no repeatedly. You needn't blame them and you don't have to respond to their attempts to persuade you that this time is special. You don't buy real friends and real lovers.

• *Poor judgment.* You may have a serious debt problem because of poor judgment. You may invest your money in cocoa bean futures and in swamps in Florida. This may be due to gullibility (you believe whatever others tell you) or greed (you want to believe what others tell you). The solution is to develop your intellectual independence. You can use the solutions outlined in chapters 14 and 15 to help you solve this problem.

Many people who make a lot of money are able to see into the future a little easier than the rest of us—they can see beyond the headlights. Others have rearview mirror vision—they jump into the rising market just before it drops. If you have this type of vision, don't engage in rickety financial investments; instead, take a more conservative approach.

Ten Steps to Getting Out of Debt

Being in debt can make you feel even more helpless and dependent. If you are continually receiving overdue notices and phone calls from creditors, chances are you probably feel less than an adult. No matter how good you are at what you do in your profession, debt can make you doubt your worth.

Above all, remember that you are not your debt. You are you.

Debt is only one aspect of your life and it can be controlled by you. Here are ten steps to getting out of debt.

Accept the Reality of the Situation. Choose to set up a reasonable budget and stick to it. Know how much money comes in and how much money goes out. If you are not single, decide as a couple that you are going to work together to get out of debt. If you can't agree on this, seek help from a third party (counselor, clergy, financial counselor).

Acceptance is tremendously important. You are in debt because you have not accepted some realities about money—how much you have and how much you can afford to spend. You will find that living within the confines of a budget is liberating.

Put Away All Credit Cards. You can give them to a friend to keep. You can put them in a safety deposit box. You can cut them up. Do whatever you need to do in order not to use them anymore. Accept that you abused your credit card privileges. You probably considered them instant money. Because you had the card in your pocket, you thought you could afford to buy the dress or the couch, or the plane trip to Hawaii. Remember, everything you purchase has to be paid for eventually in cash. Until you learn to live within a budget, put the credit cards out of sight and out of reach. Don't tempt yourself.

Make a "Payback" List and a "One-Time-Needs" List. On your payback list, write down everyone to whom you owe money. Number one on the list is the place to which you owe the least amount of money. Number two is the place to which you owe the next smallest amount of money and so on down the line. As you begin to pay off bills, you will pay off the smallest first and so on.

Make a list of one-time things you know you will be needing. For example, your car may need new tires. Or your child may need dental work. Put them in order of greatest need first. As new needs arise, put them in the proper place on your list.

As you accumulate extra money, attack number one on your payback list, then number one on your one-time-needs list. Next, attack number two on your payback list, then number two on your one-time-needs list.

Examples of a payback list and a one-time-needs list are in *table 1* (p. 149).

Set Up a Budget. Write down all your monthly expenses. Be realistic. You may wish that your monthly electric bill were $10. But if you find that it regularly runs between $25 and $35, put down $35.

Be sure to include entertainment in the budget. You will do activities for yourself anyway, like going to the movies, eating out or buying a book. Therefore, allow for this in your budget from the beginning. If you don't, you will open the door to cheating on your budget and the more you cheat, the easier it is to cheat. A reasonable amount for entertainment for a couple trying to get out of debt is $125 a month. A couple I know divides this down the middle and each gets an allowance of $62.50. However you handle your entertainment money, do include it in the budget. It is easier to stick to a budget if you are enjoying life at the same time.

An example of a budget can be seen in table 1.

Every Time You Get a Paycheck, Choose to Pay Your Bills. If you are paid weekly, pay your bills weekly. If you are paid biweekly, pay your bills biweekly.

For example, if you owe $25 a month on your credit card and are paid weekly, every time you get a paycheck, write out a check for $6.25 and put it in an envelope marked "credit card." When the bill comes due, you will have $25 to pay it. Either send in all the little checks (they won't care) or cancel them out and write one big check.

If you are paid monthly, sit down and pay your bills as soon as you are paid. You begin to think you have a lot of money in your pocket if you don't take care of the bills first.

Write Down All Sources of Income and Take Appropriate Steps If Your Income Is Less Than Your Monthly Expenses. Your budget won't work unless your income equals your monthly expenses. After you make up your budget, you will know how much income you need to bring in. If you are short, there are a number of options you can choose.

- Call your creditors and ask if they will take a smaller amount per month until you are able to pay more. Make sure they know you have every intention of paying. Most creditors simply want to know that you are honest and intend to meet your debt. Most of them want to work with you.
- Take a weekend part-time job. You will be working hard, but remember, an end is in sight and you're working for a cause—to get out of debt.
- Look for a new, higher-paying job. If you do get a higher-paying job, don't think you suddenly have money to burn. You must live frugally until you get out of debt and then you must live wisely.
- Look into job advancement or the possibility of a raise.
- Look into jobs you can do on your own time, such as direct selling, typing in your home, and so forth.

Set Up a "Payback" Savings Account. You need to set up a savings account at your bank. This account is where you put extra money that will eventually be used to pay back your bills or meet your one-time needs. For example, if you budgeted $35 for your electricity bill and your monthly bill only came to $30, put the extra $5 in the account. When you have accumulated enough in the account, pay off the first creditor on your payback list. The trick here is to get the money out of your checking account and therefore out of your reach.

When You Do Pay Off a Bill, Put the Former Monthly Payment Into the Savings Account. For example, if you've managed to pay off your credit card balance and you had been paying $25 a month, you now put that $25 in your payback savings account. This money will then be used to attack number one on your one-time list or number two on your payback list.

Set Up a New Plan When You Have a Significant Amount of Extra Money Every Month. This new plan takes into consideration Christmas, vacation, clothing, permanent savings and other needs that can now fit easily into your budget. For example, if you now have $300 extra every month, you might divide it up: 40 percent to payback savings account; 10 percent to vacation fund; 10 percent to Christmas fund; 20 percent to clothing needs; 20 percent to permanent savings.

However you set up your percentages, remember that a significant amount should still go to your payback account and that it is important now to start a permanent savings account. Christmas and vacations are events for which you will spend money anyway. Now is the time to include them in your budget. If you have the money saved, you will not be tempted to spend money that you don't have.

You may find it simpler to add categories to your budget than to work on the percentage system. If so, redo your budget, adding the new categories such as Christmas, permanent savings and so forth. However, make sure you save a large portion of your extra money for payback.

If you don't want to deal with setting up separate savings accounts for each of these categories, make an envelope for each one. Each time you have extra money, write out a check and put it in the envelope. For example, we have friends who budget on this system. They have an envelope marked "Santa Claus," and when they get their paycheck they write out a check to "Santa Claus" and slip it into the envelope. When Christmastime comes, they add up all the checks in the envelope and know how much they can spend on Christmas.

Remember, it's important to take the physical step of writing out the check and subtracting it from your account if you are using the envelope method. If you leave the money in your checking account and try to remember that $20 goes to the Christmas fund, you will probably be tempted to use that money to eat out or to go to a movie. If you write the check to "Santa Claus" or to "vacation," you assume the money is gone because you have subtracted it from your checking account balance.

When you have reached this point and have paid off three or four bills, watch out for danger signals. You can't go out and splurge now. If you do, you'll put yourself right back in the same boat you were in before you started.

When You Are Out of Debt, Celebrate in a Way That Won't Put You Back in Debt. Fix dinner for friends and family, for example. You can use your credit cards again, but don't let them use you. For example, you may need a new refrigerator. Figure out how you can fit it into your budget. Maybe you can afford to pay $100 a month for four months. Charge the refrigerator and then pay the $100 a month until it is paid off.

Maintain your one-time-needs list. This will keep you from splurging. If you want a new lamp for the living room, put it on the list and save your money for it.

You have worked hard to get out of debt. Stay out. Determine to stick to economic independence for the rest of your life.

TABLE 1

EXAMPLES

Debt	Balance
Payback List	
VISA	$ 400
Sears	$ 750
Penney	$ 900
Mastercard	$1,000
Student loan	$2,000
Bank loan	$2,000
Credit union	$3,000
One-Time-Needs List	
Repair stove	$ 70
New car engine	$ 600
New glasses	$ 125
Winter coat	$ 100
Bus ticket (sister's wedding)	$ 85
Example of a Budget	
Rent	$ 450
Telephone	$ 35

TABLE 1 (continued)
EXAMPLES

Debt	Balance
Example of a Budget	
Gas	$ 35
Health insurance	$ 40
Food	$ 400
Entertainment	$ 125
Doctors	$ 20
Student loan	$ 30
Credit union	$ 40
Mastercard	$ 45
Sears	$ 40
Electricity	$ 35
Gasoline	$ 100
Car insurance	$ 75
Renters' insurance	$ 15
Supplies	$ 75
Cable TV	$ 20
Church	$ 50
Bank Loan	$ 50
VISA	$ 25
Penney	$ 65
Total equals monthly expenses	

CHAPTER NINE

Emotional Independence

INDEPENDENCE IS ABOUT OWNERSHIP. When you're independent, you're claiming ownership of your life ("I thought it, I felt it, and I did it"). When you're dependent, you're giving up ownership of some part of yourself ("He makes me feel" . . . "It was her idea" . . . "It was his fault"). You can see the importance of ownership most clearly when you look at your emotions.

When you're emotionally independent, you take responsibility for your emotions. You acknowledge that others may set the stage for how you feel but you accept that you're the actor in the drama. And you believe the same goes for others. You may play a walk-on part in their emotional drama, but the leading role belongs to them.

In many families a great deal of confusion exists over who owns whose emotions. Look at a typical family scene.

WIFE: You hurt my feelings when you said I was rude to the neighbors.

HUSBAND: You're making me feel guilty. I was only trying to help you.

WIFE: You're trying to make me feel guilty, and that's making me mad.

HUSBAND: Well, you're making me mad now.

And on it goes.

Not claiming ownership for your emotions is one of the biggest problems between people. Many people are so used to pushing their unpleasant feelings off onto others that they have trouble knowing who owns what. Problems like this don't exist when you're emotionally independent.

Dr. Campbell believes you can operate out of two different emotional systems. In the first, you believe, "Others are responsible for my feelings and I'm responsible for theirs." In the second system, you believe, "I'm responsible for my feelings and you're responsible for your feelings." (I prefer the coinage *choice-able*.)

Dr. Campbell points out that you'll run into some definite drawbacks when you operate out of the first system. First, you have to *wait* for the other person to change so you'll feel better. Next, you become *frustrated* when he or she doesn't. Then, you start to feel *helpless* to change the situation, and then *hopeless* that anything will change. Eventually, you become *dispirited* and *resentful* toward the other person.

He adds that when you and another person are operating out of the first system, communication breaks down. When you believe that what you say is responsible for how the other person feels, you won't say anything meaningful. The other person will think the same way. As a result, intimacy disappears.

When you're emotionally independent, you choose to operate from the second model: "I'm choice-able for my emotions and you're choice-able for yours." One of the main lessons in growing up is learning to shift from the first model to the second. If people would really believe that "sticks and stones can break my bones, but names can never hurt me," most therapists' offices would be empty.

Painful emotions aren't mysterious. They are simply signals from your brain that you need to make different choices in the way you're thinking or acting. Painful emotions aren't trying to punish you, but rather to wake you up and get your attention. Your mind wants you to take the situation seriously. If the pain weren't sharp, you would ignore the signal and not make the necessary choices.

What messages are your emotions trying to send you? Remember, there are always two possibilities: *you need to act differently*, or *you need to think differently*. Each specific group of emotions has distinct messages.

When you're *anxious*, the message is either that you're in danger and should protect yourself, or you're exaggerating the danger and should think more realistically. With *guilt*, your mind is telling you either that you're acting against your values and should act differently, or you're evaluating your actions against others' values and should not buy into their values.

Anger is an indication either that you need to take action against someone who is infringing on your domain, or that you mistakenly think that an infringement is occurring. *Sadness* signals either that you need to accept a real loss so that you can get on with your life or that you think you've lost something that you haven't.

Emotional pain is like physical pain. Both tell you something is wrong that needs to be corrected. If you ignore either, the pain persists and the problem usually gets worse. The first step in being emotionally independent is to acknowledge and accept your emotions. By doing this, you send the message back to your brain that you realize something's wrong but that you'll take care of it. Once you do this, the severity of the pain immediately starts to lessen.

You may try to ignore your emotions because you don't want to admit anything is wrong with you ("I shouldn't be afraid to speak up, I'm a professional" . . . "I shouldn't feel guilty, I didn't do anything wrong" . . . "I shouldn't be depressed, I have a lovely family"). A lack of independence leads to not owning your emotions. Maturity isn't the absence of flaws and mistakes, but the owning up to them.

When you're emotionally independent, you don't say, "I'm not depressed," nor do you say, "You're making me depressed." What you do say is "I'm depressing myself today." When you take responsibility for how you feel, you can start to make choices in your favor.

Creation of Feeling

If you want to be able to choose how you feel, you need to come to terms with two issues: *who creates your emotions*, and *what do you get with your emotions?* Once you see that you create your own feelings and that you don't need the emotional payoff, you can start to choose more freely how you feel.

Your Role in Your Feelings. Your thinking creates your emotions. If you think you have to feel bad about something, you will. Similarly, if you choose to think you don't have to feel bad, you won't. Your brain, like the rest of your organs, is neutral to what it processes. Your stomach will digest unhealthy food as well as healthy food; your lungs will take in cigarette smoke as well as clean air. You have a choice in what you want your brain to process.

You're the one who generates your own internal experiences, so you're the one who can choose what experiences you want to have.

Before you can choose how you feel, you have to realize you're the one who creates your feelings. When you see that you're an emotionally free agent, you're then able to make choices. Because you create your own emotions, you can always choose new ones. If you're angry, depressed, sad, jealous or guilty, instead of saying, "I shouldn't feel this way," you can say, "I have a choice in how I want to feel."

You have much more control over your emotions than you realize. Has there ever been a time when you decided not to be guilty? Unhappy? Afraid? Jealous? Angry? Ashamed? If so, how do you account for this, if you didn't choose how you felt?

You can simply refuse to feel bad if you choose to. Take shame, for example. Shame is one of the biggest obstacles to becoming independent. You can be so heavily burdened with shame that you hide from people.

Where does your shame come from? Because you feel shame in social situations, you're prone to think that shame comes from others. In reality, you create shame yourself; this means you can choose not to feel ashamed if you want to. Is there something you were ashamed of in high school—your ethnic or religious background, economic status or the way you looked? If you once felt this way and no longer do, what happened? My guess is that you chose not to feel ashamed any more. Ellen was ashamed of the way her body looked. Because of her feelings of shame, she refused to look for a job or try to meet new people.

I told Ellen that it didn't matter whether she could convince herself she didn't have anything to be ashamed of. I said it was more important for her to realize that she could simply refuse to feel ashamed about what she once felt bad about. She could tell herself, "I'm not going to feel bad about my flaws." If you tell yourself, "I choose not to feel bad about this," stick to your choice and act on it; you can transform how you feel.

Ellen also felt guilty much of the time because she was partly supported by her elderly parents. She presented herself to others with a plea of "guilty with explanation." I told her, "In America you're innocent until proven guilty." She said, "Well, what about those times I really do screw up—what if I don't keep a promise, or something like that?"

I told her she could admit to herself and others that she did something that she (or others) thinks is wrong without having to feel guilty. Guilt actually encourages you to repeat the action you don't want. You use guilt to punish yourself and erase your action. It's a subtle way of not owning up to your choices. Guilt exaggerates the wrongness ("I'm an awfully bad person"). Exaggeration is one way of discrediting your mistakes. Ellen used guilt so that she would not have to accept her real mistakes. By showing herself and others how repentant she was about living off her parents, she didn't have to act differently. Guilt cushions you from owning up to your own actions.

Taking Choice-ability. You have to believe that you cause your own emotions or else you won't be able to do much about them. Recently, I heard a psychologist interview a married couple on the radio. The woman said she felt invalidated because her husband was going out with other women. The psychologist turned to the man and said, "Why do you *make* her feel invalidated?" Our language and culture is full of such examples. We're falsely taught to believe others create our emotions.

If you want to be emotionally independent and have the ability to choose how you feel, you have to see that you create your own emotions. Learning that you're choice-able for your own feelings is a developmental process. Children have a difficult time seeing how they create their own feelings. If children feel bad after being teased, they think the person doing the teasing caused them to feel bad. They can't see that it's their own doing that's causing their bad feelings. As you grow up you're better able to see that you're upsetting yourself, and that sticks and stones can break your bones, but names will never hurt you.

People who are psychologically dependent have the same difficulty children have in seeing how they're choosing their own feelings. One woman I saw said, "My husband promised that he would make me happy when we got married and he failed miserably." She falsely assumed that her husband was right when he said he could make her happy. However, her happiness was her choice-ability, or responsibility.

The fact that you're choice-able for your own emotions is good news. Would you want to live in a world where others could control your happiness? Where others, by a flick of the wrist, could determine your emotional fate?

Following are some common reasonings that prevent you from seeing how you create your emotions.

• *Sequential reasoning.* You may believe that because some event (your husband criticizing you) happens right before you feel bad, this is what causes your feelings. One of the problems with being human is that we often believe that an event that comes just before other events caused them. And if the other events don't come right after, then the first event isn't a causal factor. For example, it took me a long time to figure out that if I stayed up an extra two hours I felt tired the next morning; or that eating a few more calories at a meal adds up to fifteen pounds of extra weight at the end of the year.

In the same way, people are prone to consider two events that occur together as causal. This is primitive thinking ("Every time we do the sun dance, the sun comes up") and superstition ("I wore my blue dress and got a job"). Similarly, it's primitive and superstitious behavior to think others cause your emotions just because sometimes their action precedes your action of upsetting yourself.

• *Correlational reasoning.* Ellen said, "I've read where if you're under a lot of stress, you're more likely to have emotional problems. So doesn't that mean that the stress causes my emotions?" People often confuse correlations (events that vary together) with causal relationships. One study found a correlation between the number of storks in an area in Norway and the number of babies born—the more storks in an area, the more babies born. Does this mean storks *do* bring babies? There often is a third variable that accounts for any correlation. In this case, most storks in Norway are in rural areas and people in rural areas have more children.

Ellen's ideas about stress is an example of correlational reasoning—while it's true that high stress is correlated with anxiety and depression, this isn't the cause of it. Many people with low stress become depressed or anxious, and many with high stress don't. The third variable here is how you handle stress and whether you choose to let it bother you or not. If you have the right coping tools, you can handle high stress. Without any tools, low stress can cause problems.

• *Folk reasoning*. You may believe that it's natural and normal to feel bad when bad events happen to you. You've heard this your whole life. This may be natural and normal, in that this is how most people respond. However, civilization has been advanced by people going beyond what is natural and normal. Just because many people believe others cause their feelings doesn't mean that it's true. At one time bloodletting was considered natural and normal.

Your old habits feel natural and normal, but this doesn't mean that you can't choose new ones or that you have to continue with your old patterns.

• *Reasoning by analogy*. You may believe that emotional pain is the same as physical pain. Because others can cause you physical pain, you may think they can cause you emotional pain. This is an analogy—psychological pain *is like* physical pain. While you can find a number of similarities, there are crucial differences between the two. Someone can *physically intrude on or enter* your body, but they can't intrude psychologically. Others' thoughts and words can't kill you. As an adult, no one can emotionally harm you unless you give them this power over you. You are always psychologically self-contained.

Along the same lines, don't use physical pain as a metaphor for emotions: "He hurt me" . . . "She's a pain in the neck" . . . "The job's a headache" . . . "They really stuck it to me" . . . and so on. Listen to yourself. Using pain as a metaphor can stop you from seeing that you create your own emotions.

• *Emotional reasoning*. You may believe that because you feel that others cause you to be anxious, angry, depressed, lonely, jealous or guilty, this must be the truth. Your feelings aren't facts, only reflections of what you're thinking. You need facts or experiments to see if your thinking is true or not.

You can try an experiment right now. Take your book and turn it upside down for a moment. Go ahead and do it now. After you do this, come back and start reading again.

Did you do it? Suppose you did. Who is responsible or choice-able for your action, me or you? Suppose you didn't do it. Who's choice-able for your noncompliance, me or you? The person who's choice-able is the one who has the choice to do the act or not to do it. You might say, "You told me to do it, so you're choice-able."

What if I asked you to sell all your earthly possessions and send the money to the Rockefellers and you did it? Would I still be choice-able for your actions? What if you didn't do it? Who would be responsible then?

This experiment has to do with behavior. What about your feelings? With your feelings it's even clearer who's in charge. Right now you're having some emotional reaction to what you're reading. Who's causing this, me or you? Me, because I wrote it? Suppose you felt bored the first time you read this, angry the next time, and happy the third time. How can I have the power to make you swing your moods around like this? You're attributing the choice to me, but this doesn't mean I choose your feelings.

Just because you're choice-able for your own emotions doesn't mean you have to let others treat you any way they want. Instead, hold them accountable for their actions by replacing "You hurt my feelings" with "When you come home late, I feel bad." This sets the stage for discussing how the behavior can be changed or some compromise can be reached.

Seesaw of Control. By taking ownership for your feelings, you can start to choose how you feel. When you believe others or outside events are controlling how you feel, you have little choice in the matter.

Those times you work at controlling only your own feelings and not others', you feel 100 percent in control. You're at the top of the seesaw. As you try to control others' feelings, you lose your own sense of control. When you try to take 100 percent control of the other person's response, you're 100 percent out of control and down at the bottom of the teeter-totter.

To illustrate this, let's take the most common fear in America—fear of speaking in public. People's fear of giving a speech is greater than their fear of death. The reason people scare themselves is that they believe they are responsible or choice-able for whether the audience likes them or is entertained. The larger the group, the more people they believe they are responsible for or have to control. The truth is that each member of the audience is 100 percent choice-able for how he or she responds. You might say, "What I do affects that choice." That's not necessarily true. You can give the exact same speech and have tremendous variation from audience to audience. The solution to the fear? Think about the audience when you prepare the speech and then forget about their response or choice when you're giving the speech. Focus on the speech itself and turning yourself on—enjoy the speech and be glad you came. Whether they like you or the speech isn't your choice. By doing this you stay on top of the seesaw and fully in control of yourself.

As I said before, there are only four things in the world: how you think, how you feel, how you act and the rest of the world. When you focus on controlling the first three things that are under your control and let the fourth take care of itself, your life goes along harmoniously.

Payoffs. You don't want to stack the deck against yourself. To be able to choose freely how you feel, you'll have to stop believing that you'll lose something when you give up negative feelings. You have to ask yourself, "What am I giving up when I let my bad feelings go? Revenge? Attention? Sympathy?" Some writers believe your negative emotions are somehow not real and that you have them only to manipulate others.

While your emotions are real—you do feel bad—you often have benefits or payoffs for negative emotions. One of the reasons you may choose not to get rid of your negative feelings is because you don't want to lose the payoffs. Your emotions can bring you something you want. This isn't to say you feel bad just for the payoff; however, the payoffs can be a factor in why you don't let them go. You may be aware or unaware of the payoffs, and the consequences can be wanted or unwanted.

Advertisements. Your emotions have the same influence on others as advertisements do. The goal of advertising is to get your *attention*, *interest* and *action*. Advertisers first want to get your attention; then they want to get you interested; and finally they want you to take some action. Your emotional payoffs have the same characteristics. Often what you're doing with your negative emotions is trying to get someone to buy something from you.

Attention. The most notable characteristic of your emotions is that they draw attention to yourself. This attention may be wanted ("I wanted to let them know I was mad") or unwanted ("I didn't want to let them know I was nervous"). Your emotions are a rapid form of communication. You may be communicating danger, pain or a warning. Your emotions are effective attention-getters—they call out for attention. With your emotions, you're using your facial expressions, voice and body language to call attention to yourself. There is some research showing that you release emotional "odors" (called phermones) to call attention to yourself; thus, you can even smell scared. Just as in advertising, you often have to vary the attention-seeking strategy over time to make this effective.

Interest. Attention isn't enough in advertising—you have to keep the person reading or tuned in. Your emotions are often instinctively interesting to others; most of the time people want to know what's behind your emotions. A typical conversation goes:

"What's wrong?"
"Nothing."
"There must be something wrong."
"No, there's nothing wrong."
"Come on, there must be something wrong."
"I'm telling you, nothing is wrong."
"What is it? Is it your mother?"
"Yes, it's my mother."
"What about your mother?"
"Oh, it's nothing."

You can get people interested in your emotions fairly easily. Often they believe that they are somehow the cause (this is similar to when money is stolen at a party—many of the innocent people at the party feel guilty). A surefire way you can get someone's interest is to get the person involved in the drama.

"What is it about your mother?"
"Well, it's something you said about her."

Action. The reason advertisers work hard to get you to care is that they want to move you in some way. They may want you to buy their product or service, or to vote for their candidate or send money to their cause. Your emotions often have the same effect. This emotional request can be specific ("I want you to stop coming home late"). At other times, the expected action is vague. When someone is upset and you ask, "What do you want from me?" he or she often can't say exactly what he wants.

The expected action varies with each emotion. When you're *angry*, you want the other people to change how they are acting, thinking or feeling. When Ellen became more independent, her husband became angry. He wanted her to go back to the way she was. When you're *ashamed*, you want others not to look at you; thus you try to appear small and inconspicuous. When you're *anxious*, you want someone to come to your rescue or not to hurt you. With *depression*, you want someone to fix it for you, and when you're *guilty*, you want others' forgiveness.

Many times you don't know you're putting out this advertisement. You may find it helpful when you're having an emotional reaction to ask yourself, "What am I advertising now? Helplessness? Hopelessness?" Similarly, when you're about to buy into another's emotional package, you can also ask yourself, "What are they trying to sell me with their emotional advertisement?"

To be free to choose how you feel, you have to come to terms with the payoffs. You have to ask yourself, "Is the gain I get worth all the pain?" Your negative emotions, considering their cost, usually give you little in return. One of the catches of the payoffs is that you continually have to up the ante—you have to be increasingly more dramatic and interesting to get people's attention, interest and action.

You can get the benefits of the payoff without the liabilities by being direct with people. Tell them up front what you want. This is more effective than the indirect method. One of the reasons you may not be direct is that you fear they'll say no. You'll find it's better to endure the occasional no than it is to endure the painful feelings.

Another reason you may not want to be direct is because you may know that what you want is unnecessary. This might be help you don't need, a favor you could better do yourself or some unrealistic, inappropriate concessions you may want from another. When you stop and question yourself, you'll often see that you don't really need this action from others. In fact, the payoff you get is often exactly what you don't need—unnecessary help, forgiveness or continuation of the status quo. What you think you need (approval, recognition, love of another) is usually the exact opposite of what you need in order to grow (tolerance of disapproval or rejection, tolerance of your own company).

The Difficulty of Acceptance

One of the reasons you don't want to choose to feel okay about events is that this leads to acceptance. Because your mind doesn't want you to accept the situation as it is without judgments, your mind can't tolerate your feeling okay. This would mean accepting the situation.

You may hang on to your negative feelings as a way you can keep from losing control. You may think choosing to accept unwanted events and feel good is giving in and letting others or the world win. You may use your bad feelings as a method to not let others or events get away with what they did to you.

David Shapiro, a psychologist, has written about this use of negative emotions: "To forget an injustice or humiliation is to allow it to stand unrectified, to accept it, to 'give in,' to take the easy way out, to abandon protest and therefore, altogether to abandon one's rights and self-respect. It would be, as one such person put it, 'To allow myself to be a doormat.' "

Have you had this experience? You felt bad but didn't want to get over your bad feeling, because this would mean the other person or event would win? One of my clients said, "Arguing back and forth with my neighbors is exhausting me and making me hate being in my yard—but if I make peace, it would mean they were right to do what they did." Ask yourself the following questions to see if this applies to you.

- Are you staying mad at someone because you didn't want the person to get away with what was done? ("I'm not going to forget that my roommate started calling the girl I was going out with—he'd think he could do it with every girl I date.")
- Are you nursing hurts because this proves how uncaring and unfair the world is? ("I didn't get into the graduate school I wanted because I'm not a minority or female. It'd be the same no matter where I applied.")
- Are you keeping yourself scared to remind yourself and others how important and dangerous something is? ("I have to take it very easy while I'm pregnant, anything could happen.")

To choose freely how you want to feel you have to stop stacking the deck against yourself; don't make feeling bad seem so important. The gain from your emotions is rarely worth the pain. Most of your moral victories are hollow. You don't get much for your pain. You're usually cutting off your nose to spite your face. When you use your emotions as a defense against the world, you have trouble freely choosing how you want to feel. The irony is that you don't need to defend yourself emotionally against the world.

Often you don't want to accept what you believe is bad because you believe that after accepting it you'll be in worse shape. This is rarely true, but it takes almost a "leap of faith" to believe you'll be better off by accepting it. Once you do believe it and let your bad feelings go, you can start to choose to feel the way you want. Full acceptance is the absence of good or bad judgments. When you stop making these judgments, the problem melts away.

The quicker you can get over bad feelings, the better. I remember once, when I was maybe seven or eight, I was mad at my mother about something. A little later she was offering cookies to me and my brothers. My first reaction was "I don't want any of your cookies. I'm mad at you." I saw taking the cookies as a sign of giving in and a moral loss of some kind.

I then thought, "That's stupid, I'd better get some cookies while I have the chance." My mother looked at me as if to say "That's not like you." I remember then thinking something like "I'm not going to let how I feel get in the way of getting something I want." Over the years I remembered this lesson some of the time but forgot it many times. I was always much better off when I remembered the lesson.

Guidelines

You can use the following strategies to help you choose how you want to feel.

- Make a list of twenty specific times that you've felt bad over something. This could include the times you've felt scared, sad, angry, jealous. After you've made this list, ask yourself, "How much good did these feelings do me? Were they necessary or was it needless suffering? Where did it get me? Was it worth it?" Periodically review the list. (Michael listed the time he had to borrow money from a date to help pay for dinner; he felt embarrassed and ashamed. He questioned how much good it did him to feel that way. All the suffering he could muster for a lifetime couldn't make it not have happened.)
- List some of your traits or beliefs that you've chosen to feel differently about—politics, people, yourself, your family—to show yourself that you do have a choice. (Michael listed his belief that only a lazy bum would be laid off from work; he chose to think differently about this belief after being laid off from the factory where he worked.)
- Try it. Choosing is just a matter of doing it. The next time you feel bad, decide you're not going to feel bad, then see what happens. Talk to yourself out loud, in the mirror, or into a tape recorder. Say, "I refuse to feel bad." (Michael practiced this when a pedestrian yelled "Jerk!" at him. Immediately, at the first twinge of feeling bad, he said in a loud voice, "I refuse to feel bad about this." At first, he could do this for short periods only. Eventually he was able to make the choice stick.)

• One of the best ways to see your choices clearly is to exaggerate them. Blow your choice up. This helps you to see more clearly what your choices are. Michael thought about his choice to not feel bad about being called a jerk by a stranger. He asked himself how his day would have gone if he'd chosen the opposite—to feel embarrassed, ashamed and angry about what had happened. He imagined himself crying in the car right after the insult. He then saw himself walking into his office, slump-shouldered and depressed and thinking about jumping out the window. He completed the fantasy by seeing the end of the day in his mind—he was drinking himself to sleep. This exaggeration enabled him to see how much better his choice had been.

Quitting

Arthur Deikman, a psychiatrist, has written on ways Eastern and Western psychologies can be combined. He has described a technique called *quitting* that is one of the best relaxation methods available. This is also a good method to use when you want to choose how you want to feel.

How many hours a day are you involved in some purposeful action? This might be working, eating, watching TV, talking. There are probably very few moments when you're not doing something. Dr. Deikman's method is simply to quit doing everything. The following are the steps you take to practice quitting.

• Stop whatever you're doing and just sit (glance at a clock or watch).

• For ten minutes, quit reacting to any internal or external stimuli (if a truck goes by outside, let it go; if you feel like scratching, say "The heck with it, let it scratch itself").

• Don't pay any attention to your thoughts. If you start a thought, don't even bother to finish it. Let it drop on the floor.

• Stay awake and let the outside world come in. I suggest you try this right now. Whenever you become overly focused on your concerns and thoughts, just quit for ten minutes; after you do this, you have greater choice in how you want to feel.

• Tell yourself that whatever you're doing you're either going to choose to do it and with pleasure or you're not going to do it at all. Make yourself enjoy it. If you can't enjoy it, quit until you can. Michael had some old bills to sort and file. After quitting for ten minutes, he chose to feel good about doing it, instead of not doing it or doing it resentfully.

- See what kinds of excuses you have for not doing it. You'll often say that you don't want to stop and feel good now but you *can* stop waiting and start feeling good now.

In the next chapter I'll talk about the beliefs you have that lead you to feel bad.

Emotional Independence Inventory

Emotional dependency refers to letting others' actions determine how you feel. It also involves the mistaken belief that you're responsible for others' emotions. Emotional dependency can take a number of forms.

Read each group of statements carefully. Then circle the number beside the statement that best describes *you*. After you have completed the questionnaire, add up all the numbers circled. Check your total with the totals given at the end of the chapter.

1. 0 I don't feel like I'm waiting for something or someone to make me happy.
   1 I sometimes feel like I'm waiting for something or someone to make me happy.
   2 I often feel like I'm waiting for something or someone to make me happy.
   3 I am waiting for something or someone to make me happy.
2. 0 I feel happy most of the time.
   1 I sometimes feel unhappy.
   2 I feel sad all of the time.
   3 I'm so unhappy that I can't stand it.
3. 0 I don't feel afraid.
   1 I feel afraid.
   2 I feel afraid all the time and can't snap out of it.
   3 I am so afraid that I can't stand it.
4. 0 I don't feel angry.
   1 I feel angry.
   2 I feel angry all the time and can't snap out of it.
   3 I am so angry that I can't stand it.

5. 0 I don't feel guilty.
   1 I feel guilty a good part of the time.
   2 I feel quite guilty most of the time.
   3 I feel guilty all the time.
6. 0 I feel equal to others.
   1 I am critical of myself.
   2 I blame myself all the time.
   3 I blame myself for everything bad that happens.
7. 0 I sleep soundly most of the time.
   1 I usually sleep through the night but often wake up tired.
   2 I sleep fitfully and wake up in the night.
   3 I have trouble falling asleep and staying asleep and often have bad dreams.
8. 0 I almost never feel bored.
   1 I usually don't feel bored.
   2 About half the time I feel bored.
   3 Most of the time I feel bored.
9. 0 I don't feel disappointed in myself.
   1 I am disappointed in myself.
   2 I am disgusted with myself.
   3 I hate myself.
10. 0 I get as much pleasure out of life as I used to.
    1 I don't enjoy life the way I used to.
    2 I don't get real satisfaction out of life anymore.
    3 I am dissatisfied with everything.
11. 0 I can work about as well as before.
    1 I need extra effort to get started doing anything.
    2 I have to push myself very hard to do anything.
    3 I can't do any work at all.
12. 0 I'm tolerant of others.
    1 I'm somewhat critical of others.
    2 I'm often critical of others.
    3 I'm highly critical of others.
13. 0 I rarely blame others for my problems.
    1 I sometimes blame others for my problems.
    2 I often blame others for my problems.
    3 I'm constantly blaming others.
14. 0 I'm rarely fearful when out by myself.
    1 I'm sometimes fearful when out by myself.
    2 I'm often fearful when out by myself.
    3 I'm nearly always fearful when out by myself.

15. 0 I'm rarely shy with others.
    1 I'm sometimes shy with others.
    2 I'm often shy with others.
    3 I'm usually shy with others.
16. 0 I'm rarely lonely.
    1 I'm sometimes lonely.
    2 I'm often lonely.
    3 I'm usually lonely.
17. 0 My feelings aren't easily hurt.
    1 My feelings are sometimes easily hurt.
    2 My feelings are often easily hurt.
    3 My feelings are very easily hurt.
18. 0 I rarely worry about hurting others' feelings.
    1 I sometimes worry about hurting others' feelings.
    2 I often worry about hurting others' feelings.
    3 I always worry about hurting others' feelings.
19. 0 I'm rarely suspicious of others.
    1 I'm sometimes suspicious of others.
    2 I'm often suspicious of others.
    3 I'm highly suspicious of others.
20. 0 I'm rarely self-conscious.
    1 I'm sometimes self-conscious.
    2 I'm often self-conscious.
    3 I'm nearly always self-conscious.
21. 0 I rarely have urges to beat or harm someone.
    1 I sometimes have urges to beat or harm someone.
    2 I often have urges to beat or harm someone.
    3 I nearly always have urges to beat or harm someone.
22. 0 I rarely have to check and double-check what I do.
    1 I sometimes have to check and double-check what I do.
    2 I often have to check and double-check what I do.
    3 I always have to check and double-check what I do.
23. 0 I rarely feel uncomfortable eating or drinking in public.
    1 I sometimes feel uncomfortable eating or drinking in public.
    2 I often feel uncomfortable eating or drinking in public.
    3 I always feel uncomfortable eating or drinking in public.
24. 0 I rarely resent others.
    1 I sometimes resent others.
    2 I often resent others.
    3 I always resent others.

25. 0 I nearly always trust those close to me.
    1 I sometimes don't trust those close to me.
    2 I often don't trust those close to me.
    3 I never trust those close to me.
26. 0 I never feel inferior.
    1 I sometimes feel inferior.
    2 I often feel inferior.
    3 I always feel inferior.
27. 0 I never feel jealous.
    1 I sometimes feel jealous.
    2 I often feel jealous.
    3 I always feel jealous.

RESULTS:
Score of 0–6 = high level of emotional independence.
Score of 7–17 = moderate level of emotional independence.
Sore of 18–25 = low level of emotional independence.
Score of 25 or above = severe problem with emotional independence.

CHAPTER TEN

Discovering Underlying Beliefs

YOU NEED THREE PIECES of information before you can start systematically to increase your emotional independence. First, you need to know the specific areas where you're having emotional problems. Second, you need to identify the automatic thoughts that are sustaining them. And, finally, you need to know the beliefs that are generating the thoughts. This information will allow you to start becoming more emotionally independent.

Discovering Your Problem Areas

Problem Reduction. The first order of business is to discover your specific areas of emotional dependency. To do this, you need to reduce the many problems and symptoms of your dependency to the core issues.

Problem reduction involves distilling a host of problems down to a few specific ones. For example, your anxiety on the job and shyness with friends and relatives may be due to an exaggerated need for approval.

When you trace your problems back to their cause, you'll find that most roads lead to Rome. Often your problems are due to the pebble-in-the-shoe syndrome. Relatively simple problems, if not corrected, can lead to more serious problems. If you don't take the pebble out of your shoe, adjusting to it can cripple you. One woman's loneliness and lack of personal satisfaction was due to her fear of driving. Once she started to drive again, her life opened up for her. When you boil your problems down to a few basic issues, your problems become clearer and more manageable.

Questions to Ask Yourself. One way to help reduce your emotional problems is to *develop a self-questioning program.* You may now be asking yourself questions that don't have answers ("Why me?" . . . "How come nothing ever works out for me?"). Rhetorical questions don't help you learn anything about yourself. You need to know the *who*, *what*, *where*, *when* and *why* of the situation. Good questions can help you identify specific areas of emotional dependency that you want to change. Take about thirty minutes right now to answer the following questions. Write the answers down in a notebook. Don't think too much about your answers, just start writing them out.

- *Who* or *what* intimidates me?
- *Who* or *what* do I attribute my feelings of failure to?
- *What* am I afraid of doing?
- *What* don't I want to do?
- *What* times and places bring on my feelings of inferiority?
- *Where* do I feel inferior?
- *When* does my confidence disappear?
- *When* do I want to run away?
- *What* do I attribute others' feelings to?
- *What* makes me feel small?
- *What* do I avoid?
- *What* do I have trouble starting?
- *What* do I have trouble finishing?
- *What* have I been procrastinating about?
- *Which* of my personal problems am I ignoring right now?
- *What* educational, social, money or emotional problem am I putting off thinking about?
- *What* do I feel helpless to change?
- *Who* do I resent?
- *What* am I waiting for?

After you have answered these questions, summarize the answer. Read over your answers and then answer the following five questions in one sentence.

- Who am I the most emotionally dependent on?

- What is my biggest area of emotional dependency?
- Where in my life am I the most emotionally dependent?
- When am I the most emotionally dependent?
- Why am I dependent at these times and places?

Your dependency is often difficult to pin down. Often you're the most *dependent* in those areas in which you believe you're the most *independent*. I told one client I was writing a book on independence. He said, "I could write that book. I'm really independent." He said this despite the fact that he was thirty years old and was being put through school and supported by his parents.

You need to explore in as many ways as possible to see where you lack independence. The following are some other ways you can detect your areas of emotional dependency.

Ask Others. Others know a great deal about you. You can use this as a resource. Ask people close to you, "How do you think I could be more emotionally independent? What could I do better for myself?" Tell them to be honest with you. (When Martha asked her best friend, Beatrice, she was surprised by her answer. Beatrice said, "I've known you for thirty years, and for thirty years it has irritated me that you can't go to the ladies' room without asking me if I have to go. I feel I can't say no to you because you obviously are afraid that you can't make it there and back on your own.")

Write Your Autobiography. Write a personal history of your movement toward or away from emotional independence. Start with how you felt about independence as a child. Describe what it was like the first day your mother left you alone at school. Cover the high points of your life. Describe the times you had your independence and the times you lost it.

As you do this, a pattern will start to emerge. You'll find many of the problems you had in being independent when you were fourteen are still problems. (Martha realized that even as a young girl she'd always expected another girl to accompany her to public restrooms.)

After you've written your autobiography, list five lessons

you've learned from it. (Besides the obvious one about going places on her own, Martha learned that she had always thought she needed people around her, that she'd always agreed to her husband's schemes because she thought she should, that she'd encouraged her children's dependencies by doing too much for them and, finally, that she expected them to reward her by always being around her.)

Analyze Dislikes. Ask yourself what you don't like in others' emotional responses. The answer to this question can be particularly helpful if you're so consumed with "outsight" (analyzing and observing others' mistakes) that you don't have any time left for insight. This is a common problem for those in the helping fields; they avoid looking at themselves by analyzing others. (Martha did not find the question bad, but the answer was painful. She disliked women who were anxious about aging, those who tried to dress and act younger than their age. When she began to think about this, she realized that, at fifty-five, the loss of her own youth and looks was unpleasant to think about. She began to realize that a great deal of her dependency behaviors had to do with outward appearance.)

You project onto others what you don't like or suspect in yourself. You can use your projections to find out more about yourself. Get a piece of paper. On it, list six people that you know fairly well. Then draw two lines and in one column write what you like about them. In the other column write what you don't like about them. The information you write down about these people will tell you more about yourself than it will about the six people.

Start a Dream Journal. Your dreams can let you know where you're overly dependent. The purpose of dreams is to help solve your daily emotional problems. Your stresses and problems are sorted out in your dream world. So the problems you are trying to solve in your dreams are hints about where you need to become more independent.

Put a notebook and pen next to your bed. As you go to sleep, tell yourself, "I'm going to remember my dreams." Before getting up in the morning, lie there for a few minutes with your eyes closed. Then start writing them out as fast as you can. Think of the dream as a movie you want to remember. (At first, Martha said she couldn't remember her dreams. She knew she had them, but they were fuzzy fragments. When she began training herself with her dream notebook beside her bed, she had trouble recalling the whole dream. But as she wrote down more of her dreams, it became easier. During the day, when fragments came to her, she would write them down.) Learning to recall your dreams is a skill you can learn to develop. For Martha, developing this skill was good for two reasons. First, she began to know more about her dreams, and second, developing a skill she thought she didn't have made her feel better about herself.

After you write out your dream, you can analyze it. Write out the *emotional problem* ("I was panicky and couldn't find my way home"). What was your *attempted solution* ("I was trying to find someone to lead me home")? A pattern will start to emerge. The ending of the dream is the most important part. *This shows how you handled the emotional problem.*

Your dreams can also help you know when you're increasing your independence. Before working on your independence, your dream might have ended, "I was crying for help, but no one came." After working on your independence, it might end, "I remembered I had a road map in my coat pocket."

Dr. Brian Shaw, of the University of Western Ontario, and I have been doing a study of dreams and emotions. We have found that when people start becoming more independent they start having more independent dreams—this appears to be a way to incorporate new experiences into their general self-concept.

(Tom, forty-seven, primarily had frustration dreams—he would dream he was in bad situations and was helpless. After he started taking charge of his life, his dreams changed. In one dream, he and his family were stalled in their car in the middle of a mountain road and a truck was bearing down on them. Unlike his previous passive and helpless dreams, in this one he got out of the car and pushed it out of the way of the truck by himself. Although exaggerated, the theme of the dream reflected his new, more independent life-style.)

You can use your dreams as cues to be more independent. One woman was anxious about whether to drop out of nursing school or not. She dreamed she was falling from a plane. She then noticed a parachute. She pulled the ripcord and floated safely down. Because she was encouraged by the independent theme of her dream, she decided to talk to her instructors about staying in school.

Emotions As Signposts. You can use your emotions as signposts to where you lack independence. Emotional pain, like physical pain, lets you know there's a problem. Once you learn to read your emotions, you can use them to tell you when and where you've lost your independence.

Take for example your feelings of sadness. Sadness involves a loss. In nearly every case, a large share of the loss is symbolic: the loss is something that doesn't exist in concrete reality ("I've lost my pride" . . . "I've lost their approval"). You may have lost a job, but if on top of that you believe you've lost something bigger —your pride or social standing—this sadness over abstract losses is a sign that you've also lost your independence.

By stepping back and looking at your emotions, you'll be able to see where you're dependent. For example, look back over the times you've felt sad recently. Maybe you've heard about someone in your career who has done better than you. Maybe you've found out that someone you respect is angry at you. Maybe you haven't gotten what you wanted. Each of these instances could show you where you lack independence.

If you're sad because someone else has lost something, you're projecting yourself into the other person's shoes. You're interpreting their loss as yours. You're experiencing a pseudo-loss or a non-event when you attach someone else's loss to yourself. People who get wrapped up in soap operas often do this. This is a sign that you fear whatever loss the other person has had.

You'll find that the more dependent you are, the more often you'll feel sad. Depending on approval or other forms of social reward ("I need his love" . . . "If my poem is published I'll be happy" . . . "My kids'll be there if I need them") places you in almost constant risk of being unhappy ("Why didn't he call?" . . .

"Another rejection?" . . . "Why didn't my daughter write?"). There is a bright side to this: you can use your unhappiness to find out more about where you're dependent ("I'll ask myself who, what, when, where and why").

What about a real loss? What if you lost some money or someone you love? The healthy purpose of sadness is to make it possible for you to *accept the real losses* so you can get on with your life. When you block off sadness with depression, guilt and anger, you have trouble accepting the real loss and getting over it.

Most of the time in the case of real loss there are compensatory factors—you have new opportunities, you have other chances, and you have experience, the most useful commodity of all. You tend to overlook these saving factors if you've lost your independence.

Everyone suffers real loss—dependent and independent people alike. The difference is that when you're dependent, most of the sadness is due to symbolic and surplus meaning ("I can't go on by myself . . . I've lost all hope . . . I'll fail at everything"). Your real loss plus your dependency leads to problems such as depression. Symbolic losses indicate dependency and can be used as keys to identifying your problem areas.

The other painful emotions—anger, jealousy, anxiety, shame, guilt—are nearly always signs that you've lost your independence. They can be used in the same way: consider them reminders to you to get back on track. Rather than trying to suppress your feelings, use them as cues to ask yourself questions about your emotional dependencies: *who*, *what*, *when*, *where* and *why*.

When you're dependent, you often believe that even negative emotions are needed. By nursing hurts and resentments ("I'm so angry I can never forget it" . . . "I keep thinking of him kissing her"), you prevent yourself from becoming aware of what it will take to get your life back on track ("I need to accept what happened and get on with my life").

Your emotions are your best guide to where your dependency is hidden; you need to become more aware of them. If you have trouble recognizing your feelings, you might try some of the following suggestions.

• *Pay attention to how your body reacts.* Your body tells you a great deal about the emotions you're having. A tight stomach can be a clue to anxiety. Aching limbs can be a sign of depression. Tune into your own body language.

• *Start talking about your feelings.* When you're talking to others, use more *feeling* words. Tell them about your positive and negative feelings. Describe old emotions in new ways and talk about new emotions.

• *Pay attention to emotional shifts.* When your mood switches—for example, when you go from happy to sad—ask yourself, "What's going on?" Look for the different qualities in each emotional state.

• *Start to take your emotional temperature.* Periodically ask yourself, "How am I feeling?" Put a red dot on your watch and use this as a reminder to take your emotional temperature.

• *Question your motivation.* When you don't want to do something, ask yourself, "Why? Am I guilty, hopeless, discouraged or afraid?"

• *Look for others' emotions.* As you go through the day, try to discern what others are feeling. Look beyond their words for their underlying emotions. Then check out your observations ("You seem a little worried today, are you?").

• *Ask others how you seem to be feeling.* Often others are more aware of your feelings than you are. When others tell you how you're coming across, don't discount it. Instead, tell yourself, "Well, maybe I am a little angry. Let me look and see if I am."

• *Emphasize and highlight how you feel.* By blowing up how you're feeling, you can get a clearer picture of what your emotions are. You can practice this with a tape recorder. Try expressing common emotions such as love, joy, boredom and fear in your voice. Keep practicing until you can readily tell the difference.

• *Become more objective with yourself.* Randomly record yourself throughout the day. Just talk about anything into the recorder. In a couple of days, go back and listen to see if you can tell what your emotional state was. This exercise works even better when you can videotape yourself.

After you become more aware of your emotions you need to focus on your thinking.

Two Ways of Thinking

You have basically two different ways of thinking. The technical name of the first is *primary appraisal*. This is a more immature and primitive way of thinking. You believe that the world revolves around you; your only concern is "What about me? Is it good or is it bad?" Your thoughts here are automatic, global, absolute, unorganized and closely tied to your negative feelings. Essentially you're operating in a nonacceptance framework. For example, if there is some risk, you exaggerate the danger and minimize your ability to handle the danger. The only options you see are fight or flight ("I've got to get home, there are too many weirdos on the road after dark").

The second way of thinking is called *secondary appraisal*. Here, you're thinking in more mature ways. You make more realistic appraisals of your world and discriminate real from unreal dangers. You process information in a much more sophisticated and refined way ("Before I decide, let me weigh the pros and cons"). In primary appraisal, you're connected to the world with a string and tin can. In secondary appraisal, you're using an advanced computer.

Primary appraisal leads to emotional dependency, secondary appraisal leads to emotional independence. Primary appraisal is made up of automatic thoughts that keep you dependent ("I can't" . . . "He should" . . . "It's dangerous"). If you think you're helpless, you'll act in a helpless manner.

Your mind is the control tower that directs you to be dependent or independent. In the case of dependency, your primary thinking creates a nonreal world—a world where you see yourself as smaller and more helpless than you are. Your thinking stops you from acting and thus puts your goals out of reach ("I'll never be accepted at nursing school, so why try?").

What did you think when you started something new in the past—when you learned a new skill or went on your first job interview? You probably thought that the experience would be overwhelming and that you wouldn't be able to handle it. You probably also thought that it was much more important than it was. In short, you minimized your ability and exaggerated the danger.

Independence usually requires doing something you haven't done before. The push toward increased independence is a push into the unknown. Your mind can't accept not knowing so it fills in the void with frightening and discouraging possibilities. Your thoughts dispirit you by distorting reality in a negative direction ("If I break up with him, I'll be alone forever").

Stop, Look and Listen. Your automatic thoughts play a significant role in keeping you emotionally dependent. Such thoughts are misperceptions of who you are and what you can and can't do. To become more independent, you need first to become *aware* of these thoughts, so you can answer them. The basic strategy for identifying your automatic thoughts is to *stop*, *look* and *listen*. When you catch yourself acting in a dependent way, stop what you're doing, look at yourself and listen to what you're telling yourself.

Suppose you're jealous over a coworker's promotion and you're moping over it. First, *stop* moping, then *look* at yourself the way a friendly investigator would. Next, *listen* to what is running through your mind ("She shouldn't have been promoted . . . I deserve it more . . . It's not fair . . . I can't stand not being recognized . . . No matter how hard I work it doesn't do any good").

You can put the stop, look and listen strategy into practice in a variety of ways. Below are some techniques that others have found helpful.

- Use your emotions as cues to stop and listen to what you're thinking ("I hate him").
- Use your avoidances as cues to look at what's going through your mind ("I'll wait and call them tomorrow").
- Force yourself into new situations and listen to your resistance ("I don't belong here" . . . "They're all laughing at me").
- Start writing your automatic thoughts out and don't stop until they are all out.
- Speak your automatic thoughts into a tape recorder; then go back and listen to them.

• Give yourself a goal of stopping and looking for your thoughts in at least two situations every day for ten days.
• Imagine a dialogue going on inside your head between an adult and a child. Listen to words the child is saying ("It stinks" . . . "I won't . . .").
• Set an alarm to go off randomly during the day. When it goes off, stop what you're doing and look for your automatic thoughts.
• Make a date with yourself to search out your thoughts at a specific time and place ("I'll meet you at the dinner table, 7 PM").
• Use an instant-replay technique. Replay the situation over and over until you catch your thoughts.
• Look for the meaning in the situation. Ask yourself what it means to you and to your future.

Many of your automatic thoughts will be in the form of visual images. You want to see these images as clearly as you can. To help you do this, ask yourself the following questions.

• Do I see a picture as I'm thinking about it?
• Can I describe it?
• What color is it?
• Is there sound?
• Am I or others moving in it?
• Can I smell or feel any part of it?
• Can I make it more vivid?

Beliefs: The Deeper Level

Have you ever run into people you haven't seen in years and discovered that they haven't changed all that much? Their consistency is caused by their belief system. Your behavior patterns and daily comings and goings are an outward show of your underlying beliefs. Your beliefs play the largest role in the kind of life you choose to lead. If your beliefs stay the same, so do you.

After you're able to identify your automatic thinking, you can go to a deeper level and discover which of your beliefs are generating your automatic thoughts. In the final analysis, your underlying beliefs are your biggest barrier to becoming more independent. The main reason you want to identify and correct your distorted beliefs is because they hinder your *acceptance of reality*, the first step in the ACT formula.

You need rules to make order out of life and to survive. Your beliefs give meaning and consistency to your life. They allow you to set and reach goals and give you standards by which you can evaluate your experiences. Without them, life would be chaotic. However, you need useful rules that are in line with reality. They need to be flexible enough to adapt to a changing world.

Given the importance of beliefs, it's surprising how few people know what their basic beliefs are. The more emotionally dependent you are, the less you know about yourself. Eric Hoffer observed, "To become different from what we are, we must have some awareness of what we are. . . . Yet it is remarkable that the very people who are most dissatisfied and crave most for a new identity have the least self-awareness." When you're dependent and dissatisfied, you turn away from yourself before really knowing who you are.

You're more likely to change the content of your beliefs than the beliefs themselves. I went to college with Rick, an outspoken student. His basic beliefs were something like "I should go all out in whatever I do . . . I should be passionate about my ideals . . . I need recognition . . . I should be a leader." In his first three years in college he was radically conservative and the president of a small Young Republicans group. In his senior year he switched and became radically liberal, and a leader in the antiwar movement, which by that time had a much larger following. He changed affiliations, but not his basic beliefs. He was still seeking the recognition he wanted.

As a child, you developed many beliefs and rules about life, most of them unwittingly adopted from others. You took them on before you had the ability to think them out logically. As you grew older and had more experience, you added new beliefs and discarded and modified old ones.

We are much like onions, with layers of beliefs upon layers of beliefs. We never completely get rid of our immature beliefs; we just layer them over with more mature ones.

The beliefs that cause you to be emotionally dependent today are leftovers from your childhood. They are the ones that had never been fully thought out when you adopted them. Many of your beliefs and rules come from parents and other authority figures. Eric Berne says the whole process of becoming more independent "consists of obtaining a friendly divorce from one's parents (and from other parental influences) so that they may be agreeably visited on occasion, but are no longer dominant."

You'll have trouble in those areas where your map, or beliefs, doesn't match the way the world is. You'll keep getting lost and running into dead ends because your coordinates are out of line. Instead of redrawing your map, you'll act as if the lay of the land should be changed. When you're more concerned with trying to get the terrain to fit your map, rather than the other way around, you're bound to have trouble.

Beliefs that are flexible and based on common sense are often helpful. For example, common sense tells us that while it's good to have people like us, we can't expect everyone to like us. However, beliefs that are rigid, excessive, absolute and based on private sense (as opposed to common sense) are self-defeating. When you believe "I need to have everyone approve of me," you set yourself up for disappointment and discouragement.

Where you're the most dependent is where your beliefs are the strongest. This is the area where you know the least about yourself. People believe the most in what they know the least about. You can tell an expert by his degree of skepticism and an uninformed person by his degree of certainty. The more certain you are about something, the more likely you are to be wrong. It's to your benefit to question what you're absolutely certain about. Rigid beliefs can only frame a small part of reality. They exclude much more than they include. When you believe you have an exclusive on The Big Truth, you ignore everyday truths. Dogmatism of any kind limits your vision and stops you from moving ahead. Any social or religious movement that doesn't change its belief system soon becomes extinct.

Identifying Beliefs. You operate on your beliefs daily, automatically and without awareness. Once you know what your beliefs are you can then decide to keep them or discard them. Unless you know what they are, you don't have the choice of keeping them or not. Setting out to discover your beliefs can be an interesting and enlightening journey. The journey can take a while, but what you discover can change your life.

I have outlined seventy-five of the most common beliefs associated with dependency in *table 2* (pp. 188–90). I suggest you read each item and then rate how much you believe it (from 0 to 100). If you believe the item slightly you might rate it 5, and if you believe it very strongly you might rate it 90.

After you have gone though all the items, put in order the ten you believe most. If some of the ten are similar, you may be able to consolidate a few. This list will form the basis for discovering your belief system. As you go through the following exercise, add to and modify this list until you come up with a clear idea of what your beliefs are.

You can find out what your beliefs are in a number of other ways. How difficult you find the exercise will depend on how well you know yourself. Here are the standard methods I use in therapy to help people discover their underlying beliefs.

- *Trace your automatic thoughts to their source.* Your dependency-producing thoughts rest logically on one or more of your beliefs. Automatic thoughts are messages sent out from your belief system. By retracing the steps, you can discover what your beliefs are.

  For example, suppose you're afraid to ask someone for a letter of recommendation. Your automatic thoughts might be "She won't want to do it. She won't have anything good to say about me. She'll get mad at me for asking. I couldn't stand the rejection." Once you trace your thoughts backward, you might find that they come from two basic beliefs: (1) "I'm inferior to others," and (2) "Others can hurt my feelings."

  The best way to do this is to write out your thoughts. Another alternative is to talk them through with someone; however, writing is the best way you can do it yourself. The trick is to keep writing until you get to the basic belief. When you get stuck, ask yourself a question that keeps you writing.

  For example, say you have been putting off taking a class. When you first start writing out your thoughts, you'll get a lot of rationalizations ("I don't have the time; I'm too busy right now"). Ask yourself, "Why am I making these excuses?" The answer will lead you into fears ("I'm afraid I won't measure up"). At this point, ask yourself, "Where do my fears come from?" You then will get to the basic beliefs ("I'm not smart enough . . . I don't want to go anywhere alone that's dangerous").

Write out your thoughts for twenty-five or more situations; you'll notice patterns emerging. The themes may have to do with issues about health, approval, acceptance, status, achievement, attractiveness, fairness or morality. By noting recurring themes, you'll be able to tell which of your beliefs are most pronounced, and which get you into the most trouble.

• *Use a standard projection method.* By filling in the following blanks you can see which of your beliefs are most pronounced at any one time. The theory of projection tests is that you project your ideas and beliefs into the unknown blank. You can use this test at different times to see which belief system you're operating out of. If you fill out the first one ("I'm unhappy when ____") when you're upset, you might say "when others let me down." And if you fill it out when you are content, you might write "when I let myself be."

Fill in the blank with the first word that comes to mind. Don't take time to stop and reflect, just write your thought down.

1. I'm unhappy when ____________.
2. If I ____________, others should ____.
3. I can't ____________ because ____________.
4. I won't ____________.
5. Others should ____________.
6. I'm unhappy when ____________.
7. ____________ makes me feel ____________.
8. I don't ____________.
9. I must not ____________.
10. I must ____________.
11. Life should be ____________.

• *Use life as a projective test.* I have always thought that one of the best ways to get to know someone is to have a few drinks with the person and play Monopoly. Some players will almost refuse to win; they give their money and property away as quickly as possible. Others will almost kill you to get Park Place and may even cheat—if that's what it takes to win. Some will take the whole game as just that, a game to be enjoyed for its own sake. How they react when the game is over can also tell you a lot about them.

Some will gloat, others will mope, some will make excuses and a few might even congratulate the winner.

How do you play Monopoly? Throughout the day you project your beliefs onto persons, places and things around you. In Monopoly you project certain beliefs about your relationship to the world onto the game. For example, if you believe others won't like you if you win, you won't play to win. By paying attention to whatever activity you're engaged in, you can learn much about your belief system.

To detect your projections, you can ask yourself the following questions:

What television or movie figures do I identify with and why? Do I like Captain Kirk of *Star Trek?* If so, what do I like about him?

What sports figures do I like and dislike? From which of my beliefs is this coming from?

When I see someone in public who is exceedingly happy or unhappy, what do I attribute their mood to?

In soap operas or novels, what types of characters am I drawn to? What does this tell me about myself?

You can also discover what your beliefs are by looking at the world you have created for yourself. What do you wear? What kind of house do you live in? What does your circle of friends tell you about your beliefs? Take your work for example; the quality of your work is your personal signature. If one part of your work area is immaculate and another is a complete mess, what does this tell you about your beliefs? This might mean that you believe you have to be in perfect control of your life or else you're totally out of control.

• *Discover where your beliefs come from.* The general rule when you get lost is to go back to where you took the wrong turn. By going back and seeing where you adopted your beliefs, you can often make them clearer to you. When you first learned these rules, they were much more dramatic and obvious. Over the years they haven't lost their power, even though they have been covered over.

Following are some of the ways you can do detective work on where your beliefs come from.

List 5 of your family's most common sayings as you were growing up.

1. ______________________________
2. ______________________________

3. ______________________________
4. ______________________________
5. ______________________________

Fairy tales and other bedtime stories can be the basis for your present beliefs. Which stories did you identify with most and why?

Many of your beliefs are passed down for generations. We traced one patient's fear of going broke back three generations to immigrants from Russia who were very poor. Write out what you think were your parents' (and if possible your grandparents' as well) basic beliefs related to dependency.

Consolidating Beliefs. After you have a long list of possible beliefs, consolidate them into the ten most troublesome. Next to each, leave a space for the degree of belief. In *table 3* (p. 191) are one person's ten basic beliefs. Next, make photocopies of this list. You can then use this list to pinpoint your most troublesome beliefs. Rate your degree of belief for each of them right now. Then do it whenever you're acting in a dependent way. If you do this for a couple of weeks, you'll find that in some of the situations you'll hang on to several beliefs much more than to others. These are the beliefs you want to make the biggest effort to replace. The general strategy is to *accept* that this is what you now believe ("I can't stand rejection"); then *choose* to replace it with a more mature belief ("I can tolerate rejection"); and finally, *take action* to support your new belief (put yourself in situations where you're likely to be rejected). In the remaining chapters, I'll talk about other ways you can strengthen your new beliefs.

TABLE 1

GUIDELINES TO GREATER SELF-AWARENESS

1. Own you own actions and feelings.
2. Approach what you want to avoid.
3. Force yourself to think through what's unpleasant.
4. Fully experience your feelings.
5. Keep your mind open.
6. Develop new friends and associations.
7. Become more active.
8. Be more honest.

TABLE 2

DEPENDENCY BELIEFS

BELIEF	Degree of Belief (0–100)
1. I don't measure up to others.	______
2. Bad things happen to me when I stand up for myself.	______
3. I have to do everything perfectly or I don't do anything at all.	______
4. The world is a dangerous place.	______
5. Other people always seem to let me down.	______
6. If I do something for others, I'm indebted to them.	______
7. If people find out too much about me, they'll use it against me.	______
8. I have to be loved to be happy.	______
9. It's best to give up my interests to please other people.	______
10. I can't be respected unless I've achieved something (have a good education or occupation) or am especially talented.	______

11. If other people dislike me, I can't be happy. ______
12. If I'm alone, I'll be lonely. ______
13. I have to do more than other people to be as good as they. ______
14. If people know what I'm really like, they won't like me. ______
15. My happiness depends more on other people than on me. ______
16. If a person I want to love me doesn't, that means I'm unlovable. ______
17. To be nice, I have to help anyone in need. ______
18. I can't cope on my own. ______
19. My group (women, blacks, Jews, poor, old, uneducated) is inferior to other groups. ______
20. It's my fault if those I love (husband, friend, children) are in trouble. ______
21. I should think of other people first, even if I have difficulties. ______
22. I should always be modest about my abilities. ______
23. I have no right to ask other people to help me. ______
24. I should never hurt anyone's feelings. ______
25. I'm basically bad (stupid, ugly, phony, immoral, lazy, a bitch, demanding). ______
26. I must have total control. ______
27. I should give up my own interests to please others. ______
28. I have to feel bad when I'm criticized. ______
29. I find my greatest enjoyment in pleasing others. ______
30. I should never be selfish. ______
31. What others think of me is crucial to my happiness. ______
32. I can't stand people being indifferent to me. ______
33. My happiness is the result of how others treat me. ______
34. I have to please everybody. ______
35. I have little control over what I think. ______
36. I have to be especially talented to be worthwhile. ______
37. Some people are more worthy than others. ______
38. I'm responsible for what others feel. ______
39. When I deserve something, I should be able to have it. ______
40. It doesn't make any sense to take risks. ______
41. I have to control my feelings. ______

42. If I do well it's probably due to chance. ______
43. I should help others cope with their life problems. ______
44. If I ignore problems, they tend to go away. ______
45. I'm nothing if someone doesn't love me. ______
46. If I don't have people to support me, I'm bound to be unhappy. ______
47. If I help others, they should help me when I need it. ______
48. If people know my flaws, they will reject me. ______
49. I can't accept the way I am. ______
50. The way to get people to like you is to impress them. ______
51. If I'm alone, I have to be unhappy. ______
52. It's easier to get someone else to do what's difficult for me to do. ______
53. I can't accept bad news. ______
54. If I'm on my own, I flounder. ______
55. I need someone to take care of me financially. ______
56. Life should be fair. ______
57. I need to get others to do most of my work. ______
58. I should take care of others when they're in need. ______
59. I can't say no to others. ______
60. Being rejected is the worst thing that could happen to me. ______
61. I need to have a lot of friends in case I lose some of them. ______
62. I feel rejected when others don't take my advice. ______
63. I'm wasting my life. ______
64. I'm afraid I'll end up living alone. ______
65. I don't have enough will power. ______
66. I need help from others to survive. ______
67. I'm afraid of losing my looks. ______
68. I know I can always count on others to help me out. ______
69. I need a steady relationship to feel secure. ______
70. I feel safe only when I'm with others. ______
71. I don't like to be too far away from people I know. ______
72. Life is meaningless without love. ______
73. I'm inferior to others. ______
74. I can't change my situation. ______
75. Others have control over me. ______

TABLE 3

SAMPLE OF ONE CLIENT'S BASIC BELIEFS

BELIEF	Degree of Belief (0–100)
1. The world should be fair.	80
2. I am responsible for the poor of the world.	75
3. If I help someone in my family, they should help me.	90
4. If I'm not careful, I'll end up unloved.	99
5. I am losing my good looks.	90
6. My children owe it to me to care for me in my old age.	85
7. I shouldn't hurt other people's feelings.	70
8. I should have been born rich.	99
9. My forte is ideas, not carrying them out.	80

CHAPTER ELEVEN

Social Independence

ONCE YOU OWN YOUR OWN LIFE, you're able to move closer to others. You approach others with an attitude of giving and acceptance. Because you can accept yourself, you're free to accept others. Love is accepting others for what they are, not for what they could be or what you would like them to be. When others feel this acceptance, they want to be around you. The absence of your expectations and corresponding judgments frees them to be themselves.

When you're socially independent you meet others as equals. You don't see them as superiors or inferiors who need to be manipulated to your benefit. Because you're self-sufficient, you're able to deal directly with others. You don't need a go-between. The more independent you are, the less you need any form of intermediary. When you're direct with others, they are direct with you in return. As a result, you know where you stand with the people who are important in your life.

Once you're socially independent, you can give freely of yourself, your time, your services and your care. This is why social success follows social independence. You set up a positive force in others. However, when you're socially dependent you give with strings attached. This eventually works against you because it's not a gift, but a manipulation. And people don't like to be manipulated.

By believing that you can take care of yourself socially, you don't feel compelled to maneuver people into taking care of you. Manipulation may get you what you want in the short run, but in the long run you end up with people tending to avoid you. Most people will only allow you to manipulate them once or twice.

Socially dependent people approach others timidly. Because they feel helpless, they are constantly looking for people to take care of them. The problem is that others may reject them and rejection feels worse than being alone. So you may often feel caught in the middle. A further problem is that as you get older, fewer people want to come to your rescue. The solution is to develop your social independence now.

You probably lack social skills because you're afraid. Social fear, more than anything else, stops you from owning your own life. The more dependent you are, the more fears you'll have. You may fear being *abandoned*, *rejected*, *deprived*, *criticized* or *ridiculed*. These fears cause you to seek someone else to do your confronting for you, and it causes you to avoid social encounters and intimacy.

Social fears may mean constant worry about the future. You spend more time anticipating what others are going to do than you spend with them. Your constant anticipation is an interference: you have trouble listening to what others are saying and seeing what they are doing. You aren't fully there, so they don't know who you are either.

On the other hand, when you're socially independent, you appreciate what's going on now; you don't bother to judge it, good or bad. You just accept it as what it is. You have more confidence to live in the present because you aren't panicked by the future. Being in the present allows you to connect better with people. Because you can extend yourself if you choose to, you can become part of a large social network; or, if you choose, you can focus on a few intimate relationships.

People will also move toward you when you're socially independent because they enjoy being in your presence. A friend has said that he considers people as plumbing fixtures. He believes you can be either a radiator—people move toward you for warmth and comfort—or a drain—people move away from you to avoid being sucked down. When you feel empty and are continuously taking from others, people feel drained when they're with you. And when you feel full and giving, people feel comfortable when they are in your presence.

Others will also move toward you when you're socially independent because they know they can count on you. They know you'll keep your promises and will follow through on what you say. Because you can keep your bargains with yourself, you can keep them with others. You're at the place you say you'll be and you do what you say you'll do. Integrity pulls people toward you. Dependent people, on the other hand, are undependable.

Social Isolation

Your relationships with others can easily go out of whack. You may lean on others or you may shy away from them. The result is often the same: you become more socially isolated. Social isolation is usually the result of the dependency cycle. When you believe you need others to support you, you drive them off. A vicious cycle begins. The more they move away from you, the more you try to grab on.

The opposite happens when you're self-sufficient. You're at ease with yourself. You don't feel you have to act in ways calculated to please others. People in turn are less guarded and more relaxed when you don't want something from them; they feel more comfortable and move toward you.

How you really are—your true self—is nearly always more attractive than your social façade. I've noticed this in therapy. I'm not Will Rogers and there are plenty of people I've met that I don't like. However, I end up liking nearly everyone I see in therapy. The reason is that people can be themselves there; they let their guard down.

When you're socially independent, you feel free to be yourself and this allows others to feel free to be themselves. The end result is that you are closer to others.

You may voluntarily choose to isolate yourself. Many people take this route. You can do this for a variety of reasons. You may feel people usually let you down. You may think you can't be what others expect you to be. You may believe you don't have what it takes to deal with others; or because of the pain brought on by past experiences, you may be afraid of all relationships.

Charles came to see me with a problem with loneliness. When

he moved toward people in social situations, he felt like a phony. At his sister's wedding, he kept saying to himself, "I hardly know these people. All this smiling and saying 'how are you' to them is phony." Immediately after the ceremony he left, deciding that the reception would be too awkward and painful. He acted and felt this way again and again, at most social situations. By refusing to wait out the discomfort, he fueled his old habit of withdrawal and drove himself into further isolation.

He learned to overcome this block by saying to himself, "Okay, here come some of those feelings, just as I expected. Only this time I'll accept them. I'm going to choose to stay at the party and see if I can turn them around." Instead of using his feelings as reasons or excuses to avoid the uncomfortable social situation, he chose to stay and endure them. He was eventually able to become more socially active.

Intimacy

Your social independence is crucial in close relationships. A relationship based on mutual independence has a better future than one based on mutual dependency. Many dependent people have what the psychoanalytic writer Helmuth Kaiser calls *the illusion of fusion:* the belief that you can become one with another. The illusion that you can fuse with another into one organism hinders intimacy because it feeds dependency. The illusion of fusion causes you to search frantically for perfect understanding from the perfect person. However, you're doomed to be frustrated for the rest of your life because you can never become one with another. No matter how close you become with another and no matter what you think, you always remain a separate individual.

Everyday Social Dependency Checklist

You may not be aware of all of your forms of social dependency. The following are some common examples found in everyday life. Check off those that apply to you.

1. You ask someone else to confront your problems for you. YES __ NO __
2. You ask someone else to make your phone calls for you. YES __ NO __
3. You ask someone else to resolve your conflicts for you. YES __ NO __
4. You ask someone else to ask a third party for a favor. YES __ NO __
5. You lie to others. YES __ NO __
6. You don't tell what's on your mind because you fear the consequences. YES __ NO __
7. You're usually late for social engagements. YES __ NO __
8. You don't return phone calls. YES __ NO __
9. You have to continually ask for permission ("I'll check with my husband"). YES __ NO __
10. You continually complain about other people. YES __ NO __
11. You're judgmental of others ("Poor [or rich] people are no damn good"). YES __ NO __
12. You stay silent rather than tell others what's on your mind. YES __ NO __
13. You say yes to every social request and then inevitably wish you had said no. YES __ NO __
14. You don't speak up when you feel you've been taken unfair advantage of. YES __ NO __
15. You don't ask others for a favor that you would normally do for them. YES __ NO __
16. You go along with others' criticism ("Blacks are no damn good") when you don't believe it. YES __ NO __
17. You can't end phone conversations even though you want to. YES __ NO __
18. You don't tell others what movie or restaurant you would like to go to. YES __ NO __
19. You let others interrupt when you are talking, and give up the floor. YES __ NO __
20. You're afraid to ask for the return of something you've loaned. YES __ NO __
21. You can't say no to someone who wants to borrow something you don't want to lend. YES __ NO __

22. You don't speak up to watch the TV program you want to watch. YES __ NO __

23. You don't speak up when you've been stood up. YES __ NO __

24. You don't say no when you're continually asked to bring food back to others from lunch. YES __ NO __

25. You don't speak up to professionals. YES __ NO __

26. You don't ask for a ride from someone who's going where you want to go. YES __ NO __

27. At a group meeting, if anyone disagrees with any of your ideas, you clam up. YES __ NO __

28. You let people patronize you ("Here's the most important cog in the wheel, my secretary"). YES __ NO __

29. You never talk positively about your accomplishments. YES __ NO __

30. You don't let anyone in on your inner feelings. YES __ NO __

31. You discount others' compliments. YES __ NO __

32. You become defensive if anyone criticizes you. YES __ NO __

33. You accompany others to avoid hurting their feelings. YES __ NO __

34. You're constantly role playing with others instead of being yourself. YES __ NO __

35. You use honesty as a weapon. YES __ NO __

36. You're continually worried about what topic you'll discuss when you're with other people. YES __ NO __

37. You never say anything that people might take offense at, or, in other words, you're boring. YES __ NO __

38. You can't give people positive feedback. YES __ NO __

39. You can't give people negative feedback. YES __ NO __

40. You're not free and spontaneous during sex. YES __ NO __

41. You constantly are observing and commenting on yourself when you're interacting with others. YES __ NO __

42. You can't make small talk with others. YES __ NO __

43. You're overly sympathetic to others. YES __ NO __

44. You spoil others with kindness. YES __ NO __

45. You're a poor judge of others' character. YES __ NO __

46. You become involved in other-pity and take on others' problems as your own. YES __ NO __

47. You imitate your heroes and people you admire. YES __ NO __

48. You can't trust others. YES __ NO __

49. You're uncomfortable in many social situations. YES __ NO __

50. You're a reformer and want to reform others. YES __ NO __

51. You want to police others and see that they do the right thing. YES __ NO __

52. You have trouble introducing yourself to others. YES __ NO __

53. Others arrange social gatherings for you. YES __ NO __

54. You're thoughtless of others' interest in you. YES __ NO __

When in Trouble, Think the Reverse

Ellen said, "I know how I want to act and what I need to accept, but I can't think of what action to take."

I told her that the action you need to take to become more socially independent is usually clear. *You do the opposite of what you feel like doing around people.* What you're doing now is supporting your dependency, so to undermine this support, you need to reverse the pattern and do the opposite.

You have to think in reverse, especially when you're in trouble. The person who survives an airplane crash or fire is often the one who does the opposite of the victims. Survivors of crises typically use a version of the ACT formula. First, they accept the situation: they don't deny that they smell smoke or indulge in false hope that rescue is around the corner. Second, they choose to stay calm and not become excited and panicky. And finally they take action that's often the reverse of their first instinct. They don't panic after being bitten by a snake or take off in all directions when their clothes catch fire. When you're in trouble, your instincts are usually thrown off. That's why you usually need to act against them. The same goes for social situations where your instinct is to be dependent.

Thinking in reverse is the best practical way to approach everyday problems of social independence. Those times you can't think of the answer to a social dilemma, the opposite of what you're looking for is often the best. For example, have you ever wondered what was the best lie to give—then suddenly realized that telling the truth was the best approach?

Paradox of Beliefs

Many philosophers and writers have commented on the self-contradictory nature of life. You're living and dying at the same time. You need sunlight to see, but if you get too much it blinds you. Life is full of such paradoxes. You can use the self-contradictions of life to help you become more socially independent by using the reverse principle.

Any of your rules or beliefs about how to deal with others can hurt you if you follow them to extremes. Just as the sun can both warm you and blind you, your rules can help or harm you. You're acting dependently because you have followed a set of rules that may initially have helped you but now hold you back. Wanting to be liked, for example, makes perfect sense on a limited basis, but on an extended basis, it's self-destructive.

The paradox is that when you follow any of your rules to the extreme, they work in reverse: you get the opposite of what you want. If you believe that everyone has to like you, you often end up with no one liking you. The way out of this trap is to reverse your rules when they are working against you. *To get back on track you have to take the opposite tack.* Your old solutions or strategies are usually the wrong ones. By taking a radically different perspective and reversing them, you can get unstuck.

Practicality

In day-to-day social living with people, thinking in reverse has its practical advantages: it's easier going shopping Sunday morning than Friday evening; it's easier to get a dinner reservation Tuesday night than Saturday night; it's easier to look for a job when you already have one; it's easier to learn something when you're teaching it; and it's easier and more effective when interviewing for a job to interview the interviewer.

Two of my own guiding principles have to do with reversing the normal process. First, do the hardest activity first (call the person you least want to talk to first). This gives you a success experience; and everything after it seems easy. Second, tell people the bad news first and in great detail. Beating around the bush only makes matters worse.

Creativity

Being creative involves thinking in reverse. New solutions to old problems are often discovered by reversing the way you have been trying to solve them. Instead of trying to get people to like you, try to like them. Instead of trying to hide your flaws in social situations, expose them. Instead of trying to defend yourself from criticism, agree with the kernel of truth in the criticism.

Peggy would go to parties and throw herself into trying to make people like her. She believed that unless she went all out ("Gee, you're looking great tonight . . . I just love your dress . . . Where's that handsome husband of yours"), no one would like her. She greeted new people with loud attempts to be amusing and entertaining. This would backfire when they would say, "Why did you invite *her*? She can't keep her mouth shut and she's stupid besides." Her friends would defend her with "Peg's okay. You just have to see beyond how she acts with new people." Unfortunately, few people were willing to do so.

She decided to think in reverse. She started going to parties and trying to get to know the new people, rather than trying to impress them. This worked. She found that by taking an interest in and listening to new people, they became interested in her.

The way to any type of success is frequently to think in reverse. When you turn your ideas around 180 degrees, solutions start to appear. Most successful people knowingly or unknowingly use this strategy. Failures are seen and used as preludes to success. Disadvantages are turned into advantages and problems are seen as opportunities.

People who are considered lucky often use this strategy. Mark, a fellow I went to high school with, was always considered lucky. For example, he took off to Hawaii to surf for a year. Many of his friends couldn't find jobs in Honolulu and had to come home early. Mark was able to get a high-paying managerial job.

He said, "My philosophy is to do the opposite of everyone else. Because all the surfers were looking for menial jobs like busboys or gas-pump jockies, there were almost no jobs like that around. So I decided to go after the better jobs, which hardly any of them were looking for. There wasn't nearly the competition for those jobs."

When you fail you often think your best bet is to look for something less. Often your best bet is to try for something better. A friend said he was turned down for a date with a woman at his office. He said his family's rule was if you fail at something you should try for something better, so he asked out and was accepted by a more attractive woman in the office.

If a Dog Runs at You, Whistle

You can use this principle in social-conflict situations. By doing the opposite of what's expected of you, you throw others off. For example, one of the benefits of turning the other cheek is that others don't know how to respond to this. When someone is criticizing you and you say, "Is there anything else wrong?" this often takes the wind out of their sails.

The Russians beat the Germans in World War II by losing. The more territory the Germans captured, the longer their supply lines became. They won so much territory that their supply lines eventually collapsed and they lost the war.

This is the principle of judo. You *can* win for losing. President Reagan, for example, used political judo with his age. In his presidential campaign, his age started out to be a political liability. During the campaign, he celebrated his birthday openly and had five or six different birthday parties. This had the effect of making his age seem less important. If he had hidden or downplayed his birthday, his age might have been a much more significant factor in the election. The color of his hair was an issue. He probably could have avoided this by dyeing his hair completely white.

To be socially independent, you often have to defy logic and do the opposite of what you feel like doing. By thinking in reverse you can change the momentum when it's going against you. For example, in social situations you typically let up after you've suffered a setback (you didn't get invited to a party) and psych yourself up only after a good turn of events. The best approach is to get yourself up after a setback to halt the momentum. After a social defeat, you may start cutting back and creating a failure cycle.

What you do affects others and their actions in turn can affect you. By acting the opposite you can break this cycle. If a coworker is always saying how bad everything is and you continually argue with the person about this, you'll keep the pattern going. However, by agreeing with some of the truth in what he or she says or even by blowing up the other side ("You're right, the country's going to the dogs . . . I can't see one thing right with this whole country"), you can stop the pattern.

Because reversing your strategies is often the best strategy, you can use this when you're in trouble and don't know what to do. Thoreau's advice, "If a dog runs at you, whistle to him," is along the same lines. An interesting phenomenon occurs when you're willing to face the naked truth: the fear and the danger disappear. You don't have to face it even, just be willing to face it ("Okay, if they think I'm a fool, I'll accept that").

When you try to change the direction of your life, you usually follow strategies that have some logic and have worked for you before. However, following this method often stops you from getting what you want. For example, trying not to make mistakes is logical and may work in some areas of your life. But if you apply this rule to areas where you want to become independent, it backfires. Being afraid to make mistakes stops you from taking risks. You don't get the experiences (another name for mistakes) to become competent in new areas.

Often the reverse action is *the action* you *least* want to take. This is why it's probably the one in your best interest.

I've outlined some rules that are the opposite of common beliefs, and I'll talk about how they can help you to become more independent. You can often get more mileage by reversing them.

Anything Worth Doing Is Worth Doing Poorly

Marian was invited to talk about her trip to South America for a local women's club. She was stopped by fears that her presentation wouldn't be perfect. She had the belief that she had to do everything supremely well. Because she was afraid that she couldn't meet her high standards, she didn't do anything. Once she changed her belief to *if it's worth doing, it's worth doing—no matter how well it's done*, she was able to start working and finish the project.

You can use this idea to become more socially independent in some of the following ways.

- Don't wait to find the perfect date or set of friends.
- Speak up, even if what you say isn't brilliant.
- Don't try to find the perfect opening line. "Hi, how are you?" will do.
- Call people on the phone, even if you're not good on the phone.
- Don't expect or try to make every social encounter go smoothly.
- Don't wait for a "better" time to invite friends to your home.
- Don't discount a new friend because he or she is too short . . . too tall . . . too old . . . too fat . . . too poor . . .
- Don't choose not to do something because your friends think it sounds dumb or foolish.

Stop Trying So Hard. Have you noticed that when you try to get something, it's difficult to get, and when you stop trying, it often comes right to you? The most common example is a couple that tries and tries to have a baby unsuccessfully. Finally they adopt a child. Then, after they've quit trying, the woman almost immediately becomes pregnant. The belief that the more you want something the more likely you'll be to get it is often wrong. When you want something too much, you create resistance that gets in the way.

John was prone to talk himself into many problems. Once he was reading about impotence and said to himself, "My God, I wonder if I could get that. That sounds like something I might get." He rushed home to check this out with his wife. He tried like mad to get an erection. Of course he couldn't get one. Most forms of sexual dysfunction are caused by trying too hard. You try yourself into knots. The trick of sexual counseling is to reverse the normal procedure. Typically, a counselor asks the couple to have sex without trying to have orgasms.

There are reasons why trying gets in the way. Laurence Morehouse, director of the Human Performance Lab at UCLA and an expert on how to maximize human performance, has talked about this. His basic message is that you'll accomplish more and have more fun doing it if you stop trying so hard. "At stake in learning to be a better performer are some cherished notions of how excellence is achieved. Foremost among them is the idea that the harder we struggle the better we'll do. That's almost always wrong." He says you'll achieve more if you don't overload yourself with projects, concerns and goals. Your over-effort spoils the act.

When you try hard you tense up; you then have to untense to get moving. A relaxed muscle can be stretched to a greater length than a tensed muscle.

Part of this relates to levels of motivation. If you want something too much you often use more energy than you need to. This throws the whole process off. If you try with all your might to thread a needle, you'll have more trouble than if you don't try so hard. Each task has its proper level of motivation. That's why trying too hard often becomes counterproductive. The following are some ways you can put this principle into action.

- Stop trying to make people like you.
- Stop trying so hard to please others.
- Stop trying so hard to get others (children, husband or wife) to do what you want them to do.
- Stop trying so hard to get people to understand you.
- Stop trying so hard to solve others' problems.
- Stop trying so hard to improve others.
- Stop trying so hard to hide your flaws.

I've found that when people say, "I'm trying to change," they haven't yet made up their minds what they are going to do.

Make Yourself Vulnerable. You may have learned that you have to protect yourself at all costs. This is often the wrong strategy. Take social anxiety, for example. When you believe you have to protect yourself from it, the anxiety persists. What you resist often persists ("I shouldn't be anxious around others" . . . "Don't be anxious, you won't know how to act") makes you more anxious. The way to control anxiety or panic attacks is to make yourself more vulnerable by experiencing it. Allan Watts refers to this principle as "The wisdom of insecurity."

Jane, for example, was anxious about her appearance. She tried constantly to protect her looks by never making facial expressions —she wanted to prevent wrinkles. She would refuse any invitations that involved getting out in the sun or wind. She bought nearly every face cream on the market. She was scared that someday she would lose her attractiveness.

She spent more time believing she was unattractive than attractive. To get over her fear of losing her looks, she needed to reverse her strategy and go out in public over and over without trying to look her best. She was eventually able to do this, and her anxiety disappeared.

Whatever you base your self-worth on is your area of greatest weakness. Trying to protect this is what causes you your trouble. If you overvalue good looks, status, money, you'll get depressed and anxious around these areas. For example, I saw a patient who said, "My biggest strength is my honesty." His biggest fear? He was afraid people would think he was dishonest. He would try to be overly honest by qualifying what he said and feeling guilty if he wasn't 100 percent honest. To overcome this fear, he had to reverse his strategy and allow himself to cut some corners and accept that what others thought of him was their concern, not his.

A major block to social independence is social anxiety or fear. This is caused by trying to protect yourself. Below are some ways you can reverse the process and get a different result.

- Openly expect that you will get anxious around others. Don't be surprised when you are.
- Look at your anxiety in a detached way—watch it go up and down.
- Don't fight it. Accept it and let it be.
- Don't focus too much on your fear. Instead, focus on something real that's around you—such as what others are wearing.
- Don't hide your anxiety; tell others when you're nervous.
- Don't try to protect yourself by bragging or hiding behind others' achievements, your looks, achievements or social status. This only makes you more fearful in the long run.
- Self-disclose about yourself. Tell the good as well as the bad.
- Don't blame others. A wrong strategy is to make yourself feel more comfortable by putting down the event or people involved in it.
- There often are other people present in a social situation who feel uncomfortable too—rather than trying to help them feel more relaxed, accept them as they are.

Don't Just Do Something, Sit There. Often your best action is to take no action. The belief that you always have to do something can cause you to keep your dependency going and cause you problems. Often you need time to sort issues out before you take some action. To become more independent you have to stop seeking reassurance, others' company and attention. For example, it may be more important for you to stay home than to go out. Below are some ways you can use this in becoming more independent.

- Instead of impulsively asking for help, think through what you can do for yourself.
- Instead of overreacting to others, stop and see what *you* can do that's more constructive.
- When you start to panic and want to leave a frightening situation, force yourself to stay.
- When you're about to give up on a project, give yourself some time to think about it. Most of the failures in the world are caused by not doing quite enough. After you think about it, you may be able to come up with something more you can do.

It's Easier to Do Than to Say. In talking about independence, people frequently say, "It's easier to say than to do." But is it really? One of the hardest tasks is to have long conversations with yourself about what you're going to do. This takes so much energy you don't have any left to do the job.

One of the reasons you'll find it harder to say than to do is that for each of your reasons why you should do something your mind comes up with rationalizations or reasons why you can't do it. Have you noticed that those tasks you just *do* are the easiest? One of the reasons people often do a job themselves rather than have others do it is that it's easier to do than to explain how to do it: thus, saying it becomes more difficult than just doing it. The following are ways you can put this reverse principle into practice.

- Don't focus on the task—going to a party where you don't know anyone—just do it. Live dangerously.
- Don't overexplain to yourself what you're going to say. The content of the task will take care of itself. Don't overprepare.
- If you have trouble following through on what you tell others you're going to do, don't tell them, surprise them—and yourself.
- Whenever the thought comes to your mind to do something you've been putting off, do it right then—make that phone call or write that letter.

You Get More with Less. Nearly any activity reaches some point of diminishing return. This applies to your actions that are keeping you socially dependent. Too much help makes you more helpless. Doing too much for your children can make them into social cripples. Seeking constant reassurance makes you more insecure. The following are what you'll get when you apply this principle to social independence.

- More respect with less selling of yourself.
- More clarity with less explaining.
- More achievement with less ambition.
- More closeness with less demand for it.
- More comfort with less work at trying to get it.
- More understanding with less apologizing.

Much of dependency is paradoxical. You try to protect yourself and this makes you feel more vulnerable. You try to feel more secure and this makes you more insecure. You try to get people to help you and you end up more helpless. You try to get people to connect with you and people move farther away. You try to make yourself feel better and you end up feeling worse.

To become independent, you often have to use this paradoxical truth to your advantage and think in reverse. My job as a therapist is often to get people to stop doing what they want to do ("I want to call him one more time in case he's changed his mind") and start doing what they don't want to do ("I don't want to go to the meeting"). Doing the opposite often appears to be the hardest action, but it turns out to be the easiest.

To see where you stand in terms of social independence, you can take the following inventory.

Social Independence Inventory

Social dependency refers to your interaction with other people—your way of approaching others, your style and intent, and what others mean to you. This also includes your ability to form intimate relationships. *Partner* in the questionnaire refers to your husband, wife, or the person with whom you're in a relationship. If you're not in a relationship now, answer the way you have acted in relationships in the past, or the way you imagine you would act.

Read each group of statements carefully. Then circle the number beside the statement that best describes you. After you have completed the questionnaire, add up all the numbers circled. Check your total with the totals given at the end of the chapter.

1. 0 I'm direct when I talk to others.
   1 I'm usually direct when I talk to others.
   2 It's difficult for me to be direct when I talk to others.
   3 It's impossible for me to be direct when I talk to others.
2. 0 I don't overcompliment others.
   1 I occasionally get carried away and overcompliment others.
   2 I often overcompliment others.
   3 I always overcompliment others.
3. 0 I rarely feel shame around others.
   1 I occasionally feel shame around others.
   2 I often feel shame around others.
   3 I feel shame around others.
4. 0 When I want to do something for enjoyment, I can usually find someone to join me.
   1 I often end up doing things alone even though I'd like to have someone join me.
   2 There's no one right now I can go out and enjoy things with.
   3 There hasn't been anyone I could go out and enjoy things with for several years.
5. 0 There is someone I am intimate with now on a regular basis.
   1 I am not intimate with anyone now on a regular basis.
   2 I am often disturbed that I am not intimate with someone on a regular basis.
   3 I have never been intimate with anyone on a regular basis for several months.
6. 0 I have seen or spoken to friends three or four times in the last two weeks.
   1 I have seen or spoken to friends two or three times in the last two weeks.
   2 I have seen or spoken to one friend in the last two weeks.
   3 I have not seen or spoken to a friend in the last two weeks.
7. 0 I can always talk about my innermost feelings to friends if I choose to.
   1 About half the time I feel able to talk about my innermost feelings to friends.
   2 I am usually not able to talk about my feelings.
   3 I am never able to talk about my feelings.

8. 0 I haven't had any open arguments with my friends in the last two weeks.
 1 I usually get along well with my friends but have minor arguments.
 2 I have many arguments with my friends.
 3 I am constantly in arguments with my friends.
9. 0 My feelings were not hurt or offended by a friend in the past two weeks.
 1 My feelings were hurt or offended, but I got over it in a few hours.
 2 My feelings were hurt or offended, but I got over it in a few days.
 3 My feelings were hurt or offended and it will take me months to recover.
10. 0 I have not felt shy or uncomfortable with people in the last two weeks.
 1 I sometimes feel uncomfortable but can relax after a while.
 2 About half the time I feel uncomfortable with people.
 3 I always feel uncomfortable with people.
11. 0 I have not felt lonely and have not wished for more friends during the last two weeks.
 1 I have felt lonely a few times.
 2 About half the time I felt lonely.
 3 I always feel lonely and wish for more friends.
12. 0 I'm married or in a relationship, but I enjoy going out alone.
 1 I go out alone but prefer to go with my partner.
 2 I rarely go anywhere without my partner.
 3 I do everything with my partner.
13. 0 I always get along well with my relatives.
 1 I usually get along well with my relatives but have had some minor arguments.
 2 I have many arguments with my relatives.
 3 I am constantly in arguments with my relatives.
14. 0 I contact my relatives regularly.
 1 I wait for my relatives to contact me.
 2 I avoid my relatives but they contact me.
 3 I have no contacts with any relatives.
15. 0 I have not depended on my relatives for help, advice, money or friendship during the last two weeks.

1 I depended on my relatives three or four times during the last two weeks.
2 I depended on my relatives about half the time during the last two weeks.
3 I depended completely on my relatives during the last two weeks.

16. 0 I don't feel that I've let my relatives down.
1 I usually don't feel that I've let my relatives down.
2 Most of the time I feel I've let my relatives down.
3 I always feel I've let my relatives down.

17. 0 I don't feel that my relatives have let me down or been unfair to me.
1 I feel that my relatives usually don't let me down.
2 I feel that my relatives let me down most of the time.
3 I am very bitter that my relatives are unfair to me and let me down.

18. 0 I can always talk freely about my problems and feelings with my partner.
1 I usually talk freely about my feelings with my partner.
2 I usually am not able to talk freely with my partner.
3 I am not able to talk freely with my partner.

19. 0 I am almost never bossed around by my partner.
1 I am bossed around by my partner occasionally.
2 I am bossed around by my partner most of the time.
3 I am always bossed around by my partner.

20. 0 I am not dependent on my partner.
1 I am occasionally dependent on my partner.
2 I am often dependent on my partner.
3 I am dependent on my partner for everything.

21. 0 I always feel affection for my partner.
1 I usually feel affection for my partner.
2 I seldom feel affection for my partner.
3 I never feel affection for my partner.

22. 0 I don't get upset when my partner acts like a different person.
1 I sometimes get upset when my partner acts like a different person.
2 I get pretty upset when my partner acts like a different person.
3 It is upsetting when my partner acts like a different person.

23. 0 I feel pleased about my interactions with my partner.
    1 I sometimes feel unhappy about my interactions with my partner.
    2 I often feel unhappy about my interactions with my partner.
    3 I am unhappy about my interactions with my partner.
24. 0 My partner is not dependent on me.
    1 I feel my partner may be a little dependent on me.
    2 I feel my partner is too dependent on me.
    3 My partner is too dependent on me.
25. 0 I have as much privacy as I'd like.
    1 I could use more privacy from my partner.
    2 I want more privacy from my partner.
    3 I don't have enough privacy from my partner.
26. 0 I don't feel uncomfortable when I go out in public.
    1 I sometimes feel uncomfortable when I go out in public.
    2 I often feel uncomfortable when I go out in public.
    3 I feel uncomfortable when I go out in public.
27. 0 I'm not particularly afraid of strangers.
    1 I'm sometimes afraid of strangers.
    2 I'm often afraid of strangers.
    3 I'm terrified of strangers.

RESULTS:

Score of 0–6 = high level of social independence.
Score of 7–17 = moderate level of social independence.
Score of 18–25 = low level of social independence.
Score of 25 or above = severe problem with social independence.

CHAPTER TWELVE

Escaping Social Straitjackets

EDWIN HAD WORKED for the same large Philadelphia insurance company for twenty-five years. One summer his church was sponsoring a group tour of Europe. He and his wife Eleanor had always wanted to go to Europe, since both of their parents had been born there. They signed up and bought their tickets. Edwin requested vacation time for his trip. A week later, his supervisor called him into his office to say that he couldn't let him have the time off. The supervisor said that Edwin would be needed in the office during that time.

Edwin's coworkers said the supervisor was being ridiculous—the work could be easily be done by others and he should take the matter to the personnel department; they believed that the personnel manager would override the supervisor and give him the time off. Edwin agonized for days over whether to go to the personnel department or not; he finally decided that it wouldn't be right to go over his supervisor's head. He turned his ticket in and Eleanor went to Europe alone.

Your Best Interest

Like Edwin, you may be afraid of authority figures. What makes you so intimidated by authority? What causes you to endure great discomfort rather than risk the chance of public shame or humiliation? What causes you to be so fearful of strangers? In short, why did you put on these social straitjackets in the first place and why do you continue to wear them?

To find the answers, you have to keep in mind a basic principle of human behavior: *you always act in what you think is your best interest*. You don't do anything for others; there's no such thing as altruism. When you give without strings attached, you do this because you believe it's in your best interest to do so. You always do what you do because you believe it's in your best interest to do so.

What you see as your "best interest" can be broken down into three areas: your *material* best interest ("I'm going to get as much for my house as I can"), your *psychological* best interest ("I'm going to give my son five hundred dollars because it makes me feel good to do it and I'd feel guilty if I didn't"), and your *social* best interest ("I'm not going to litter the streets because I don't want to live in a dirty city").

It is in these three areas that you run into most of the conflicts in your life—"Should I tell the prospective buyer the house has a bad roof" . . . "If I don't give my son the money he wants I'll feel guilty" . . . "There's no trash barrel around and I don't want to put this soda can in my purse."

Leading a healthy, independent life means achieving a working balance between your material, psychological and social best interests. Many people act in what they believe to be their best interest in one area at the expense of their best interests in the other two.

Edwin sacrificed his material best interest (going on the trip) to protect his psychological and social interests (not having his supervisor mad at him). Often what we think is our best social interest is really a rigid social straitjacket.

Extended Childhood

The reason that we buy into so many excessively restrictive social straitjackets is our long childhood. Dr. James Brain, an anthropologist, says, "With humans, a child *has* to be totally dependent on adults for at least seven years and would find it difficult to survive by itself for about seven more years."

A long childhood and adolescence makes us vulnerable to a host of social straitjackets—we learn to bow to authority pressure, earn rewards by being nice, hold ourselves back with needless shame and fear strangers.

For example, during this time you are subject to the almost complete authority of your parents and other grownups. You learn that you have to follow this authority or pay the consequences for not following it. You also learn that authority over you can be easily transferred to others: babysitters, big brothers or sisters, teachers, uncles or aunts, police officers and a host of other grownups. The authority figure holds over you the threat of severe consequences if you don't follow his or her wishes. For many people, this fear of authority continues—even after they grow up and there are no longer severe negative consequences for not going along with the authority. In short, you can carry your unreasonable fear of authority into adulthood.

Shame. Excess shame is another carryover from your childhood. One of the ways that children are controlled and molded into socialized adults is through the use of shame. Many parents intentionally use shame to help toilet train a child ("Big boys don't wet their pants"). Even well-meaning parents find it difficult not to show some disgust over their child's soiled clothes; this unintentionally makes the child feel shame. Your shame (the experience of being seen as bad or wrong by others) quickly spreads to a variety of other areas ("Shame on you, Sally, you shouldn't talk to your friend like that" . . . "Billy, you should be ashamed of yourself for saying that word"). You may carry this feeling of shame with you throughout your life. Any time that you stand out or are different from others can cause you to experience shame. Your early experiences of shame were so painful that you'll do just about anything to avoid shame.

Nice. Niceness can be another straitjacket carried over from our childhood. Most parents want above all that their children be nice to others. The parents themselves feel shame when their children aren't nice in public. Parents reward their children for being nice and punish them for not being nice. Most children, because of their dependency on their parents, are often quite fearful, and so they work hard at being nice.

What is the most outstanding characteristic of fairy tales? What kind of people are Cinderella, Jack of "Jack and the Beanstalk," Sleeping Beauty, Hansel and Gretel? They are all nice people. The explicit and implicit messages of childhood are that niceness will protect you from evil. Many people grow up believing that if they are always nice, they won't have any problems and nothing bad will happen to them.

Fear of Strangers. Recently in Los Angeles (due to several brutal murders of children) there has been a rash of publicity on why children should avoid all strangers. Local schools have been putting on plays showing children how to avoid strangers. Because parents are frightened, they are passing this fear on to their children. While children need to learn a reasonable degree of caution, too many warnings about strangers cause people to be afraid of strangers through the rest of their lives. (I think a better approach is to teach children to go only with people they know or those who know the secret family password. The emphasis is on approaching *only what is safe*, not on avoiding everything that could be dangerous—which is just about everything. This way children can learn caution without taking on excessive fear.)

Fear of strangers is a fear that can socially cripple you. If you have this fear, it's to your advantage to learn how to overcome it. Next, I'll talk about how you can loosen these straitjackets and start to live.

Overcoming Fear of Authority

Dependency, in essence, is looking for parents to take care of you. I read recently about two children from an abusive foster home; they were walking up and down a beach asking people to adopt them. Excessively dependent people, like these two kids, are continually looking for someone to adopt them and take care of their every need.

You may feel like an orphan, wandering helplessly and in need of protection. Occasionally, you'll find a parent figure who will take care of you. This has the effect of sealing the "child" inside you. Emotionally, you become like an invalid child: your parent figure pushes you around in a wheelchair while you watch adults run free on the beach.

"Honor thy father and thy mother" makes perfect sense. For our own good we need the approval and acceptance of the authority figures of our childhood. However, carrying this over into adulthood and making other adults into mother and father figures can cause you a great deal of difficulty. Honoring a father-figure and a mother-figure can make you overly submissive or self-defeatingly rebellious. You are caught in a bind where your only options are to obey or disobey.

Go over the authority-problems checklist in *table 1* (pp. 236–38) to see if you have a problem with authority figures. You may not know to what extent you're intimidated by authority figures. This checklist will help you to better spot these areas. After you have completed the checklist, ask yourself how your problems get in the way of your desire for more independence. You might never even have questioned how you feel about authority figures until now.

At times, the signals that trigger your feelings of dependency in the face of authority are obvious and at other times they are subtle. While such signals may be unintentional, they are often used intentionally by people to try to keep you in a dependent, submissive role.

Nonverbal Signals

- *Use of uniforms or badges.* The person you're talking to or working with wears a white smock.
- *Use of furniture.* The person you're talking to or working with has a large desk and gives you a chair to sit in that's five inches shorter than his or hers.
- *Use of status symbols.* The person you're talking to or working with dresses in expensive clothes and looks your clothes over appraisingly.
- *Use of space.* The person you're talking to gets up and leaves while you are still talking or won't leave until you agree to his or her request.

• *The person makes no reaction to what you say.* After presenting your case or argument, the person just looks at you. The person simply tries to outwait you.

• *Use of body language.* The person looks out the window when you talk to him or her.

• *Use of time.* Calling the meeting and then coming late.

Verbal Signals

• *The person pulls rank.* "I'm the boss. You work for me."

• *The person makes you a low priority.* "I don't have time to talk to you right now."

• *The person outtalks and snows you.* You leave the person asking yourself, "What happened?"

• *The person makes vague threats or promises.* "I wouldn't do that if I were you," or "It might be to your advantage to go along with me."

• *The person speaks down to you.* "I guess you wouldn't understand," or "If you knew what I know, you'd agree."

• *The person relies on social position to keep you in place.* "Because I say so."

• *The person discounts your competency.* "I don't pay you to think."

• *Use of third parties.* "My assistant will give you the details."

• *Use of communications media.* "Give me your request in writing."

• *Use of titles.* "Tell her Dr. Brown called."

To overcome problems with authority figures, you can use the ACT formula.

Acceptance of Your Own Authority. Accept the following:

No one is innately better than me. In the final analysis, I nearly always know what's best for me. No one can discount or invalidate me, unless I allow them to. When I stand up to an authority figure I may act, sound and feel childish, but I'm still an adult. No one is more grown up or bigger than me.

And finally, accept nonjudgmentally that you presently have a problem with authority figures.

Choose to Be Independent. Throughout the day you'll be confronted with situations where you can choose to take the dependent submissive role or choose to be independent. You can refuse to let your mother pressure you into doing something you don't want to do. You can refuse to let your boss put the whammy on you. You can decide to hold your ground with an authority figure instead of giving way. You can refuse to let your doctor overwhelm you. You can decide to confront your teacher. You can refuse to agree automatically with instructions you doubt. You can refrain from asking permission to do what is your business in the first place.

Take Action. You have to start having different experiences with people to whom you give your respect in order to overcome your fears. You can use the authority-problem checklist (*table 1*) as a guideline; start acting the opposite of how you normally do. True independence is having full choice, and acting contrary to your nature for a while will show you that you do have a choice.

One action people find helpful is the *third time is the charm* method. You can use this to step out of the submissive role when you're dealing with people trying to take authority over you. You stand up for yourself at least three times.

- To a waiter who is rude, make three specific requests ("May I have more water? . . . Will you take this back, it's cold? . . . Will you put cheese on my apple pie?").
- Tell your boss what you want at least three separate times ("I need next week off . . . I can't come in next week . . . When I'm gone next week . . .").
- Tell the police officer at least three times why you believe the ticket is unwarranted. This may not change the officer's mind, but you're learning to stand up to authority.
- Ask the doctor to explain three times what the problem is and what the cure entails ("I want to be sure I understand this . . . Now, tell me again").
- Ask the teacher three times to reconsider your grade. The rationale for this method is that after three requests or assertive actions, you're moving out of the submissive role.

Shame

Shame Can Kill. I was once in a restaurant with a woman who almost choked to death. Someone in our party noticed she was turning blue and helped her dislodge the food. Later she said that even though she knew the international signal for choking (placing your hand at your throat in a choking gesture), she was too ashamed to use it. She didn't want to make a public scene.

People cooperate with assailants and rapists because they're too ashamed to scream and fight—they often think they can handle the situation quietly. Someone suffering chest pains refuses to call the rescue squad because he or she would be ashamed of the commotion if it weren't a heart attack. Shame is one of the most powerful emotions, and yet it is one of the least recognized.

I believe that shame plays a large part in the lives of many assassins and mass killers; they seem to have a large problem with social acceptance. Many of them talk about the humiliation of having others see them as losers. One fact has always stayed with me about one mass killer. The sniper climbed to the top of a college tower and started shooting. When he was finally captured, they found, among his cache of arms and ammunition, mouthwash and deodorant. Apparently, he didn't mind killing people, but he didn't want to offend anyone and experience the shame of bad breath and body odor.

Shame has other costs, too.

Shame Costs You Money. Shame is a billion-dollar business. Many of the products on the market today have one purpose: to protect you from shame. Take hair for example. You wouldn't think there is anything inherently shameful about hair. Yet men spend millions to get it and women spend millions to get rid of it. And both spend millions to make it publicly acceptable in some way, believing that no one will sit next to someone with dandruff or fly-away hair.

If you think about it, you'll see that shame costs you money in many ways—when you don't return shoddy merchandise, when you don't refuse to pay for poor service, when you don't file claims with insurance companies, when you don't ask for what's yours, when you let others shame you into business deals that aren't to your advantage and when you don't ask for a cut in price or try to bargain.

Shame Costs You Income. Shame not only costs you money, it also prevents you from making money. Over the years, I've worked with a number of salespeople, and one of their biggest problems in selling is that they are ashamed of their profession. They are ashamed to knock on doors, make calls, and tell people what they are selling.

My next-door neighbor is in the top 1 percent of insurance salespeople in the country. Why? I believe the main reason is that she has no shame about selling insurance. She'll try to sell insurance to just about anyone she meets. Obviously, many of them buy it. As a result, she has a condominium in Hawaii and two Mercedes cars in her garage.

Shame Costs You in Unsolved Problems. When you have a problem you're ashamed of, you rarely try to solve it. You're ashamed of your weight, so you don't exercise in public; you're ashamed of your drinking problem, so you hide it. One man with a slowly failing business was a close friend of another man whose business is saving failing businesses. However, because of the first man's shame, he never asked for advice that might have saved him from going bankrupt. One of the most therapeutic aspects of Alcoholics Anonymous is that members, by outwardly talking about their drinking problems, overcome the shame associated with it: this frees them to do something about it.

Shame Costs You Enjoyment. Shame steals your enjoyment and can ruin your days. Do you shudder today when you remember a particular run in your stocking, the time your fly was down, a stain on your clothing that you thought your boss noticed or the third marguerita at the office party? Most of your shameful experiences are never noticed or remembered by others, yet you suffer from them over and over again. Not only have you lost the pleasure of the moment, but you have to repeatedly suffer when you don't accept your "shameful" behavior.

Shame Costs You Comfort. You wear tight shoes because you're ashamed to take them off in public. You don't lie down in the airport lounge even though you're bone tired. You don't ask where the bathroom is, even though your bladder feels ready to explode. You can't hear because you don't want others to see you wearing a hearing aid and you endure blurred vision because you don't want others to see you need glasses. The cruel irony is that the pain of shame is a drop in the bucket compared to the pain we put up with to avoid it.

Shame Costs You Self-direction. You let others shame you into doing activities that you don't want to do or that you don't believe are in your best interests. This might be working for a charity, going along with a project you don't approve of, or working overtime. Once people know you have a shame phobia, they can always pull that string to get you dancing their way.

Shame Costs You Sleepless Nights. The worst part about shame is the anticipation of it. You fear that you'll make a public fool of yourself and feel ashamed. This dreaded anticipation obsesses you and you ruminate about the upcoming event. You die a thousand deaths anticipating the shame. The second worst part of shame is the post-shame period; here you replay in your mind over and over how shameful your behavior was. Compared to the anticipation and the replays, the actual experience of shame is relatively painless. You can have heightened and painful self-consciousness, but this isn't a severe pain like having your toenail ripped off. This should give you a cue to how to get rid of shame.

Shame As a Backup System. Before I talk about how you can get rid of this shame, you first have to see if you have any reason why you *don't* want to get rid of it. Lester had a number of severe shame phobias. He said, "I'm afraid if I get rid of my shame, I'll have no control over myself. I might start urinating against walls in public places."

Most of your reasons for not wanting to get rid of shame come down to the belief that you somehow need shame. This isn't true. Shame is a backup system. You can decide to act in socially appropriate ways without having the experience of shame to keep you in line.

I told Lester that I had in fact urinated in public places many times without feeling any shame. What is considered shameful is based on what any particular culture says is good or bad. Countries such as Afghanistan or Nepal have almost no public and few private toilets. As a result, people relieve themselves discreetly but in public places. I felt no shame when I did the same when I was in these countries.

I also told Lester that while I might now feel shame to urinate on the corner of Hollywood and Vine, I'm sure I could learn to do it without shame. I told him, "Suppose I did work at it and learned to overcome this shame. Would that mean I would be urinating wherever I felt like doing it? . . . No, I don't need shame to stop me from doing that. First, it's a social taboo that I happen to agree with (I don't like the smell of places where people relieve themselves). Second, it's against the law and I don't want to be arrested." Shame is needless baggage.

Antishame Program. The best way to overcome shame is to purposely go out and experience it. Put yourself in situations where you're likely to experience shame or, when you find yourself experiencing shame, tell yourself "Okay, I'll use this situation as an antishame experience." You use the ACT formula. First, you *accept* the shame, next *choose* to fully experience it, and then you *take action* by staying in the situation until the feelings of shame disappear or are significantly reduced.

I have been using this procedure with clients for several years. They have found it to be an almost miraculous way to cure themselves of crippling shame.

I picked up the idea of antishame exercises from psychologist Albert Ellis. However, the same process of densensitization is used in many areas of psychology and medicine. Suppose you have allergies. The allergist will give you therapeutic doses of the pollens you're allergic to; this has the effect of desensitizing you to these very same pollens.

To rid yourself of shame, you have to give yourself therapeutic doses of shame. After you've received the correct therapeutic dose, your shame (painful self-consciousness) will go away.

At times I will go out with clients who are afraid of making fools of themselves in public and deliberately make a fool of myself. For example, my office is near the crowded corner of Western and Wilshire in Los Angeles. I'll go out with a client, who will watch as I scream out the time of day or the letters of the alphabet. The clients then do it themselves. Inevitably they find that the world doesn't come to an end when they behave this way; and they find their shame starts to go away when they face the public humiliation they fear. The naked truth often is the best cure.

My psychological assistants also go out in public with clients and help them experience the shame they dread. One woman, for example, was afraid of fainting in public. The therapist lay down in the middle of a busy supermarket to show her that this wouldn't be the end of the world. By pushing the limits, you can begin to see how much freedom you have. You begin to get a clearer perception of your place in the world and how unimportant what others do is to you—and how unimportant what *you do* is to them. You'll find that you really have to work to get others' attention in America today.

You don't necessarily have to make a spectacle of yourself to get over shame (although this may be the quickest way). You can use shameful events that occur naturally or gradually repeated exposure to shame to get the same results. The following is a ten-point program you can use to get over your shame.

- *Set a weekly dosage schedule of 500 shame units.* Rate each experience of shame from 0 to 100. For example, you might rate going to the store in curlers as a 50-unit shame experience. You might rate buying a dollar's worth of gas at a full service pump, asking for full service, and then driving around to the cheaper self-service pump to fill your tank as a 90-unit experience. You can't get the points unless you experience the shame. Later, as you become desensitized to a particular shame, you'll have to do a more shameful activity to get the same effect. Write down when and how much shame you experienced. A weekly planner is a good place to write this down.

• *Make up a shame list.* Write down all of the public behaviors that you feel especially ashamed about. You'll find some examples in *table 2* (pp. 238–39). They aren't difficult to think of; we have so many shameful taboos. Be sure to add items that you're particularly sensitive to. One woman, for example, was extremely sensitive to looking "cheap" in public. She listed such activities as sitting next to her husband when riding in the car and giving him a hug and a kiss in public. Make sure you do at least one antishame activity a day until the problem is beaten. If you don't have any naturally occurring ones, pick one from your list.

• *Use models.* If you have trouble getting started, ask someone who's not bothered by a particular shameful act to do it in your presence ("If you scream out the time of day first, then I will"). You can use television or movie actors as models. I believe that comedians such as Steve Martin and the cast of *Saturday Night Live* are popular because they thumb their noses at social taboos. Much of their humor is really antishame exercises—dressing up like a bee, wearing arrows through their heads, or portraying "coneheads." People like this because they would like to be free from social taboos, too. Watch how they do it and then imitate them.

• *Fully experience the shame.* Don't try to shut your feelings off; rather, fully experience and accept them. Stay in the shameful situation as long as you can without running away from it or backing down. If you're drinking or using drugs such as Valium, you'll get little benefit from acting shameful. While you may need to use mental props when first experiencing your shame ("This is only a game"), drop them as soon as you can. You'll have to force yourself at times to get this experience.

• *Increasingly expose more vulnerabilities.* At first you may want to experience shame in areas that don't impinge on your strong fears of social disapproval. Later, you'll want to expose these too. For example, if you're ashamed of your age, you can start telling people your age—you can get more shame units by adding a couple of years to it. If you're ashamed of your toupée, you might want to start by telling someone about it and eventually take it off in front of people. You might make a list of some of your most shameful experiences ("I had an abortion" . . . "I served time" . . . "I had a bad drinking problem" . . . "I had a baby out of wedlock"

. . . "My son is homosexual" . . . "I once worked as a prostitute") and tell someone about them. The reason you're still bothered by them is that you haven't accepted them. By talking about them you start to accept them.

Use some common sense in doing this. Don't tell your boss you served time for robbery, or tell your parents or husband or wife every one of your indiscretions. Pick someone you believe is understanding and accepting. However, if you pick someone who is shocked, you do get more antishame units.

- *Choose to accept your shame.* By choosing to accept the shame, you transform the nature of the experience. The experience goes from one of pain to one of mastery. Rather than discounting yourself, you accept yourself. Give yourself credit for going through the process.
- *Watch yourself.* Pay attention to how you protect yourself from shame. This might include lying ("I didn't do it"), being evasive ("I'm not sure I know what you mean"), diversion ("I don't know about that . . . by the way, you didn't tell me how your evening went"), covering up (wearing elevator shoes), denial ("I don't care"), excuses, omissions, disguise, avoidance, silence, stonewalling, self-deception, bragging, reassurance, blinders, and so on.
- *Turn your evasions into antishame units.* "I lied the other day when I said I'm forty-five. I'm really forty-nine." Give yourself double credit for revealing deceptions.
- *Use antishame experiences to check out your thinking.* Make predictions of what will happen when you do the shameful act ("Everyone will stare") and then see what really happens. Ask yourself, "Even if people do look at me in an odd way or make a remark about me, is it really important?" Make predictions about how much pain will be involved in your antishame experience ("I'll break down and cry") and see if it turns out to be that painful.
- *Continue the 500-unit program on a weekly basis.* Most people find that within two to three weeks most of their shame is gone. You need to periodically give yourself booster shots of antishame. Every couple of months check yourself and see if your shame allergies are acting up again.

Shame-Free. If you systematically follow this plan and get rid of your shame, what will happen to you? First, people won't be able to intimidate you so easily. Therefore, you'll feel freer, looser, lighter, when you're out in public. You'll be able to deal with life directly—without the help of a go-between to buffer the shame for you. You'll be able to go more places on your own without it.

You'll also find that you'll like yourself more. You'll see that you can be a fool and still accept yourself.

Shame Keeps You in Bondage. What you don't accept in yourself is what you feel shame over. By getting over the shame you move toward self-acceptance.

The shame or embarrassment you feel for others is a clue to what you don't or won't accept in yourself ("Mary must really be ashamed, everyone knows she got pregnant on her vacation" . . . "How can he stand to show his face after we all saw . . ."). So the less shame you have, the more you'll be able to accept others ("Mary, I'd like to give a baby shower for you" . . . "Heck, Bill, who cares what happened?").

Hiding. When you find yourself starting to hide or conceal some misfortune or flaw, stop yourself. All you'll be doing is creating more shame for yourself. One teenager hated to show his big belly but wanted to go on a church beach party. He went but he wore his T-shirt, even in the water. All the other kids kept asking, "Hey, why don't you take your shirt off?" By trying to hide his flabby belly, he actually drew shameful attention to himself. If you don't accept your mistakes, they come back to haunt you: what you resist persists.

Maturity. Right now, you probably have a backlog of shameful experiences you haven't accepted about yourself—layers of immaturity. Start now and turn your flaws around and advertise them—you'll begin to add layers of maturity. (The boy at the church beach party would have done better to take his shirt off like the other guys and could even have patted his belly and laughed.) As an adolescent your friends may have shunned you for your nonconforming behavior or appearance. And your adult friends with adolescent values may still do this. But you can accept that by facing the naked truth and not hiding is the way to grow. By enduring public humiliation you can grow.

Choice. Most of the experiences that usually precede feelings of shame are beyond your control—like falling on the ice or having the elastic in your underwear break. However, what is in your control is deciding where and when to feel ashamed or not to—that's your choice.

Pride. Pride is on the other side of the coin—it's shame's twin. Those traits you feel the most proud about (your talents, brains, competence, appearance) are the same traits that you're going to have the most shame over. The beauty queen is the most ashamed over lost looks, the actor or writer over bad reviews. To get rid of shame you also need to start to get rid of your pride (perceptions of mob approval) as well as shame (perceptions of mob disapproval). Don't brag or oversell any of your traits; this comes back to haunt you.

Niceness

To become socially independent, you often need to undergo *antinice* as well as antishame training. What's wrong with being nice? In and of itself, nothing. However, being nice *is a problem* when you do it because you think you have to. You're nice not out of independent free choice but because you believe you have no other choice. Believing you always have to be nice keeps you in a dependent child role in relation to others. Most of the problems of fear of authority and shame apply equally to being compulsively nice.

With niceness you have additional problems as well. Trying to be nice all the time is an unnatural state. You cover up the real you. As a result, you break out of your niceness straitjacket with an inappropriate meanness. The backlash to your compulsive niceness can come out in a variety of ways. This is the "*When You're Nice you're very nice, and when you're bad, you may be horrid*" *syndrome*.

One man said he decided not to marry a girl because she treated him with sugar and spice but treated service people like dirt. I know another man who is the nicest and sweetest husband and father you could imagine but a tyrant with his employees. I've known others who were the reverse; they were real sweethearts at their jobs and abusive at home.

Your niceness may result in indirect hostility toward others. You probably know a number of nice guys who become devils once they are behind the wheels of their cars.

Trying to be nice all the time can lead to poor mental and physical health. I've noticed an unusually large number of nice people who are bothered by chronic depression and recurring anxiety. One study found that overly nice compliant older people die much earlier than cantankerous older persons. Trying to be nice all the time can be a great physical and mental strain.

If you're highly constricted by your niceness, it's to your advantage to loosen yourself up. In *table 3* (pp. 240–41) I've listed some of the more common "nice" rules. You may want to add some of your own to this list. The goal of antinice training is to make being nice a free choice, not a compulsion. And you can only do this by seeing that you don't have to be nice on command.

Antinice training involves acting the opposite of each of these rules for at least one day. For example, the first one is "always be cooperative with everyone." If this is the one that you decide to work on, you make a point of being uncooperative as many times as you can that day *on purpose*. You have to be in a cooperative mood to make it count. You could start by telling your husband that he'll have to make his own breakfast. You can tell your son you won't drive him to the Cub Scout meeting that night. Of course, if you're just in an angry mood, this won't count. You can tell your boss that you don't have time to type the report right away. If you stop at the store on the way home, have the checkout clerk check one of the prices for you.

The next day work on another nice rule. You can cut the rules up and put them in a jar and pull one out each day and use that one. Or you can check off from the list one that is most appropriate for that day. You can reward yourself for each one of these injunctions that you act upon. One woman gave herself five dollars for each day she did the antinice activity. She treated herself to some new clothes at the end of the program.

Again, the purpose of this training isn't to make you into a rude, socially inappropriate person. We all know people that could benefit from *niceness training*—they usually are dependent people stuck in the childhood mood of rudeness and disobedience. The purpose of *antiniceness training* is to help you gain greater independence—which means greater self-accepting and greater freedom of choice.

Like the antishame exercises, the purpose of this is to see that the world won't come to an end if you're not nice and you'll be much freer and looser as a result. This gives you the independent choice, which you don't have when you're overly dependent.

Be Leery of Strangers

Around the world you can find an almost universal fear of strangers. People in each primitive tribe say, "We're friendly, but the people on the other side of the hill are vicious killers." When you get to the next tribe over the hill, they say the same thing: "We're friendly, but the people on the next side of the hill . . . watch out." Frightening myths about other people is one of the most confining social straitjackets you can wear.

George was a student I went to graduate school with. He had, as far as I could tell, absolutely no fear of authorities. Within a week of starting his program he was calling all of the professors by their first names and inviting them out to have coffee with him. He, however, was petrified of anyone who wasn't middle class or white. He took a room right on campus and wouldn't wander more than two blocks from campus because of his fear of Blacks. He refused to take the subway anywhere in Philadelphia and wouldn't drive his car in any neighborhood that was made up of minorities.

He never had any bad experiences with minorities, he just was afraid of them. He arranged his life so he only had to interact with white middle-class people. Many people are like George. They have frightening myths about people that keep them locked into a dependent role.

Dr. Aaron Beck and I have been doing research in what causes people anxiety. We have found most people's fear of strangers is based on erroneous beliefs. Here are some common myths we've come up with that revolve around this fear of strangers:

Myth 1: People Are Basically Unfriendly. The majority of people are in fact quite helpful and will respond positively to you—especially if you approach them in a positive way. People in New York are supposedly among the most unfriendly in the world. However, if you approach them and ask them for directions, the majority will respond in a friendly way. I've found this to be true with people all over the world. The truth is that people in the village over the next hill are friendly.

The neighborhoods around the University of Pennsylvania are mostly black; people in each area will tell you their neighborhood is safe but the next one is bad. The university is on 36th Street. Those at 36th Street say, "You can't live safely past 40th Street"; those on 40th Street will tell you you can't live past 45th Street. We lived at 46th Street and our neighbors said, "You can't live past 50th Street." We have some friends, the Larimees, who now live near 57th Street and they say their neighbors are the friendliest they've met in the ten years of living in West Philadelphia.

Myth 2: If a Person Is Unfriendly, He or She Can't Be Helpful. Even if someone is unfriendly, he or she can still provide practical help. For example, even if you meet an unfriendly New Yorker, he or she can tell you the information you need to know. When people are unfriendly you can still push to get the information you need. Sometimes it helps to say "You don't seem to be feeling too well today." If said in a real and compassionate way, this can break the ice. One waitress I told this to said her feet were aching and she didn't mean to be unfriendly.

Myth 3: If Others Are Friendly to Me, I Have to Take Whatever They Say. Con artists and people that are giving you news you don't want to hear are often overly nice after they have taken advantage of you. Con artists call this "cooling out the mark." After they have defrauded you, one of the accomplices talks nicely to you so that you won't make a fuss to the authorities. When someone has taken advantage of you, it's usually to your advantage to make a fuss whether they are friendly or not.

Myth 4: If Others Are Unfriendly, You Have to Let Their Behavior Control You. Many people who provide services use your fear of anger as a way to control you. Nearly always when someone has been rude to you they will sooner or later sing a different tune if you push the matter. One of the secrets is not to let the person provoke you into anger. When you're angry you're out of control. Wrestlers and boxers often try to make their opponents angry by such taunts as "Your mother eats cat litter." Once you're angry your judgment and whole system are off.

You don't have to be afraid of people's anger. You can simply hold your ground and continue to repeat calmly what you want. You make what they say or do irrelevant to your goals. Don't be reactive to what they say. You may have an anger phobia. This is another legacy from your childhood when grownups really could harm you. If this is your case, you can use the same procedure as in the antishame training; the only difference is that you provoke others' anger until you can become comfortable with it.

Myth 5: I Can't Bother Others. This is another result of your ideas that you developed as a child. Just because you have these ideas doesn't mean that they are true.

You may believe that you can't encroach on others' territory. You can't call up someone in authority or speak up. You need to test these out. How do you know what someone's boundary is until you test it out? Stop people on the street and ask the time of day. Ask if you can use a store's facilities or phone.

My grandfather was something of an eccentric; he never minded asking people for favors. For example, when I was a child and drove with him, he would often say, "I've got to call home." He then would see a woman watering her lawn. He would pull up and say, "I've got to call home, can I use your phone?" The lady would say, "Sure." Perhaps it was because he was an old man in more innocent times, but he would repeatedly have the favor granted.

Many people are afraid to ask others to do them favors because they believe that people won't like them. This is the opposite of a basic principle of psychology: if you want to get someone to like you, get them to do you favors. The more good someone does for you, the more they will like you. The less they do for you, the less interest they have in you, and the worse they treat you the worse they'll feel about you.

Myth 6: Others Will Harm Me If I Act Differently Than Expected in Public. This is similar to shame, but it's fear of mob retaliation, not mob scorn. Stop and think what will really happen if you don't follow the expected; you can even test it out. You'll find out that nothing ever happens most of the time.

While people in America may have become more mistrustful in the last few years, they have also become more tolerant. You have much more latitude in how you act in public than you believe. If you feel very constricted in public places, you might start by going to sports events where yelling and outlandish behavior are expected and accepted. Go and scream.

Myth 8: If Others Are Bad to Me in Public, I Should Be Bad to Them in Return. This rarely works. Even if you can think of the perfect cutting remark in return, this only causes the person to feel bad and act badly to two more people—you in return act badly to two more. This is how you get negative pyramid schemes going. Often your best bet is to turn the situation around and say, "You really seem to be having a hard day." This sympathy can often transform the situation.

A large part of being socially dependent is caused by being oversocialized. The solution is to become less reactive to others. This doesn't mean that you should throw intimate relationships and friends out the window. In the next chapter, I'll talk about how you can improve your close relationships.

TABLE 1

AUTHORITY PROBLEMS CHECKLIST

NOTE: AF = Authority Figure

1. React to store clerks and service people as if they are AFs. YES __ NO __
2. I often believe AFs (doctors, teachers, bosses, police) have supernatural powers. YES __ NO __
3. I'm often hesitant to intrude on AF time ("I just want a minute of your time"). YES __ NO __
4. I'm often hesitant to intrude on AF space ("I'm afraid to go by my boss's office"). YES __ NO __
5. I'm afraid to ask the AF for a favor. YES __ NO __
6. I'm glad to do a favor for the AF. YES __ NO __
7. I feel guilty when I go against the wishes of the AF. YES __ NO __
8. I feel fearful when I go against the AF. YES __ NO __
9. I often believe the AF can read my mind. YES __ NO __
10. I believe the AF has control over my privileges. YES __ NO __
11. I believe the AF's wishes come first. YES __ NO __
12. I believe I have to do all the compromising with the AF. YES __ NO __
13. I often call the AF by titles (Mr., Dr., Father) while he or she calls me by my first name. YES __ NO __
14. I feel I have no protection against the AF's fire power. YES __ NO __
15. I'm inarticulate and can't speak when I'm in the presence of the AF. YES __ NO __
16. I always show great deference to the AF ("Thank you and forgive me for the traffic ticket, Officer"). YES __ NO __
17. I feel completely dependent on the AF. YES __ NO __
18. I don't believe the AFs are sensitive to what I tell them. YES __ NO __
19. I'm overly sensitive to what the AFs tell me. YES __ NO __
20. AFs don't fear my reprisal. YES __ NO __
21. I often feel that AFs can do whatever they want with me. YES __ NO __

22. AFs always expect me to conform to their wishes. YES __ NO __
23. I often do the opposite of what AFs want me to do. YES __ NO __
24. I never express my anger to AFs. YES __ NO __
25. I put off seeing or calling AFs. YES __ NO __
26. I'm often tongue-tied around AFs. YES __ NO __
27. I have great difficulty saying no to AFs. YES __ NO __
28. I readily give into AFs' desires. YES __ NO __
29. I enjoy giving in to AFs. YES __ NO __
30. I believe I'm lucky just to be able to work with the AF. YES __ NO __
31. I often act like a child in front of the AF. YES __ NO __
32. I often talk very harshly about the AF behind his or her back. YES __ NO __
33. I don't like to take on leadership or authority roles. YES __ NO __
34. I identify strongly with an AF. YES __ NO __
35. I have trouble asking questions of speakers in large groups. YES __ NO __
36. I feel like a phony in the presence of the AF. YES __ NO __
37. The AF can always out-debate me. YES __ NO __
38. AFs are always confident and in control around me. YES __ NO __
39. The AFs often discount me. YES __ NO __
40. I have trouble confronting AFs. YES __ NO __
41. AFs nearly always talk down to me. YES __ NO __
42. AFs always take complete control of the situation. YES __ NO __
43. AFs' logic always seems better. YES __ NO __
44. I need the AFs more than they need me. YES __ NO __
45. The AF has higher self-respect than me. YES __ NO __
46. I have low self-respect around the AF. YES __ NO __
47. I'm filled with self-doubt around the AF. YES __ NO __
48. I'm overconcerned about how the AFs are feeling. YES __ NO __
49. I overapologize to the AF. YES __ NO __
50. When an AF does something nice for me, I brag about it. YES __ NO __

51. I brag about my association with the AF. YES __ NO __
52. I save up positive things to tell the AF. YES __ NO __
53. I'm the one who likes to give the good news to the AF. YES __ NO __
54. I don't like to give the bad news or tell problems to the AF. YES __ NO __
55. I say I agree with the AF, even if I really don't. YES __ NO __
56. I try to use a go-between to get to the AF. YES __ NO __
57. I practice the halo effect with the AF (everything he or she does is great). YES __ NO __
58. I hide my mistakes from the AF. YES __ NO __
59. I always ask permission from the AF. YES __ NO __
60. I always seek forgiveness from the AF. YES __ NO __

TABLE 2

ANTISHAME EXERCISES

1. Go to a gas station and ask for full service after buying a dollar's worth of gas at the self-service pump.
2. Go to self-service pump first, then go to full service for last dollar to top off and get service.
3. Talk loudly in elevator.
4. Go places alone—such as a fancy restaurant.
5. Wear inappropriate clothes (formal clothes to an informal gathering).
6. Confess weakness ("I can't sing, dance or swim").
7. Make a scene in a store.
8. Cry in public when you feel like it.
9. Scream out the time of day in public places.
10. Lend book in which you've made personal markings.
11. Demand a lot of service.
12. Lie down in a public place.
13. Ask up front for money that's owed to you.

14. Brag if you usually don't.
15. Give an unpopular opinion ("I think Mothers' Day should be abolished").
16. Go out if you look less than perfect.
17. Go out in public places with someone you're ashamed of.
18. Panhandle—ask a stranger on the street for some change.
19. Go out without your false teeth.
20. Go out without your toupée.
21. Go out with a mudpack on your face.
22. Tell people your age.
23. Wear a Halloween mask.
24. Go out without your makeup.
25. Go into a sex shop.
26. Have a drink in a gay bar.
27. Raise your voice inappropriately in a public place.
28. Talk about private matters where others can hear.
29. Exaggerate your losses ("I really blew a deal today").
30. Tell people you're going bald.
31. Say loudly at a social gathering that you have to go to the bathroom.
32. Go get a massage.
33. Wear a bathing suit in front of strangers.
34. Go to a grocery store and buy one pea.
35. Go to a hardware store and buy one nail.
36. Tell people how much you weigh—add a couple of pounds.
37. Wear two different-colored shoes.
38. Go into a store and say, "I'm not buying anything, but I'd like you to validate my parking ticket."
39. Ask a store proprietor to break a hundred-dollar bill.
40. Go to a gym if you're ashamed of your body and walk around naked.
41. Buy a *Playgirl* magazine if you're a man.
42. Buy a *Playboy* magazine if you're a woman.
43. Buy a Yo-yo and play with it in public.
44. Tell someone that you masturbate.
45. Tell someone a family secret ("My uncle is a peeping tom").
46. Pin a sign on the back of your shirt that says "I have almost no shame."

TABLE 3
NICE GUY LIST

1. Always be cooperative with everyone.
2. Always go along with what everyone else wants.
3. Always be sensitive to others' desires.
4. Never interrupt others when they are speaking.
5. Always ask others how they are.
6. Always be tactful when speaking.
7. Always thank everyone at all times.
8. Always have a pleasant look on your face.
9. Never look depressed.
10. Always sound enthusiastic.
11. Always agree with everything others say.
12. Never sound angry.
13. Always apologize for upsetting people.
14. Always speak softly.
15. Always look neat—dress conservatively.
16. Always smile when talking to or greeting people.
17. Never get upset if someone appears to be angry with you.
18. Always accept what others say without question.
19. Always worry about your help being adequate when offering help.
20. Always agree with salespeople's advice.
21. Never ask anyone to do you a favor.
22. Never upset a waiter by moving to another table if service is slow.
23. Never use bad language.
24. Always call right back if someone calls and leaves a message.
25. Always worry about how others will react to what you say.
26. Always remember to ask about someone the next time you see him or her.
27. Always entertain everyone all the time.
28. Always say please.
29. Always tell people they look nice.
30. Never criticize another person.
31. Never be irreverent.
32. Always cheer others up.
33. Always compliment others.
34. Never let others think you don't like them.
35. Always laugh at others' jokes, especially if they aren't funny.

36. Never tell another to leave if you're busy.
37. Never give someone the brush-off—on the phone or in person.
38. Always tip, no matter how bad the service.
39. Never brag.
40. Always explain when you make a mistake.
41. Never deliberately tell a lie.
42. Always apologize for being late.
43. Always let people cut in front of you in line.
44. Never tell people how you really feel when they ask.
45. Always use mouth wash and deodorant.
46. Always ask about what's important to others (kids, health).
47. Always make small talk with others you see.
48. Never complain to anyone about anything.
49. Always say good-bye when you leave people.
50. Always offer others something to drink or eat when you see them.
51. Always let others go first.
52. Never ask others to lend you lunch money.
53. Always tell people you had a good time—even when you didn't.
54. Always tell people to come to see you, especially when you don't mean it.
55. Always tell people the food tastes good and ask for the recipe.
56. Never say bad things about other people.
57. Never make a pest of yourself.
58. Never ask others to repeat themselves for a third time.
59. Always have good table manners.
60. Always tell people how sorry you are about their bad news, especially if you aren't.
61. Always excuse yourself when you leave others.
62. Never disagree with others.
63. Always bring gifts when they are expected—wine to dinner, food to funerals, hostess gifts to parties.
64. Always thank people in writing or by phone after you've thanked them in person.
65. Tip people even when you don't want to.
66. Compliment what you don't like in others.

CHAPTER THIRTEEN

Friends and Lovers

YOU MUST FIRST HAVE a good relationship with yourself before you can have a good relationship with others. You have to feel worthwhile and acceptable in your own eyes. The more independent you are, the better you'll be able to connect and relate with others. Your social self-interest is on a continuum that runs from how you meet the public to how you handle your most intimate relationships. In this chapter, I'll talk about how you can use independence as a way to form closer and more intimate relationships with others.

How do you become more independent with your friends? You should first determine if they are friends or not. The person may be a pseudo-friend who takes but doesn't give. In true friendships, there is a balance. If there's not a fair trade-off, this is usually a sign of pseudo-friendship.

In a normal two-way friendship, you have value for value. What you give is equal to what you get. This may involve helping another person with his or her personal problems—in a sense, cocounseling. The key is that it's reciprocal; you get something in return. One of the signs of a deeper friendship is that you let the other person in on your personal problems. The best indicator of the quality of your friendship is how well the other person handles your successes, not your failures or problems. Only your best of friends will be able to enjoy your successes.

Pseudo-friendship

Sometimes what you think is a friendship is really a pseudo-friendship: the other person is getting all the benefits of the relationship and you're paying all the costs; this is a taking relationship.

To see if it's a true friendship or not, look at the context of your relationship. If it's usually in balance and shifts over and you're doing all the giving, it may be temporary and mean that the other person is going through a bad patch. However, if it has been a chronically one-way street, you probably have pseudo-friendship.

Ask yourself, "Is this unbalance a continual problem, or does it only happen every so often?" Does the person continually want to talk about his or her problems, or are they just a small part of your interactions? Does the person always get very emotionally wrought up? Does he or she not want to hang up the phone or not want to leave? Does the person call often and at inappropriate times? Does the person ignore your problems and interests? Does the person continually seek your advice and then not follow it? Does the person follow the suggestion in a way that guarantees that it won't work? Does the friend have a new problem each time he or she calls? Do you want to avoid talking to him or her? Do you dread it? Do you feel drained afterward?

One of the best ways to tell if you're in a pseudo-friendship is to pay attention to how you feel. The general pattern is that at first you feel good because you're helping someone. Next, you start to feel guilty, as if you're responsible for the other person's life. And finally you get angry. Pay particular attention to guilt: with exceedingly dependent people, you often feel guilty about *their* problems.

When you do all of the feeding in the friendship you're being just as dependent as the one who's doing all of the taking. Once you're socially independent, you don't stay in pseudo-friendships. Remember, it's your choice to stay or not to stay in pseudo-friendships.

Being a Friend

You may be the one who is doing all the taking in your friendship; your constant need to take from others chews up your friendships and leaves you more isolated. If you have a string of unfulfilled friendships, this probably is your problem. You may be the one who's draining others: the only gift you give to others is your problems. After you have completed the friendship dependency checklist in *table 1* (pp. 268–69) you may find that you have confused exploitation with friendship. The way out of this is to start giving rather than taking.

Giving

One of the signs of being independent is the ability to give of yourself, of your time, of your energy, of your material goods. Because you're self-sufficient, you feel complete and thus able to give to others.

When you're dependent, you're focusing on receiving. You feel empty and helpless. As a consequence, your focus is on wanting others to take care of you. You attempt to get others to buy into the illusion that you're not going to make it on your own. Because of your mental set, you never feel free to give of *yourself* to others: your focusing on receiving blocks you from giving. Once you get used to receiving, it can be difficult to switch to giving—you become prey to the "give me an inch and I'll take a mile" syndrome.

This is too bad. It's your loss; most of the joy of living comes out of true giving—giving without strings attached. Take children for example. The joy of raising children is the joy of giving. This is giving in its purest form. You don't give with any ulterior motive involved—you just do it for the child. Giving with strings attached is trading when it's stated and manipulating when it's not.

Mood Lifting

A number of studies have found that when your mood goes up (someone gives you a cookie), you're much more inclined to give of yourself (you mail a letter you find on the sidewalk). In the same vein, giving of yourself raises your mood. Giving and your mood are interrelated; when one goes up, the other does too. And both are contagious. When you're around giving people, you feel better and you're more inclined to give of yourself.

Holiday and Anniversary Blues

You may, like others, become depressed and blue during public and personal holidays (Easter, Christmas, Mothers' Day, birthdays). You may become unhappy just thinking about birthdays, anniversaries and other special occasions. If so, you've fallen into the trap of believing it's better to receive than to give. When you buy into this belief, you can never get enough (presents, compliments): each gift only makes you want to have more. Like a drug addict, you want more and more.

Your whole focus is one of "What can you give me?" If you go through enough holidays when you expect to be given wonderful gifts and aren't, you may eventually become cynical, antiholiday and antianniversary. This is your defense against being let down again.

The real problem is that you are asking to be given something that you believe you're entitled to. By turning this around and starting to give to others, your mood changes and the holidays become full of joy and a time you look forward to, not days you dread.

I have worked with many people who become emotionally sick during holidays; they inevitably have major problems with dependency. I suggest to them that they switch their focus from getting to giving. The more personal your giving, the better. Give a gift certificate of your time. For example, you can give your son or daughter a gift certificate of yourself ("Good for one day with your father to go anywhere you want to go"). Give what you make and put time into (a poem, a painting, a piece of woodworking); give gifts that you've thought about; give of your time; give your personal belongings: rather than waiting until you die you can give those close to you something you really like that's part of you. For example, one woman gave her daughter a favorite vase she had always admired.

Blueprint for Emotional Health

Giving isn't only the antidote to holiday blues, it's the way to emotional health. Once you start becoming involved in helping others, you start to forget about your own problems. Giving is also the key to keeping relationships alive. It's to your advantage to make a contribution to others rather than constant withdrawals. You start liking yourself better when you're contributing to others—your self-respect and confidence start to go up.

Joan of Arc Syndrome

What about the woman who gives to everyone all the time and is constantly stepped on? This is what psychiatrist John Rush calls "the Joan of Arc depression"—the person is being burned at the stake while she tries to make everyone happy. This isn't true giving; it's either a misperception of an obligation or a form of manipulation that's not working.

You have to give without expecting anything in return if giving is to work. If you give because you're supposed to or are duty-bound by social custom, you don't get the benefit—you only become more tied to social bondage. Giving is the clue to having better relationships with all people, not just with friends.

Here are some specific ways you can give of yourself.

- *Give of your knowledge.* Teach your son how to tune a carburetor, or show a friend how to fix a special dish.
- *Give of your time.* Take your mother-in-law shopping.
- *Give of your energy.* Paint your grandmother's kitchen.
- *Give your material things.* Give an art object that your new daughter-in-law admires to her.

- *Give your honest feedback.* Tell your friend if you think his jokes are inappropriate for a speech he's giving.
- *Give of your concern and love.* Send a note to your cousin when her husband has surgery.
- *Give of your wisdom.* Tell people what lessons you've learned in life.
- *Give spontaneously.* Next time you have an urge to give something, do it right away and then don't second-guess your act.
- *Give anonymously.* Give something big to someone and don't tell anyone.
- *Give of your tolerance.* Next time a friend does something you don't like, tell yourself you give the person your acceptance of this as a silent gift.
- *Give others a break.* If someone does something you don't like, let it go without criticizing.
- *Give others credit.* One omission that strains relationships more than anything else is when people aren't given credit for their contribution. Acknowledge others' contributions.
- *Give of your experience.* I greatly appreciate it when clients tell me, "Here's something I learned, you might use it with your other patients." (Not too long ago there was a movement in professional psychology to give psychology away. The notion is that ideas on how to be happier and more productive belong to everyone.)
- *Give way in a dispute.* If you believe you always have to be right or be first, give way to someone else. Let them win for a change.
- *Give back with interest.* When someone does you a good turn, repay them plus.
- *Give an ear to someone.* You can often help out by listening to someone.
- *Give to a stranger.* If someone does you a good turn and you want to repay it, but can't, do a good deed for a stranger.
- *Give your best.* You will be happy and better off by giving the best you can of yourself to what you're involved in. Your best is never perfection and only you know what it is.

I've noticed that some people are always being given things by other people. If you look, you'll see that they are the ones that more often give of themselves to others in honesty, in enjoyment, in laughter, in help. Gifts come back to you if you don't expect them to. One of the great paradoxes of life is that by giving to others, you end up receiving more yourself. The opposite of a giving person is a person who withholds. You may withhold your wit, wisdom, love, knowledge. The paradox is that you end up the loser by withholding this. According to Marguerite and Willard Beecher, to become self-reliant you need to be "a host instead of a guest in life." Above all, what you want is to give to others close to you a relationship that is nonjudgmental and fully accepting.

Acceptance

By giving to others, you're showing acceptance of them. This gift comes back to you in the form of greater self-acceptance. When you're accepting of others, they move closer to you. To see the power of acceptance, ask yourself how you feel when you feel accepted by others and then contrast this with how you feel when you don't feel accepted.

The following are some excerpts from John Wood's book, *How Do You Feel?*, on ways ordinary people feel about being accepted.

> *Terry Van Orshoven:* "How does it feel to be accepted? . . . good, warm, comfortable, relaxed. It feels secure, important; takes away demands and expectations. With acceptance I give myself the opportunity to be with someone without demands or with a great lessening of demands on me. When I don't feel accepted I will place demands on myself to be something other than I really am or want to be."
>
> *Howard Saunders:* "It seems like the good times take care of themselves and in the bad times I really need the acceptance of people around me that I care about: that's when it's most important."
>
> *Ralph Keys:* "When I feel like I'm accepted, it feels like an emotional sauna. It feels good, warm; it makes me relax. I let down my guard and don't consider so much what I am saying and what effect it will have. The tension of how I'm going over with others seems to disappear. I can think of specific times when I feel like I've really blown it completely with someone, been scared to see them a day or two later, and been pleasantly surprised that they are still my friend. Not that they've liked what I did, or a way I was, but that they realized it's part of being human, or even better that they see that I did what I did because I was hurting in some way. When I'm not accepted I'm just not natural at all. It seems to

make me behave in a lot of strange ways, some of which I'm not even aware of."

John Wood: "I have this on-going fantasy to do with acceptance. I have found myself into it several times in group situations. I imagine that all of us in the group are Indian chiefs in an important council. We are all very important people and whatever we say is listened to with attention by each of the other chiefs. I value all the chiefs and their wisdom—in whatever way it is expressed—as they value me and mine. Each of us accepts the notion that whatever another says is true; we do not deny it, laugh at it or defend an opposite point of view. We *accept* each other. That kind of acceptance seems to bring out my uniqueness, my creativity, my own best self to the issue or situation at hand."

The independent way to be in relationships is to let other people be themselves. Your nonacceptance of them is a form of dependency; you're demanding that they fit your ideals perfectly in order for you to be happy with them. Thus, you're making your happiness dependent on their perfection.

Nonacceptance

If you're not accepting of much of your life ("I can't stand this city, the people in it or the way it's run"), people don't want to be around you. Your rejection of reality and other people gets in the way of how you relate to others. Most people, for example, dislike being around complainers. Complaining usually is a manifestation of dependency and nonacceptance.

By complaining, you reveal something to the world you're not accepting and are thus dependent on: "I'm too hot (or too cold)" . . . "The food is too spicy (or too bland)" . . . "My neighbors are too rowdy (or boring)" . . . "The service here is too slow (or too fast)" . . . "My husband spends too much time away from home (or at home)" . . . "My mother is too pushy (or too passive)" . . . and so on. In each complaint, you're not accepting some part of reality. Speaking up and asking for change is often the best policy. However, if you continually complain about aspects of reality you can't change (the weather) or won't change (your marriage), it's a form of dependency. Complaining and making straightforward requests are two different matters. Your complaining often causes you trouble with people you would like to be close to.

Judgments

Another sign of social dependency is constantly making value judgments of people. Your judgments turn others off and stop you from seeing the world clearly and accepting it as it is. This is partly due to feeling you have the final say about what is good and bad ("Rich, meat-eating, Southern Catholic gentlemen are better than poor, vegetarian, Yankee Protestant ladies").

The problem is compounded by how you make your judgments. You may, for example, say, "Los Angeles is a terrible place to live." This is more judgmental than saying "I don't like Los Angeles." Your judgments and complaints usually tell you more about yourself than about the things you judge. (If someone tells you she doesn't like Mexicans, does this tell you more about Mexicans or about her?)

Often this is a form of fascism—"People who can't sing are inferior" . . . "People with crooked teeth are all losers." This first judgment was made by a music teacher; the second by a dental receptionist. Such judgments come back to haunt you when your teeth go bad or you lose your voice. Ask yourself, "What kinds of judgments am I prone to make?"

Your judgments often are a form of projection. You're judging something in others that you don't want to accept in yourself. Consider some of the common judgments you're likely to make—*you are* doing exactly what you're complaining about in others.

"YOU ALWAYS YELL!!"
"I can't stand people who complain."
"I can't tolerate people who are intolerant."
"I'd like to strangle someone who is that cruel."
"You know, kind of, like, he's too vague."
"Pleeeese don't whiiine."
"I hate people who are prejudiced."
"I don't like her—she talks about other people behind their backs."
"People who make judgments are no good."

"I can't stand being around people who are closed-minded."
"That bastard is continually slandering people."

Your judgments often come back to haunt you. My mother once told me, "I can't understand why anyone would want to watch soap operas." At last count she was watching eight of them.

Slander

Closely related to being judgmental is being slanderous. Malicious gossip and character assassination are endemic throughout society. To be either the person slandering someone or to accept unquestioningly the slander is a symptom of social dependency.

Mike Geller is a communication specialist who has studied the process of slander in detail. He writes, "Children learn the value of slander at an early age. It helps them to get attention or eliminates competition in the friendship game. The extent to which slander operates among adults—in personal, business, professional, social and political situations—proves that some people don't outgrow their tendency to slander. And the frequency with which it is effective proves that few adults have learned to identify slander by *testing* accusations before reaching judgment."

People will seek you out to hear your latest piece of gossip. At first glance, the gossip appears to be the most popular person in the office. However, on closer inspection this turns out to be pseudo-popularity. If you're a slanderer, people soon become wary of you; they begin to wonder what you're saying about *them*. I've also noticed that those who do a lot of slandering nearly always end up being slandered by others. The message is clear: to become socially independent, you have to stop slandering and stop giving credibility and encouragement to people who slander.

Low Frustration Tolerance

You can tell how dependent you are by what you say you can't tolerate; the less you can tolerate the more dependent you are. How many traits of others do you tell yourself you "can't stand"?

To become more socially independent, you need to become aware of what you can't tolerate in others and learn how to increase your tolerance. Examples of low social tolerance are: "I can't stand people who like disco (classical, rock-and-roll, country) music. I can't stand pushy people. I can't stand politicians."

You'll be more socially independent if you begin to accept your friends' and associates' nonacceptance of some aspect of yourself. Take your success for example. I ran a study with a group of friends and acquaintances. To half of them I sent a letter stressing the success factors of a book I wrote (sales to book clubs and so forth); with the other half I stressed the failure factors (lack of exposure and so forth). What do you think happened? In general, those who were told I was doing well didn't want to hear about it and those who were told I was doing badly gave me great encouragement and support and helpful ideas.

I then reversed the process. I told the first group I was doing poorly and the second group I was doing well. I got the same effect: people who hadn't been interested in my success were very supportive and helpful when they heard the book was doing poorly. The lesson: friends have much more trouble accepting your successes than your failures. I think that this is something you have to accept about most people. Most people see your successes as upsetting the delicate social balance between you and them.

Making Friends

The way you make friends is by making acquaintances. You will eventually, if you're looking for friends, make friends from your acquaintances. Keep in mind that people who want to be your friends will be looking for you, too. Like most forms of success, it's a numbers game. The more acquaintances you make the sooner you'll meet those people looking to be friends with you. Many friendships can then blossom into more intimate relationships.

Close Relationships

Allowing Others to Be Independent. When I first started doing therapy I would often to go great lengths to help my clients with their problems. I went beyond the call of duty. I would have the sessions run overtime and ask clients to call me between sessions to see how they were managing their problems. I also spent a lot of time in between sessions thinking about how they could handle their problems. In short, I did much of their work for them during therapy. I had a very high success rate. I think if the therapist puts that much effort into it, people are almost embarrassed not to get better.

I found, however, that once the clients for whom I did all this work stopped therapy, many relapsed into their old problems. I'm now much more inclined to put the work back on the clients and let them choose to do it or not do it. I enforce more strictly the limits and boundaries of therapy. As a result, I find that a few people don't get well as quickly, but I also find I don't have nearly the same relapse problem.

The same applies to close relationships; when you're in an independent relationship, you allow others to be independent. The more dependent you are the more you fight the other person's attempts to be independent. You don't let your children go when it's right for them to leave. You hang on to people beyond the point of needed protectiveness. You fight your husband's or wife's attempts to own his or her own life. This ends up being destructive for both of you. You're stuck in dependency.

I saw one woman, Muriel, for one consultation. She treated her forty-year-old son more like a lover than a son. She became deathly sick if he went out with a woman more than twice. She came to me to learn how she could make her son more loyal to her. I suggested this might not be in either of their best interests. She never came back for therapy.

This is just one of many examples I've seen of mutually dependent relationships. Many people in the relationship believe they are the independent one. However, if you're truly independent, you'll let the other person be independent. If this is your problem, you can use the ACT formula to overcome it.

1. *Accept.* Accept that the other person is responsible for his or her own life. Accept the possibility that the person may fall as he or she learns to walk and that overprotectiveness can be crippling. Accept the possibility that your help isn't really a help but a hindrance. Accept that you're not responsible for the person's thoughts, feelings and actions—no matter what you did to or for them in the past. Accept that it can be painful for both parties to break off the dependency. Accept that the person who is now dependent will be ambivalent about breaking the dependency ties.

2. *Choose.* Realize you have free choice to let the other person grow. No matter what frightening scenarios your mind conjures up, you can still choose to let the other person be independent. No matter how much the other person tries to manipulate you, you can choose to let them be independent. It takes courage, but you're the one who has the free choice. The other person may not be aware that she or he has the free choice to be independent.

3. *Take action.* I read a letter in an advice column where the mother wrote that her son was in the local jail and his father was taking him daily supplies of cigarettes, potato chips, candy bars, magazines, pastry and chewing gum. The action to take in helping someone become more independent is to stop this type of dependency-producing behavior. Stop material and emotional supply lines to people who are dependent on you. They are better off developing their own responses. Stop taking care of them physically (making beds, checking their car), economically (paying their bills), emotionally (taking on guilt for their poor choices) and intellectually (telling them what they should think and do).

Resistance to Your Independence

As you become more independent, those around you often won't like it—particularly those who are the closest to you. People you've been dependent on over the years have gotten used to it. They have become comfortable with your asking their permission, advice, forgiveness and accountability. Even if they don't like the bad aspect of your dependency, they have gotten used to it. Most people don't like change, even if it's from bad to good.

You know you're moving forward when you start seeing some

resistance. Welcome this; it's a sign that you're starting to grow and become more independent. Nearly all forms of change meet with resistance. The resistance you meet may be vocal and direct, or silent and indirect. It may take the form of blackmail ("If you act like that, I won't go with you to your mother's"), or of vague threats ("That's how my first wife acted").

When you meet resistance, you need to empathize with the other person. Understand his point of view yet choose to be independent in the face of his reaction. You do have to take action that ensures you hold your ground. You will need to have some ammunition when those around you start to sabotage and undermine your actions. Following are some common examples.

- "*You don't love me anymore.*" Answer: "My independence doesn't mean I don't love you. In fact, the more independent I become, the more I'm capable of loving you. I can only tell you I still love you, but it's up to you to decide if you want to believe me or not. I can't force you to believe me."
- "*You're acting selfishly.*" Answer: "I'm making some new choices you can interpret as selfishness. I see it as acting in my own self-interest. A large degree of mental health *is* acting in what could be called a selfish way. This doesn't mean I'm not open to compromises that are equitable to both of us on specific issues."
- "*You're making a fool of yourself.*" Answer: "If I am, I am. Maybe I need to make a fool of myself for once. The fool in mythology was always the person who acted foolishly so that he could safely reveal the truth."
- "*You're too incompetent to do that.*" Answer: "The reason I want to do it on my own is so I'll make my own mistakes. My incompetence or mistakes are teaching me how to do it right."
- "*You're morally wrong: what you're doing is going against everything that's sacred.*" Answer: "In the final analysis, I'm the one who's accountable for my actions. Therefore, it follows that I'm the one who has to decide what's morally right or wrong for me."
- "*You're acting neurotic* (crazy)." Answer: "Neurosis is in the eye of the beholder. If I am, I'll be the one who's responsible for my behavior and will have to pay the price for it."
- "*You're letting the kids and whole family down.*" Answer: "The best way I can help the kids and rest of the family is by providing a model of a self-reliant person. I'll do what I can around the house,

but I'm not the only one who lives here. If the kids don't pick up their dirty clothes, I'm not going to pick up and wash their clothes for them."

- *"You're killing me,"* (says your mother). Answer: "I realize you feel bad about my breaking away and not having as much contact with you. However, I need this time to develop my independence. I have to be on my own to become self-sufficient. Although I know you're having trouble accepting this now, I believe that in the long run you'll be happier for me."
- *"You're a bad son* (daughter, husband, wife)." Answer: "Is the issue one of moral judgment about what is good or bad? I don't think so. I believe it's one of different values or of choosing different values. Are relationships ever beyond being redefined? Because I'm becoming more independent, does that mean I'm bad? Do you believe calling me bad and making moral judgments helps the situation?"
- *"You're making me angry* (anxious)." Answer: "People often react with emotions, especially with anger, to change. The purpose of anger is to try to get back to the status quo. I see this as a communication that you're sending me. I see that you're angry and want me to be the way I was. However, I still have the choice to remain independent."

Keep the ACT formula in mind for ways to handle non-acceptance: 1) Accept their resistance—if you resist their resistance you get stuck; 2) Choose to be independent in the face of it; 3) Take action to continue your independence program.

Dependent Versus Independent

To see if you have an independent or dependent relationship, you can ask yourself a key question: "Do I have a free choice to stay or leave the relationship?" If you feel like you have no choice, then it's a dependent relationship.

Dr. Aaron Stern says, "Only independent people can choose to remain in a relationship. Dependent people remain out of necessity. The most mature level of love exists only in the face of free choice. Therefore, loving can be experienced and enjoyed only to the extent that the participants are able to maintain themselves independently."

Both parties are party to dependency. Excessively dependent people, if you let them, can help to make you more dependent. Another key question is: "Do I accept the person the way he or she is?" If not, you probably want them to resemble a real or idealized parent.

Janice, for example, married an alcoholic who worked sporadically. She said he was much like her father. She wanted him to be an idealized father who didn't abuse her and was a responsible person.

To make a relationship work, you need to accept the person rather than try to mold him or her to your ideal image. Look at the person and decide if you want to have that person as a partner or not.

Acceptance of Those Close to You

The Beechers in their book, *Beyond Success and Failure*, quote some telling words from Lao-Tzu:

> The intelligent man is not wishful. He accepts what others wish for themselves as his wish for them. Those who appear as good, he accepts, and those who appear as bad, he accepts: for nature accepts both. Those who appear faithful he accepts, and those who appear unfaithful he accepts: for nature accepts both. The intelligent man treats every kind of nature impartially. And wishes good to one as much as another.

When I was living in Tokyo I read about a woman who killed herself and her two children after her husband came home and said, "You sure eat a lot" after seeing some cookies were gone from the cupboard. He wasn't accepting the reality that she was eating and she wasn't accepting his harsh and critical statement. To make a relationship work you need to accept the other person, especially the traits you don't like. It doesn't mean you have to like them, it just means that you accept them and give it to them as a gift. Often it's the traits you can't accept in the other person that are the traits you feel the worst about when the person is gone.

For example, if you can't accept that the other person likes a certain kind of music and that person someday dies or leaves, that type of music will remind you the most of how much you miss him or her. Usually there's much more to the person than just these few traits you don't like. Consider the person as a total package with traits you like and traits you don't like. No one is the same as you. Once you can get yourself to accept the other person, the relationship goes along harmoniously.

Breaking Up Is Hard to Do

A messy problem is when two dependent people are about to break up. Often they both want to, yet neither wants to take the responsibility. So one of them makes such a mess—with affairs, drinking and emotional problems—that the other person makes the decision. The more dependent person who wanted the breakup in the first place doesn't have to take responsibility and can play the injured party to boot.

If you want to break up with a person because the relationship is (a) self-destructive and (b) going nowhere, the self-reliant choice is to do the breaking up yourself.

I remember an interesting story a colleague once told me about breaking up. He said:

> I learned an important lesson about breaking up when I was in college. A girl I was going with decided to throw me over for someone else. The other guy was a hood with a police record as long as my arm. He called me up and told me to stay away from the girl. I didn't know what to do. I went to see a friend who had always given me good advice in the past.
>
> He suggested that I confront both of them in person and tell them I was bowing out of the picture and that they were welcome to each other. He also suggested that I then go out and spend a day by myself to see if I could enjoy my own company.
>
> I followed his advice. After the confrontation, I rode my motorcycle up to the mountains. I had one of my best days ever. I learned that I could be happy by myself and that I didn't need the girl to make me happy. Three weeks later she called and wanted to know if I was interested in getting back together again.

One of the basic principles of human nature is that people move toward the strong and away from the weak. Once you start acting more independently, people will move toward you. I've seen this happen many times with my clients when they start to become more independent. Others find them much more attractive. If someone wants to break up with you, the best strategy is to work on becoming more independent, not on pleading helplessness.

Independence in the Close Relationship

The independence-based relationship has a much better chance of succeeding and growing. You're closer if you're both independent. Most of the problems caused in marriage are due to one or both of the persons having excessive amounts of dependency.

Following are some typical conflicts in dependent-based relationships.

Honesty Versus Kindness. One of the most common conflicts with couples is whether to hurt the other's feelings or to be honest with her or him. Many people hold their tongues until resentment builds up or the other person doesn't get needed feedback. In most cases, honesty is the best policy. However, there are many cases in which it is better to choose carefully the type of honesty you use. There are a number of different types of honesty.

For example, there's indirect honesty. When I met Pat fifteen years ago, I had a suit that I thought was great-looking. In reality, it was out of date and looked as if it was made out of cardboard. (After my gold sports coat I quit investing in expensive clothes.) Pat didn't want to hurt my feelings, but at the same time she didn't want me going out on job interviews and other places in this funny-looking suit.

She got together with a friend and asked what to do. He suggested that they buy a men's magazine and show me some up-to-date suits and see if I could be interested, then suggest that I might get one like those in the magazine. They did and I did.

This was a way of being honest without bluntly coming out with it. Sometimes the slow truth is better. There are times when people are not yet ready to hear bad news, so you have to tell them the truth, but in a slower and more self-discovering way.

There's also the direct truth, which is usually the best strategy.

You tell people the truth directly (today Pat would tell me, "Your suit looks as if it's made out of cardboard"). If you and a friend are about to go into a party and she asks you, "How do I look?" tell her that she has lipstick on her teeth. In cases like these, the person appreciates the direct truth, rather than learning an hour later that she just met thirty people with lipstick on her teeth.

The worst mistake is to err constantly on the side of being kind rather than being open and honest. The other person never knows where he or she stands with you and you quickly lose your credibility.

Blaming Versus Ownership. Many marriages and relationships break up because people become overly involved with blaming. Whenever you get into a blame situation, the relationship deteriorates. This is not to say, however, that you shouldn't hold people accountable for their behavior. You can see the difference between blame and accountability in *table 2* (p. 270). You can use this table as a guideline for how to hold others accountable without getting into blame.

Independence Versus Manipulation. There is no such thing as true manipulation. You are only choosing to allow other people to direct your behavior. You do this under the illusion that they are controlling you ("I have to call my mother—she says she'll have a heart attack if I don't"). I talked before about how people use shame (not living up to your public image) and guilt (not owning your choices) to try to control you.

Another way you can allow people to control you is with their anger. You may not do something because of your fear of the other person's anger. This goes back to the time you were a child when someone was angry with you and you could have been hit. Now it may only be a vague fear of being harmed physically. (If in fact you are hit when the other person is angry, you need to do something about the relationship: your life is too short to spend it being knocked around by other people.)

People can manipulate you only if you choose to let them. Salespeople, relatives and countless other people will try. But you can choose not to let them. If you're the attempted manipulator, you can improve your relationships by being more direct and by taking care of yourself.

Values Conflict. Nearly everyone believes that his or her values and tastes are superior. People believe their own tastes are at the top of the taste hierarchy. Allow other people to have different values and tastes. That's what relationships are all about: not being concerned that the other's values and tastes are the same as yours. Variety is what makes life interesting. You're hurting yourself when you think your partner's taste reflects poorly on you. Accept others' taste for what it is—*their* taste.

Reasonable Versus Unreasonable. When marriages or other relationships go wrong, each person thinks the other person is being unreasonable. However, each person has good reasons for what he or she does. You need to accept that people's reasons seem reasonable to them. Often their ideas may be left over from immature reasoning, but you still have to allow them to have their reasons. Instead of arguing and blaming, tell them fully and calmly what you believe your reasons are. Try to sell them, not force it down their throats. Don't blame them and get irritated and angry. If they don't buy your reason from you, they don't have to.

When the other person isn't buying, stop selling. For example, if your husband doesn't want to go to the musical, rather than telling him how great it will be, just tell him that you're going and he can choose to go or not go. Often, when he has nothing to resist, he will end up going along with you.

The Golden Rule. The golden rule, "Do unto others as you would have them do unto you," is often the wrong strategy. People are different. A husband may like to spend his time at home and a wife may like to be more social. They may respond differently to how they want to be treated when they're upset or when they have good news. It's better to ask people how they like to be treated rather than automatically assuming how they want to be treated.

Repeat Performance. Good things don't just happen; something made them happen. Go back to when your marriage was working and find out what you were doing to make it work and then start doing more of this again.

Reverse Principle

You can use the reverse principle to remain independent in a close relationship. For example, plan for irritating behavior instead of always trying to avoid it. In many relationships the other person talks about topics that you don't like or you're not interested in (and vice versa), and you both try to avoid this. Both of you, however, continue with this line of talking because you believe you aren't being listened to. Here, rather than shouting, plan some time to talk about it for a specific period of time.

Make this theme-specific. Set a specific amount of time, say one hour, and then discuss the issue in full detail. Don't deviate. Get back on track until the issue is all talked out. Following are some programs you can schedule:

- *Wall Street This Week.* If your partner is overconcerned about money issues and continually wants to talk about them, schedule some time for a detailed discussion. One client's husband was in business for himself, and she was continually anxious about the cash flow. They would argue because he wouldn't want to discuss it three or four times a day. The husband agreed to discuss financial matters with her in great detail between 7 and 8 P.M. if she would agree not to discuss them at any other time.
- *As the World Turns.* If your partner wants to discuss the comings and goings of friends and relatives, set a timer to do this.
- *The Health Hour.* If one or both of you are concerned about your own or others' health, schedule time.
- *Mental Health Hour.* As above, if you want to analyze yourself or others, set some specific time aside for it.
- *Sesame Street.* Set some time aside to discuss specific subjects about your children. Don't pop this on the other person before going to bed.
- *Point Counterpoint.* Argue each point one by one at a specific time. Each person gets a chance for a rebuttal.

• *Family Feud.* Like counterpoint, if your family is having fights, divide up sides and have a go at it.

• *The Phil Donahue Show.* If you have some sexual concerns, give them a full and open airing. Imitate Donahue, who seems to be able to talk openly, candidly and nonjudgmentally about sex and other taboo topics.

• *Hour Magazine.* If you have a variety of topics, set aside sixty minutes to openly and frankly discuss them.

Let Others Own Their Own Moods. One of the best ways to change old habits and patterns and preserve a relationship is to let people have their bad moods. At times they'll just tease you with it ("I feel terrible"), but remember, it's their bad mood. Let them have it. Our two-year-old son has a pouting corner he goes to when he's unhappy. Set aside a place where you or your partner can sulk—preferably away from others. You may ask yourself why you're so concerned about his or her moods.

I talked to one man, Rex, about this. He let his wife's mood make him feel bad and frustrated as he tried in vain to make her feel better.

THERAPIST: Why don't you let her have her moods?
REX: I know we talked about it. I know I'm not responsible for how she feels. It's her choice. Yet I don't like it.
What don't you like about it?
She just seems to indulge herself with them.
By indulge you mean she enjoys them?
Yeah, I think she enjoys them.
Why do you want to stop her from enjoying herself then?
(Laughing) I can see what you're saying. It's her mood; she can do whatever she wants with it.

If the presence of someone in a bad mood bothers you, you can ask them to go somewhere else, or you could go somewhere else. The idea is to learn to be nonreactive to your partner's bad moods.

Disputes

In any relationship you can have a variety of disagreements and arguments. The goal of social independence isn't to eliminate disputes but rather to learn how to handle them in more independent and mature ways. You can use the following four-step program to resolve disputes in an independent way.

- *Prepare a brief for your disputes.* You need to put some time into thinking about what you're specifically disputing. Think like a lawyer and write down specific points you want to discuss. Suppose your daughter has been borrowing your clothes without asking. You want to write down specific incidents ("Last Tuesday I saw you leaving on your date wearing my new silk blouse") and specific requests for changes in behavior ("In the future, I would like you first to ask to borrow my blouse and then pay to dry clean it after you've worn it").

  Part of your preparation involves setting a time and place to have your dispute. Generally, periods of transition (coming home or going out) are the worst times for a dispute. Make sure you have enough time to discuss fully all of the issues and that you both agree on the time and place for the discussion.
- *Establish "heads of agreement."* Western Europeans have a very useful way of negotiating. Before they get into the details of any deal, they see if they can reach some basic mutual agreements. "You want to sell me a factory and I want to buy it. We both want a price that is fair, and we want this transaction to take place within six months." They call these *heads of agreements.* The details are filled in after the heads of agreement are established. If the heads of agreement can't be established, there is no deal and really no reason to talk further about one.

  You can use the same method in your disputes. Say you're in some conflict with your husband over your son. The heads of agreement might be: you both want what's best for the child; you agree there is a problem; and you both want to do something to solve the problem.

  If you can't reach a consensus on these basic heads of agreement, there's no use in discussing details—you have to do more work on reaching basic heads of agreements. Remember, you're not locked in to any heads of agreements. After you discuss the details, you may want to have different heads of agreement. For example, you may conclude that it's your problem that needs solving, not your son's.
- *Work out details.* After you have reached some heads of agreement, you can start sorting out the details. You want first to make

sure you know what the other person's points are. Keep asking questions until you think you know what the other person is saying and then offer a capsule summary to see if you do understand ("You're saying that you think I'm inconsiderate to take a nap while you do my typing").

You also want to make sure the other person understands your points. You may have to repeat yourself many times before the other person hears you.

The cardinal rule is to stick to the issues at hand—don't go into past history, off on tangents, or engage in character assassination —yours or the other person's. When you find yourself going off on a tangent (you start by discussing where to spend Christmas dinner and veer off into talking about your upcoming vacation), stop and get back to the main point.

If the other person tries to pull you in a different direction, agree with the possibility that there might be truth in the side issues but you want to stay with the central question ("I may be a complete bitch, but let's stay with whose family we are going to have Christmas dinner with").

Stay with the issue until you can come to some agreement. The agreement might be to agree to disagree or agree to discuss the matter more fully at some later date.

In hashing out the details you should expect to reach some peaks and valleys. You needn't be scared or put off by the valleys, just choose to accept them and push on.

• *Initial the protocol.* Eastern Europeans have a useful custom of ending negotiating meetings with agreeing about what was agreed upon. This is called the "protocol" and each party initials it. The protocol spells out what action each party will take. The protocol is something between an informal agreement and a legally binding contract—it's a serious statement of intent.

After you have worked out the details of your dispute, it's a good policy to write out in detail or verbalize specifically the action both of you are going to take. The plan of action may be just to get more information. The initialed protocol can be referred to in further disputes if needed.

Use the Critical Choice

You can use this method to avoid getting caught up in the dependency cycle. Do the opposite of what your inclinations are.

This is a way to show yourself that you do have free choice in how you respond.

- When you feel like criticizing your partner, give him or her a compliment.
- When you feel like giving in to your partner, stand your ground.
- When you feel like taking, give to your partner ("I'll stay home tonight and watch the kids").
- When you want to deny your feelings ("I'm not in a bad mood"), exaggerate them ("This is about the worst I've felt in weeks").
- When you feel like avoiding, approach ("Hello Bill, how are you today?").

Following are some general guidelines for a more independence-based relationship.

- *Consult with each other before making promises or commitments involving both of you.* Don't automatically assume that your partner is available and willing to accompany you to a social function.
- *Keep secrecy on any matter to a minimum.* The real problem of extramarital affairs usually isn't the outside sex but the lying. Your coverups hurt the relationship much more than the sex does.
- *Start small.* If you have a big unresolved problem in your relationship, take a smaller problem such as the type of movie you both go to. Solve this problem together and after you do, see how you did it. You may have found you used *acceptance* ("We have different tastes"), *choosing to be independent* ("I'll still own my tastes") and *taking action* ("We'll rotate movies we go to and see more of our favorite types separately"). You can then use this formula with other problem areas.
- *Empathy.* If you can't agree on an issue, at least see the matter from the other person's point of view. Reversing roles helps.
- *Compromise.* See if you each can rate 1 to 10 how important the issue is and see if you can reach a compromise acceptable to both.
- *Avoid psychoanalysis.* Don't second-guess the other person's motives. People often ask me if I psychoanalyze Pat. I tell them Pat and I only psychoanalyze each other when we're fighting ("You're the ——— type" . . . "You're doing that because . . ." "You think . . ."), which of course only escalates the argument.

People have a variety of motives and no one can know for sure what they are. No one likes to be put into categories.

• *Go back to the beginning*. Remember, you chose the person in the relationship—why did you? Do you really want him or her to be someone else? If you chose the strong silent type, don't blame him for being too stubborn and withholding.

• *Use the twice rule*. Tell people what you want only twice ("Please take the dog out"). You can give them the benefit of the doubt about the first time, but the second they must have heard. If you ask more than twice, you're nagging and not allowing the person to be independent. If he or she refuses to follow the action, then you have to act in your own best interest; this may mean going to the gathering alone, or eating the meal by yourself if the other person doesn't come home on time.

• *Don't continually police others*. Let others police themselves—pack their own clothes, set their own alarm clock, get themselves up on time.

In the next chapter, I'll talk about how you can increase your intellectual independence.

TABLE 1

DEPENDENT FRIENDSHIPS

1. I always want to talk my problems out with friends. YES __ NO __
2. I'm not a good listener to my friends' problems. YES __ NO __
3. I often spend hours on the phone talking to different people about my problems. YES __ NO __
4. I don't like to hear about my friends' successes. YES __ NO __
5. When I have a problem, my first thought is "How can someone help me with it?" YES __ NO __
6. I categorize my friends by the type of problem they can help me solve. YES __ NO __
7. Many of my friends seem to avoid me. YES __ NO __
8. I like to tell people when I'm sick. YES __ NO __
9. I often complain about the same problem over and over to my friends. YES __ NO __

10. I think my friends have the answers to my problems. YES __ NO __

11. I think the purpose of friendship is to solve the other person's problem. YES __ NO __

12. People have accused me of dumping my problems on them. YES __ NO __

13. When people give me suggestions or advice, I often find myself saying, "Yes, but . . ." YES __ NO __

14. I often seek out friends to give me counseling. YES __ NO __

15. I think the best way to get something done is to ask a friend to help. YES __ NO __

16. I'm happy when I hear my friends have had a setback or failure. YES __ NO __

17. I rate my friends in priority by what they can do for me. YES __ NO __

18. I pick my friends by their status. YES __ NO __

19. My first thought when I meet someone is "What can he do for me?" YES __ NO __

20. I get in touch with friends only when I have a problem I need help for. YES __ NO __

21. I keep up friendships because I believe I may need them someday. YES __ NO __

22. People seem to get tired of me quickly. YES __ NO __

23. People seldom come to me for help with their problems. YES __ NO __

24. I do most of the talking in my friendships. YES __ NO __

25. I'm more likely to call my friends than they are to call me. YES __ NO __

TABLE 2
DIFFERENCE BETWEEN BLAME AND ACCOUNTABILITY

Blame *versus*	*Accountability*
It's an overgeneralization.	It's specific and thus more helpful.
It comes back to burn you—the poker is hot at both ends.	You aren't in the victor role.
It doesn't take into account that they are doing the best they can.	Helps them not to do it again.
They often become defensive and thus stop listening and learning.	Gives more information. If they continue after you tell them not to, this is an indication of where you stand.
They are more likely, not less likely, to persist.	They can hear and better learn.
The blame and attention may serve as a reward.	You're more accepting.
You're setting yourself up as the moral arbiter of good and bad.	You're less likely to take on ownership of their choices.

CHAPTER FOURTEEN

Intellectual Independence

WHO IS THE BEST CANDIDATE? Which newspaper is right? What's good or bad taste in furniture? What's a right idea or a wrong idea? You may be overwhelmed by these questions, or you may never have thought about the issues. As a result, you vacillate over decisions, second-guess yourself or try not to think about the issues at all. Lack of intellectual independence makes you feel worse about yourself and creates real problems as decisions go unmade.

Automation and computers often add to the problem of intellectual dependency. You are given the answers to problems without having any real understanding of the problems themselves. When you take time to figure out something yourself, you nearly always come out ahead of the person who wants only the answer.

The trend toward relying on experts is becoming pervasive in our culture; this is a trap that leads to intellectual dependency. The TV announcer says, "It's raining outside, so make sure you wear a raincoat and boots." The financial expert says, "Buy gold." The child expert says, "Never spank your child." In the long run, you're usually better off to investigate, to question and to do your own leg work. When you take time to think out the situation for yourself, you know where you stand.

When you're intellectually independent, you follow your own gleam or hunches rather than let others define your life and options for you. You ask others for their opinions and advice, but when it comes down to it, *you* make the decision.

How many times have you let others persuade you against your own better judgment, even though you knew instinctively that you were right? I know a businessman who has had many successes and a few failures. He says, "My successes were always different, but every time I got into a bad deal, the situation was always the same. A voice inside me, a guardian angel if you will, told me, 'Don't do it.' The times I got into trouble was when I listened to others and not to myself."

Most of the time you will have trouble getting objective advice. People who are close enough to the situation to understand it usually have a vested interest in it. Few people can separate their vested interest from recommendations they give you. Those who don't have a vested interest can give you advice based only on their experiences. Because no experiences are exactly the same, this advice can easily be wrong for you.

This doesn't mean you don't want to search out information. While you want to question information that goes against what you believe, be aware that a part of being intellectually independent is the ability to yield to truth and not be devastated by it: you can accept that what you once thought true about politics, religion or life isn't necessarily so.

You have the ability to let old beliefs go and admit when you're wrong. You listen openly to other points of view before you consider the issue closed. Because you don't believe you have *immaculate perception*, you check out facts before you decide.

Problem Solving

You're more successful when you can deal directly with the problems and challenges of reality. Your efficiency drops when you ask others to interpret the world for you. Intellectual independence increases efficiency, which increases self-confidence, which leads to more independence. This is the success cycle. As you think more for yourself, you see that you can start projects and follow them through to the end.

The more you can think for yourself, the better you're able to handle difficult situations. Researchers have found that if you have confidence in your problem-solving ability, you can handle stress more effectively. You can see the stressful situation more clearly and thus increase your resources to handle it.

You may not have the specific talents or abilities that you need to solve the problem. But if you have the mental set that somehow you can handle the situation, you'll be able to come up with the talent you need to be successful.

A friend of mind was once driving in the Arizona desert. He got out of his car to have a better look at the view. When he got back in, he couldn't get his car started. He tried and tried, but it wouldn't start. It was getting dark and he knew almost nothing about cars. *But he still had confidence in his ability to think and solve problems.* Although no cars were on the road, he did remember passing a crossroads bar about five miles back.

He walked back to the bar. When he got there, he told three or four men sitting on the bar stools that his car was broken down. He got no response from them. And when he directly asked for help, they said it was his tough luck and that there was a garage about seventy-five miles down the road. However, when he said, "Would anyone here like to make fifty dollars?" he got an offer for help.

By not giving up and by using the resources he had (knowledge about what motivates people and fifty dollars) he was able to handle this difficulty. His mental set allowed him to come up with the solution to the problem and handle it.

Numerous studies have shown that the more control you believe you have over your own fate, the happier, more productive and healthier you'll be. This is true, not only for people, but for animals as well. Whether you believe you can direct your own life determines how you handle stress and meet challenges. When you believe you are subject to others or outside influences, you give up. When you believe you're the actor, you don't.

Integrity

A hallmark of intellectual independence is your integrity. The luxury of being able to tell the truth comes with being independent. When you're intimidated by others you have the urge to tell them what you think they want to hear, rather than what's true. This ranges from being a "yes person" at work to not letting those close to you in on what you really think.

Many people lie and cheat because they think this is the only way they can get what they need—others' approval or help in some way. Lies and other forms of dishonesty are a disservice to yourself. Every time you lie, you end up hurting and cheating yourself more than others. When you're independent, you realize that you don't have to manipulate others to get what you want; as a result, you can be honest with others and with yourself.

One of the important lessons of growing up is: "No one has a monopoly on the truth." Many people would like you to think they do—people on TV, in politics, and in the schools.

The Expert Illusion

When I was in grade school, I thought the teachers had all the answers. I falsely assumed this for years. I kept thinking I would get the answers from the teacher at the next level. By the time I got to be a visiting lecturer at Oxford I had finally come to realize that no one has the answers. I found a real expert is someone who has more questions than other people about some subject. In a sense experts know less, not more, about the subject. Every experiment scientists run opens more questions than it answers. If you read scientific papers, you'll see they start with one question in the introduction and end up with many more questions in the summary.

While it can be beneficial to get the experts' opinions, you have to keep in mind that what they know is overshadowed by what they don't know. Just because it's in the newspapers or in a book is no assurance that it's true. Because medical researchers or other experts say it's true, there's no assurance they're right. Just consider all the conflicting information you've heard over the years on how to handle burns or whether to spank your child.

Intellectual independence is the overriding concern in determining the shape and quality of your life. When you have it, life is enjoyable and satisfying, and when you don't, life isn't. Areas that are troublesome for you are the ones where you don't think for yourself. In these areas, you've let someone else do your arithmetic for you. You can master your difficulties and meet challenges better by starting to do your own arithmetic; you'll find your life will start to add up right.

Everyday Intellectual Dependency

You can start to become more intellectually independent by looking around you to see where you can improve. The following are some common examples of intellectual dependency. Mark off those that apply to you and then make a daily effort to let them go.

1. You count on others to be your memory ("What did I do with my keys?"). YES __ NO __
2. You count on others to make your decisions and choices ("Should I take the job or not?"). YES __ NO __
3. You count on others to do your analytical thinking ("Should I buy or rent a house?"). YES __ NO __
4. You count on others to do your concentration for you ("Read this contract and tell me what it says"). YES __ NO __
5. You count on others to make your judgments for you ("Who are we for in this election?"). YES __ NO __
6. You count on others to define reality for you ("What's going on here at the office?"). YES __ NO __
7. You rely on others to tell you what's good and bad taste ("Do you think this is the right wallpaper?"). YES __ NO __
8. You rely on others to do your investigating for you ("Call up the social security office for me and see where my check is"). YES __ NO __
9. You count on others to give you daily information ("How do you spell calendar? . . . what's the date today? . . . do you have the time?"). YES __ NO __
10. You count on others to take in information for you ("Give the directions to my wife [secretary]"). YES __ NO __
11. You count on others to give out your information ("Call Mrs. Jones and tell her why I can't come home"). YES __ NO __

12. You count on others to follow through for you ("Mary, take care of the details for me"). YES __ NO __

13. You count on others to keep you honest ("Tell me if I'm going off my diet"). YES __ NO __

14. You count on others to be totally honest with you ("I thought he really owned the Brooklyn Bridge"). YES __ NO __

15. You count on others to be totally dishonest with you ("I don't believe a word any of them said"). YES __ NO __

16. You count on others to fit into a pigeonhole ("He's just like all engineers"). YES __ NO __

17. You count on experts to have all the answers ("My brother-in-law, the lawyer, will know all the ins and outs of this"). YES __ NO __

18. You count on uneducated people to always be wrong ("My brother's a truck driver. What does he know?"). YES __ NO __

19. You count on those with outward signs of success to always be right ("How was I to know he was a crook? He had a twenty-five-foot limousine"). YES __ NO __

20. You count anything that goes against your belief system to be wrong ("The newspapers are lying"). YES __ NO __

21. You count on leaders, especially dynamic and charismatic talkers, to always be right ("He seemed so sure of himself"). YES __ NO __

22. You count on large followings to determine what's true ("Twenty thousand investors can't be wrong"). YES __ NO __

23. You count on everything you read to be true ("I read it in a medical journal; it must be true"). YES __ NO __

24. You count on others to protect you from negative consequences ("Should I wear a warm coat?"). YES __ NO __

Guidelines to Intellectual Independence

When you're intellectually independent, you claim ownership of your thoughts, beliefs, attitudes and point of view. You're not afraid to own up. The following are some ways you can put this into action when you're interacting with others and when you have a choice to think for yourself or not.

Be Direct. When you ask others for what you want in an indirect way, you're showing your fear of owning your own request. Often only by asking "Why?" can others get to your direct request.

"Does the car have gas in it?"
"No, why do you ask?"
"No reason, I was just wondering."
"Why were you wondering?"
"Well, would you please fill it for me?"

When you catch yourself being indirect, question yourself until you can get to your direct request, and then make it.

Sarcasm and cynicism are indirect ways of expressing your disapproval. You don't want to own up to giving direct negative opinions to others so you disguise it ("I'm sure every magazine will want to publish what you write" versus "It's difficult to get articles published").

Be Brief. Overexplaining is a form of not owning your opinions and actions. Suppose you've decided to change college majors. Overexplaining why you did this is a form of nonacceptance. You're trying to convince yourself you made the right decision and the harder you try, the less convinced you become.

Closely related to this is overapologizing and making excuses to justify your actions. Disraeli's rule, "Don't complain, don't explain," is often good advice.

Avoid Excessive Qualifications. You want to state your opinions and leave it at that. You might, for example, say, "Well, to me, I think . . . and I might be wrong . . . but again, don't take my word for it, but I think it might rain." "Now, don't get me wrong, but . . ." Excessive qualifications are a way of trying to avoid accountability. You don't want to take the blame if others get stuck in the rain without their umbrellas.

Let Your Opinions Stand on Their Own. You may feel that you have to provide a reference for whatever you say ("I read in *Time Magazine* . . ."). This is a disease that graduate students and many academics have. They have to support their observations with what others have said. It doesn't make any difference who the reference is, just so someone else said it before.

Don't Seek Validation for All of Your Observations. Stand on your own feet and tolerate others who do not readily agree with your observations. The following is how people seek intellectual reassurance:

"You know, I think I'm right, don't you think so, Mary?"
"I think so, Larry, don't you think so?"
"Yes, I'm absolutely positive, you know what I mean?"
"Yeah, I know what you mean, I'm absolutely sure too—I think."

Own Your Own Preferences. Usually you have some preference for what you would like to do—an activity, vacation spot, movie, restaurant. It's important for you to state these. Verbal forms of this version of nonownership are: "You decide" . . . "I don't know, you choose" . . . "It doesn't make any difference to me." The next time you're in this situation, speak up and say what you want to do. Just because others have strong opinions doesn't mean yours aren't valid. If you habitually don't say anything, mention the first one that comes to you—and stick with it.

The same applies to tastes in art, music and other cultural and entertainment activities. If you enjoy watching soap operas, reading the *National Enquirer* and eating at McDonald's, speak up and tell people.

Practice Nonverbal Ownership. You can disclaim ownership of an idea or opinion by making your outward expression contradict what you say. You may nervously laugh and smile and say, in effect, "Don't take my serious statement seriously. I'm really not that serious." You may speak softly or mumble so that others don't know what you're saying. You don't claim ownership of what you say by making a joke out of it. Say what you mean in a way that shows you mean it.

Be Clear and Strong in Voicing Your Opinion. You can escape ownership or responsibility by presenting your ideas in vague terms, double talk, or understatements. To be intellectually independent it's better to exaggerate your ideas a little more than to understate them. When you understate your ideas, you rob them of power. State your opinion in strong, forceful words and then accept the consequences. Your ideas might be wrong, but they are yours. Be specific when you talk and bring in facts to support your position.

Make Your Own Decisions. To be intellecutally independent you need to learn to make your own decisions as often as you can. With most decisions, there are no right or wrong ones. They just have different results. One decision may be the longer way around, but you still end up at the same place. What's important is that after you make a decision you follow through. People often have trouble with decisions, not because they can't decide but because they keep changing their minds after they have decided.

Keep Your Beliefs Open. The most notable characteristic of intellectual dependency is a closed mind. To keep your mind open, stop proselytizing your beliefs. All proselytizing is self-proselytizing—you're constantly trying to convince yourself.

Seek out and accept facts that go against your beliefs. Growth comes from making sense of the facts that don't add up. Avoid stereotypic thinking—no two people or situations are exactly the same.

Increase Your Tolerance. Many people, because they can't live with any degree of uncertainty, gravitate toward people and movements that claim to have all the answers. There are, however, no absolute truths. Henry Miller decided to write the whole truth and nothing but the truth. His writings were so graphic that they were banned for years. He finally concluded in later years, "I said I was going to write the truth, so help me God, and I thought I was. I found I couldn't. Nobody can write the absolute truth."

To be intellectually independent, you have to settle for continually seeking out the truth rather than to someday having it.

Stay an Adult in Serious Matters. When you don't want to be accountable, you may have an inclination to regress to more childlike behavior. One form of this is to revert to baby talk ("Me sorry, I was a bad girl"). Another form is to refer to yourself in the third person. Bill Jones might, for example, say, "Well, Bill Jones has to look out for himself." This is the way children respond. Only after they develop a sense of themselves do children use the first person.

Develop Creative Outlets. One theory of emotional disorders is that the person is a frustrated artist. (The disturbance is caused because he or she has no creative outlet.) Several studies have found that when people become more healthy emotionally they become more creative. Dr. Paul Torrance, for example, has studied this phenomenon. He concludes, "There's no doubt that using your imagination and creativity not only makes you feel better, it can also help you live longer."

Do creative things for yourself, not for others. One artist said about art, "It's very selfish. The artist does it for himself, and if somebody else likes it, that's great. Creative things demand a unique personal vision and integrity that are beyond criticism."

Take Time Out to Think. To become intellectually independent you need to take time to think and reflect. This is when your best ideas and decisions come to you. To think for yourself, you have to get away from all the distractions. Try to "check out" at least five minutes a day, one hour a week, and one whole day once a year. Plan it on your calendar and go off by yourself and do nothing but think and reflect about yourself. You need occasional periods of withdrawal, solitude and privacy to develop your intellectual independence.

Do Your Work More Intelligently. You can increase your intelligence in everyday activities. Think about the ways you do the dishes, drive to work, mow the lawn; think how you can do these tasks more creatively and more intellectually. Analyze why and how you do things now, then do them differently. Physical work can help increase your intellectual independence. Ask yourself how you can do these jobs faster, more interestingly, and yet have more fun. Eric Hoffer said, "You cannot gauge the intelligence of an American by talking with him; you must work with him."

Learn Something New. One of the best ways to keep intellectually independent is to continue to learn. Learn something that's not related to your profession. If you're a scriptwriter, take a woodworking class; if you're a carpenter, take a class in scriptwriting. Learning is what keeps you young. Older people who continue to use their brains stay young. Learning something new is one of the best antidotes for intellectual dependence.

Use the ACT Formula. You can always pull out the ACT formula whenever you feel yourself slipping into intellectual dependency. For example, you may have trouble with math. You may have avoided math in the past—not doing your own taxes, turning down jobs requiring bookkeeping, not taking math classes—so you may not have learned many basic math procedures. First, *accept* that math is as hard as it is for you, no more, no less. Next, *choose* to be independent about it. Make up your mind that you're going to master what you've been avoiding. Finally, *take action* by getting a text on basic math, take a class in it, or hire a tutor.

In becoming intellectually independent, you want above all to learn to think straighter. In the next chapter I'll talk about some ways you can do this.

To see how you now fare in intellectual independence you can take the following inventory.

Intellectual Independence Inventory

This refers to your ability to think for yourself, to make your own decisions and follow your own judgment. This also involves your spiritual and creative lives and your ability to follow your own hunches.

Read each group of statements carefully. Then circle the number beside the statement that best describes you. After you have completed the questionnaire, add up all the numbers circled. Check your total with the totals given at the end of the chapter.

1. 0 I finish projects I start.
   1 I sometimes don't finish projects I start.
   2 I often don't finish projects I start.
   3 I never finish projects.
2. 0 I rarely procrastinate.
   1 I sometimes procrastinate.
   2 I often procrastinate.
   3 I always procrastinate.
3. 0 I feel confident to make different choices in my life.
   1 I hesitate to make different choices in my life.
   2 I feel I can't make different choices in my life.
   3 I feel helpless to make different choices in my life.
4. 0 I'm committed to some ideal or project.
   1 I'm fairly committed to some ideal or project.
   2 I find it difficult to commit myself to some ideal or project.
   3 I cannot commit myself to some idea or project.
5. 0 I don't feel like a phony in my profession.
   1 I sometimes feel like a phony in my profession.
   2 I often feel like a phony in my profession.
   3 I feel like a phony in my profession.
6. 0 I'm confident in my ability to solve problems on my own.
   1 I occasionally doubt my ability to solve problems on my own.
   2 I often doubt my ability to solve problems on my own.
   3 I cannot solve problems on my own.
7. 0 I'm not suggestible.
   1 I'm sometimes suggestible.
   2 I'm often suggestible.
   3 I'm very suggestible.
8. 0 I'm creative.
   1 I'm somewhat creative.
   2 I'm very creative.
   3 I am not creative.
9. 0 If my creative work pleases me, I do it.
   1 If others don't believe my creative work is good enough, I often don't do it.
   2 If others don't believe my creative work is good, I usually don't do it.

3 If others don't believe my creative work is good, I never do it.

10. 0 I worked out my own beliefs about religion and God.
1 My beliefs about religion and God are somewhat affected by others' beliefs.
2 My beliefs about religion and God are strongly affected by others' beliefs.
3 My beliefs about religion and God were taught to me by others.

11. 0 I've developed my own philosophy of life.
1 My philosophy of life is somewhat affected by others.
2 My philosophy of life is greatly affected by others.
3 My philosophy of life was taught to me by others.

12. 0 I don't automatically believe everything I read or see in the media.
1 I don't automatically believe most of what I read or see in the media.
2 I believe most of what I read or see in the media.
3 I believe everything I read or see in the media.

13. 0 I make decisions well.
1 I put off making decisions.
2 I have great difficulty making decisions.
3 I cannot make decisions at all.

14. 0 I trust my judgment.
1 I often don't trust my judgment.
2 I usually don't trust my judgment.
3 I don't trust my judgment.

15. 0 I trust my aesthetic judgment.
1 I often don't trust my aesthetic judgment.
2 I usually don't trust my aesthetic judgment.
3 I don't trust my aesthetic judgment.

16. 0 I believe I know as much as anyone else.
1 I often believe I don't know as much as other people.
2 I usually believe I don't know as much as other people.
3 I don't know as much as other people.

17. 0 I go against group decisions if I think I'm right.
1 I often go against group decisions if I think I'm right.
2 I sometimes go against group decisions if I think I'm right.
3 I never go against group decisions, even if I think I'm right.

18. 0 I rarely doubt my decisions, actions or choices.
    1 I occasionally doubt my decisions, actions or choices.
    2 I often doubt my decisions, actions or choices.
    3 I always doubt my decisions, actions or choices.
19. 0 I rarely lie to protect my pride.
    1 I sometimes lie to protect my pride.
    2 I often lie to protect my pride.
    3 I always lie to protect my pride.
20. 0 If there is something I don't know, I try to understand it.
    1 If there is something I don't know, I usually try to understand it.
    2 If there is something I don't know, I rarely try to understand it.
    3 If there is something I don't know, I don't care to understand it.
21. 0 I investigate what and who I vote for.
    1 I sometimes rely on others to investigate what and who I vote for.
    2 I usually rely on others to investigate what and who I vote for.
    3 Others tell me who and what to vote for.
22. 0 I can concede an argument if I see I'm wrong.
    1 I sometimes have difficulty conceding an argument, even if I'm wrong.
    2 I often have difficulty conceding an argument, even if I'm wrong.
    3 I cannot concede an argument, even if I'm wrong.
23. 0 I can be friends with people who have entirely different social or religious views from mine.
    1 I sometimes can be friends with people who have entirely different political or religious views from mine.
    2 I rarely can be friends with people who have entirely different political or religious views from mine.
    3 I cannot be friends with people who have entirely different political or religious views from mine.
24. 0 I rarely get into intellectual arguments.
    1 I often get into intellectual arguments.
    2 I usually get into intellectual arguments.
    3 I am constantly getting into intellectual arguments.
25. 0 I don't worry about how intelligent I am.
    1 I often worry about how intelligent I am.

2 I usually worry about my intelligence.
3 I'm obsessed with my intelligence.

26. 0 I don't automatically believe I'm smarter than others.
1 I often believe I'm smarter than others.
2 I usually believe I'm smarter than others.
3 I always believe I'm smarter than others.

27. 0 I can tolerate not knowing something that's important to me.
1 I often have trouble tolerating not knowing something that's important to me.
2 I usually have trouble tolerating not knowing something that's important to me.
3 I always have trouble tolerating not knowing something that's important to me.

RESULTS:
Score of 0–6 = high level of intellectual independence.
Score of 7–17 = moderate level of intellectual independence.
Score of 18–25 = low level of intellectual independence.
Score of 25 or above = severe problem with intellectual independence.

CHAPTER FIFTEEN

Misperceptions of Time, Space and Motion

TO BECOME INTELLECTUALLY INDEPENDENT, you need to accept reality as much as possible. The reason you have trouble accepting it is that you have false beliefs. In this chapter I'm going to talk about some of your most common erroneous beliefs and suggest alternate ways to view your situation.

For the sake of convenience, I've divided your beliefs into three categories: *time*, *space* and *motion*. Misperception of *time* refers to seeing time in a personal way ("This pain will go on forever") rather than objectively. *Space* has to do with how you view others in relation to yourself. You may see people as being below you or above you or too close or too far from you. Misperception of *motion* has to do with how you decide to reach your goals ("I should put off anything that is difficult until I feel like doing it").

These categories can and often do overlap. For example, when you get into an uncomfortable situation, you may tell yourself, "I can't stand it." This could be a misperception of time (you think the discomfort will go on forever) and space ("I can't tolerate being in this place") and motion (if you think moving away from the pain is the best way to get what you want). Despite this overlap, I'll talk about them as if each were separate.

The alternative answers I give to these beliefs are only food for thought. The best answers are the ones you find yourself. As you read the ones I've listed, be on the lookout for your own associations. When an idea triggers some thought you can use, make note of it.

To become more intellectually independent you have to reprogram yourself. You've been indoctrinating yourself daily with your misperceptions; now you need to balance the score. To do this, get a stack of 3"x5" cards. On one side of a card write one of your distorted beliefs or ideas. On the other side, put down more realistic and useful ways of looking at the situation. Do this with all of your beliefs that you would like to replace with more mature beliefs.

Flip through the cards whenever you get a chance during the day. Look over your old beliefs and study your answers to them. It takes repetition to help you layer over your ingrained beliefs. Periodically update your cards. Get rid of old answers that don't move you and add new ones that do.

Time

The concept of time in general can cause you a great deal of confusion. Most people refer to time as though it were something concrete and real ("I'll kill some time" . . . "I'll save time"). Time, though, is nothing you can see, touch or feel. It's an abstraction; when you confuse an abstraction with what is real and concrete you often have trouble becoming independent. To become independent you need to deal with what's real and in front of you, what is, not with abstractions.

Time can become an excuse for not being independent. "I don't have the time to take care of myself" really means "I'm choosing to do something that's more pleasurable." You may use time as a way to escape looking at yourself. You may say, "I have to learn to manage my time," when what you really mean is that you have to learn to manage yourself.

I treated one man who was overly dependent on people around him to take care of his everyday functions. His rationale was "Time is the one thing that you can't change, and my time is limited." His focus was on trying to manage time instead of learning to be more effective.

Your efficiency is a result of what you do, not a result of the time in which you do it. In one week you can be three or four times as efficient as you are in another. Time doesn't exist as something real that you can manage. Thinking of time as concrete keeps you in a passive role. In *table 1* (p. 311) I've listed some of the ways you may use time as a smoke screen to mask dependency.

Everything is continuously changing. Time is a convenient way of measuring change—what changed in the past, what's changing now and what could change in the future. Time, as we use it, is better at measuring some changes than others.

Your age can be used as a misperception of reality. Babies develop at a fairly uniform rate, so considering their growth by the ages of six months, twelve months and twenty-four months is a useful way to measure their development. However, when people get older, they develop in a much less uniform way. Chronological measurement of change becomes largely irrelevant. When you say someone is fifty, this doesn't tell you very much about him or her. If you have beliefs about fifty-year-old people in general, they are probably misperceptions. This is why researchers of aging use biological age rather than chronological age as a way to measure development in adults.

I'm going to break common misperceptions of time into past, present and future.

Past. You may believe that because of the way your parents raised you, because of your religious training or because of traumas that happened in the past, you're locked in to who you are. You may think that because you've been acting the same way for a long time you, like an old dog, can't learn new tricks.

Belief: "Because of what happened to me in the past I can't become more independent."

Alternative Answers:

- "While my past plays a major role in who I am, this doesn't mean I can't make different choices."
- I'm letting go of many of my old habits; I can choose new ones."
- "While I can't transform my whole personality, I can learn new ways of how I choose to think, feel, and act."
- "Human beings are extremely pliable and can change their long-held habits and beliefs."

- "My past problems were caused by skill deficiencies. I can learn new skills."
- "What's keeping me locked in to the past isn't the past, but believing now what I believed then."
- "I'm using this as an excuse for not choosing to be independent."
- "I'm needlessly holding on to the past."
- "This is a self-fulfilling prophecy. By acting on the prophecy, I make it true."

You may have attempted unsuccessfully to make new choices in the past. Most of the time you started toward independence but, at some critical point, you failed to follow through and fell back into dependence. For example, you may have tried to leave home or learn to drive.

Belief: "I've tried to be independent in the past and couldn't, so I'll never be able to."

Alternative answers:

- "It's not true that I haven't been able to increase my range of choice. I've learned many new ways of acting."
- "I can choose to be independent—that's all it takes."
- "Even if I've always been dependent in the past, that doesn't mean I can't decide to change right now."
- "I may have needed the failure experience to see what I was doing wrong."
- "Today will soon be the past, so I'd better focus on now."
- "I can look at past experiences more objectively and see what I can learn from them, rather than use them as excuses."
- "Don't experience life by looking through the rear-view mirror."
- "The only period I can manage is right now."
- "The best way to free myself of the past is to focus on what I'm doing today."
- "Try as hard as you can to change the past. Really try, right now. Did it work?"
- "What's the point of flying backward like a goony bird?"
- "What's keeping me stuck in the past right now is my memory traces. I don't have to focus on them."

- "Life is unfolding because of my past choices. I can make different choices right now."
- "I have a free will to make choices."

When you ask yourself too many *whys* you often have trouble coming up with meaningful answers. Asking why can be a form of nonacceptance. You can spend years digging out the whys and only find yourself deeper in a hole. Right now it's more important to accept that you're dependent because acceptance is what frees you to choose.

Belief: "I have to go back to my early childhood and find out why I'm so dependent."

Alternative answers:

- "Even if I get insight to the past, this won't change anything now—unless I act differently now."
- "I don't have to know how the crack got in the bridge, I only need to fix it before the bridge collapses."
- "I can look at past experiences (which is another word for *mistakes*) as a way to help me now and not as a reason to keep banging my head against a wall."
- "So what if I've been dependent on others in the past—everyone who is now independent was dependent on someone in the past."
- "By blaming and justifying, I'm holding on to the past."
- "The past is the past, so what?"

Present. There's some symmetry to the good and bad events that happen in your life, but little is apparent when they happen. Good and bad periods run in patches: a good one is followed by a bad one is followed by a good one.

When you're in a good patch, friends and associates tell you how great you are. When you're in a bad one, that's when they decide to tell you what's wrong with you. Why does this happen? One reason is that when you're in a bad patch, people perceive you as more accepting of criticism than they do when you're in a good patch.

I was one of three supervisors watching a trainee doing therapy through a two-way mirror. I said, "I've been meaning to tell Joe some of the more basic things he's doing wrong in therapy. I think I'll tell him today."

One of the other supervisors said, "That's funny. I told him a lot of the things he's doing wrong earlier today."

The third supervisor said, "You know, he's pretty down. His wife left him last week."

Just as baby chicks will peck a deformed chick to death, we have an almost instinctual drive to kick someone when he or she is down. People in general will more likely get on you when you're in a bad period. There's a Persian folk saying, "If you see a blind man, kick him. Why be kinder to him than God is?"

When you get into a bad patch your timing is thrown off. I once watched another couple at a dinner show. Apparently their reservation was put in the wrong book. Because of this error their whole evening was spoiled. Their seating was messed up; they didn't get their complimentary drinks. This pattern continued throughout the night. Occasionally you do get "out of sync." The trick is not to assume this will go on forever.

Much of the problem in remaining intellectually independent in the face of changing conditions grows out of your expectations. If you expect present bad events to continue, you overlook rescue factors and create a self-fulfilling prophecy. And if you expect good events to continue, you set yourself up for disappointment.

I believe life is very much like a series of good news/bad news jokes. Lin Yutang quotes the famous parable of the *Old Man at the Fort*, which highlights the same point:

> An Old Man was living with his son at an abandoned fort at the top of a hill, and one day he lost a horse. The neighbours came to express their sympathy for this misfortune, and the Old Man asked, "How do you know this is bad luck?" A few days afterwards, his horse returned with a number of wild horses, and his neighbours came again to congratulate him on this stroke of fortune, and the Old Man replied, "How do you know this is good luck?" With so many horses around, his son began to take to riding, and one day he broke his leg. Again the neighbours came around to express their sympathy, and the Old Man replied, "How do you know this is bad luck?" The next year, there was a

war, and because the Old Man's son was crippled, he did not have to go to the front.

What you call good or bad often depends on what time perspective you take. A couple of days ago I accidentally backed a hired truck into a wall. At first this looked like bad news; however, the accident caused me to get the truck insurance policy out. I found the accident was fully covered and I also discovered that the policy covered some furniture that had been broken earlier in transit. If I hadn't run into the wall I would never have discovered this good news.

Distortion: "My present troubles (or successes) will go on forever."

Sample answers:

- "Because patches, good or bad, aren't frozen in time, there's little reason to get either overjoyed or desperate over them."
- "The elegant solution is to work toward enlightened acceptance of outside events and to try to keep my expectations low and my motivation high."
- "All problems are time-limited."
- "I'll have to see how the situation unfolds before I'll be able to see what the solutions are."
- "I've gone through periods like this before."
- "This too shall pass."
- "This is a good time to develop my tolerance for frustration."
- "What can I get out of the situation that's at hand?"

When you start acting independently you may think that the discomfort brought on by your new actions will go away immediately. Often, just as you are about to break through, you decide that you can't go on any longer. This is the "wall" runners talk about. It's important that you hold on until you get through the wall.

Belief: "This is taking too long."

Alternate answers:

- "It will take as long as it takes—no longer, no shorter."
- "I upset myself by using vague words like *too*."
- "This type of thinking creates boredom."
- "Focus on what I can do right now."

- "It's wishful thinking to demand things to be different right away."
- "Change goes on below the surface before it's noticeable."
- "It's not true that if it doesn't happen now it never will."
- "My lack of patience stops me from trying and then following the natural unfolding of events."
- "Giving in to this gets me further out of sync."

How you react to disappointment is a central concern in becoming more independent. Disappointments can be the removal of obstacles to a higher goal, if you see them as such—you lose one job and this allows you to take a better one. You can tell yourself, "I have an appointment with success, and this dis-appointment just means that I'm not at the right corner at the right time. Perhaps we are going to meet in a better neighborhood." However, if you see disappointments as dead ends, they often will be.

Basically, disappointments are forms of communication: they're telling you something you need to know. It might be that you're spending too much time in the wrong area; that you have lost sight of what you really want; that you haven't covered some deficiency you need to deal with (if you go on without correcting it, you'll really have problems). Above all else, disappointments are red flags that say, "Hey, here's a point where you can escalate the curve upward toward where you want to go." *(See figure 1, p. 312.)*

Your view of disappointment is the key. If you see setbacks as final, then they are. When you see them as friendly aids to help you get where you want to go, they become curves and loops and stop cutting you like zigs and zags.

Belief: "This setback means I'll never reach my goal."

Alternative answers:

- "How have some of my other major disappointments worked out?"
- "How many times have I heard others say, 'I thought it would be the end of the world, but now I can see it was the best thing that could have happened'?"
- "It may turn out that there isn't a problem."

- "After a setback, I need time to see where the partial solution will start to appear."
- "It's not possible to project the present into the future."
- "How can I use this disappointment as the removal of an obstacle to a higher goal?"
- "Emerson, in his essay on self-reliance, says, 'A strenuous soul hates cheap success.' "
- "Nothing ever stays the same."
- "Humans have a great ability to adapt to unforeseen situations."
- "Perhaps the best strategy is to work on some other project."
- "Don't compound bad events by a bad mood."

Often people use their work or other commitments as an excuse to be dependent ("You clear the table because I have work to do"). This is a way to avoid the choices that you could make for yourself. You're putting the accountability on an abstraction (time) rather than on yourself.

Belief: "I don't have the time to be independent."

Alternative answers:

- "What I can accomplish is largely irrelevant of time constraints."
- "If I'm the author of my own life, I accomplish just about everything I want to."
- "I can be more efficient by doing things for myself."
- "The issue is self-management—not time management."
- "Many of my dependent behaviors are keeping me from being more efficient."
- "If I'm more independent I can get more done."

Many people will keep you waiting in order to show their dominance over you; this is often a strategy among academic people. On the whole, they are fairly powerless people. One of the ways they show what limited power they do have is to keep students and colleagues waiting. Many academic meetings start late because a member will be late in order to show his or her power ("You can't start the meeting without me").

When you allow yourself to be kept waiting, this is a misperception of who owns the time. This is a way to lose your independence. If you're waiting for other people, you end up giving your time to them—they take control of you.

Belief: "Others are wasting my time."

Alternative answers:

- "Am I allowing others to keep me waiting without speaking up?"
- "I'll be more assertive. I'll leave if the chronically late person doesn't show."
- "I have a choice. I can take a good book to read or leave."
- "My time is as valuable to me as theirs is to them."
- "I have to keep my eye on what I'm doing and be aware of what others are doing to me."

Future. Anxiety is an unrealistic fear of some danger in the future. If you focus on what's going on around you, you can't be anxious. To be anxious you have to project yourself into the future.

Belief: "I'm afraid something terrible will happen."

Alternative answers:

- "I'm no fortuneteller. I don't know what the future will bring."
- "This is a problem of wanting 100 percent guarantees. No one can give me such a guarantee."
- "Just because something could happen doesn't mean it will."
- "There's always some probability of danger in any activity."
- "Don't confuse a low probability with a high probability."
- "I don't need certainty to enjoy life."
- "Once I know more about it, I won't have the fear."
- "Even if it is as bad as I predict, I can handle it."
- "Focus on the present, which I can control, not the future which I can't."
- "Anxiety won't prevent something bad from happening to me."
- "Is this a pseudo-danger to my self-image, rather than a real danger?"
- "I have lived through such dangerous periods before."
- "I may learn something from it."
- "Anxiety is a sign of growth, that I'm taking risks."

- "The more I focus on danger the less I am able to handle the real problem effectively."
- "Am I using this worry as a form of magic to ward off danger?"
- "Where is the evidence that it's so dangerous?

You engage in magical thinking when you believe someone or something will always come to your rescue. This is a legacy of childhood. Most of the time hope turns out to be false hope. The cavalry doesn't come, you have to save yourself.

Belief: "Someone or some event will come along and make me feel happy and satisfied."

Alternative answers:

- "Hope is a poor basis for running my life."
- "When I'm independent I try to keep my expectations of the future low and live for today."
- "I'm better off focusing on what I do have."
- "I have no evidence this will happen."
- "This is just a way of not accepting the present."
- "I can be happy without a knight in shining armor."
- "My experience is that this seldom happens."
- "On those occasions when my expectations are completely met, it's rarely as good as I had imagined."
- "I'm setting myself up for disappointment."
- "I just can't claim ownership for something I don't have."
- "Just because I want something doesn't mean I'm going to get it."

No one knows enough about the future to be pessimistic. This is one of the most debilitating beliefs you can have. It's the most common attitude of people who kill themselves. Pessimism of any kind keeps you choosing dependency.

Belief: "The future is hopeless."

Alternative answers:

- "Where's my evidence that the situation is hopeless?"
- "This reflects my thinking, not reality."
- "To believe nothing will work out is as mindless as to think everything will."
- "I'm overlooking my strengths."
- "No one knows enough to be that pessimistic."

• "I'll see what I can learn; periods of hopelessness can be the best time to learn about myself."

• "Learn to develop a tolerance for feelings of hopelessness without giving in to them."

Space

Dr. Aaron Beck and I have recently been studying personality types and their relationship to space. We're finding that people tend to fall into one of two types—*claustrophobic* or *agoraphobic*. We are expanding on the physical definitions to include social and psychological traits. The claustrophobe fears being closed in. This person usually avoids commitment and any type of social situation where his or her freedom might be curtailed. Agoraphobia means fear of open spaces. The agoraphobe fears being abandoned and left alone. This person is afraid that he or she will be cut off from social contact. You may be claustrophobic at some times and agoraphobic at other times. However, you probably experience one much oftener than the other.

Agoraphobia and claustrophobia have to do with horizontal space; you feel people are too close or too far from you. Another type of misperception has to do with vertical space: you believe people are above or below you. When you think people are above you, you give up your independence to them. And when you think others are below you, you often make it more difficult for them to become independent.

Agoraphobia. You may think that you can't function on your own in difficult areas, but you have never really tested this out by doing activities by yourself. Some people hold this belief to such a degree that they will stay home rather than go out alone.

Belief: "I can't do it alone."

Alternative answers:

• "We are born alone and die alone. We can never become totally one with another—this is an *illusion of fusion*."

• "There is a difference between being lonely and being alone. Just because I enjoy being with others doesn't mean I can't enjoy my own company."

• "Relying on myself is a habit I can learn."

• "I don't have to have a pipeline to others to take care of me. I can provide my own fuels. I'm self-contained."

• "While I can never fully fuse with another, I'm rarely completely isolated."

• "There are many rescue factors I can always use."

• "The feeling of dread I have while I'm alone is only anxiety—the natural result of fear. In time, it will disappear."

• "Anxiety is not dangerous, only uncomfortable."

To some people, the risk of being rejected is the worst possibility in the world. People with this belief may do just about anything to ensure that they're not left on their own.

Belief: "I couldn't take it if I were abandoned and left all alone."

Alternative answers:

• "Being alone will not kill me."

• "Being with someone else is not a lifeline."

• "Many people learn to live and be on their own. There's no reason why I can't."

• "By acting as if people have to take care of me, I'm stopping myself from growing. I need some room of my own to grow in."

• "When I try to engulf others, they feel trapped and move away."

• "By holding onto others, I not only slow them down, but I can never develop my own legs to keep me going."

• "I have spent time on my own and survived."

• "I can tolerate rejection; this doesn't mean that I can never have another person in my life."

The person fearful of being alone will often cultivate a large circle of friends and acquaintances. This is done largely out of fear. The person wants to make sure he or she will be taken care of in case of an emergency and won't be left alone.

Belief: "I have to protect myself from being all alone by taking out insurance."

Alternative beliefs:

• "If I'm continually going from one person to another, I'll never be able to see what I can do on my own."

• "The more secure I try to become, the more insecure I make myself feel."

- "Insurance is a poor basis for a relationship."
- "I'm overinsured. The cost of the premium is too high."
- "I don't need constant reassurance ('Do you still love me? . . . Is the pipeline still open?')."
- "The pipeline for social supplies is a self-created illusion."

You may believe you need others to tell you where you stand or to give you direction. You may believe that without this help you'd be lost. The illusion is that you *need* others.

Belief: "I'm drifting and need someone to tell me what direction to take."

Alternative answers:

- "If I'm drifting, it's because I'm choosing to."
- "I don't need other people to tell me what to do."
- "I choose my own directions."
- "There's nothing that says I can't drift. I might need this time to find out what I want to do."
- "I can survive on my own without a perfectly worked-out road map."
- "I don't always have to know where I'm going next."
- "I can tolerate some ambiguity—which is the spice of life."
- "I don't have to know with 100 percent certainty where I stand with others."

You may fear risks because you feel you'll be left out on a limb. You fear new independent choices because of the threat of being cut off from your predictable world.

Belief: "I can't take any risks because I could be left alone."

Alternative answers:

- "Since risks lead to learning, if I don't take risks, I can't learn."
- "To do what I want and to go places that I choose, I have to take risks."
- "If I can't risk displeasing others, I'll never be able to evolve."
- "I'm exaggerating both the degree of risk and the extent of the danger."
- "Others want to be paid for protecting me. Am I willing to pay the price? Is it worth it?"
- "I can get more pleasure from the unexpected than from the expected."

- "Life without surprises is dull and uninteresting. To get the most enjoyment, I can maximize my surprises by minimizing my expectations."

Claustrophobia. You may have a group of beliefs about space that's the opposite of agoraphobia. Your beliefs may revolve around being trapped and losing your freedom. These beliefs often block your independence by exaggerating the dangers of the world. If the agoraphobe's life revolves around the *illusion of fusion*, the claustrophobe's centers around the *illusion of exclusion*. You believe that you can and should separate yourself from others.

You may not start new projects or relationships because you believe your freedom will be hindered. You believe you can't get out of commitments. You underestimate your sense of control over events and your ability to choose the kind of life you want to live. You may believe people will manipulate you into doing what you don't want to do. One man, for example, had trouble getting a job because he feared most of the jobs he interviewed for would take away his freedom.

Belief: "Commitments are traps."

Alternative answers:

- "Real freedom is internal, not external."
- "The more I try to get complete external freedom, the more I constrict myself."
- "I always have a choice to be or not to be in a relationship."
- "Nothing in the environment is physically holding me now."
- "Relationships can't really tie me down—I can always leave."

You may avoid doing independent activities such as learning how to cook or balancing a checkbook because you fear that you'll be trapped in the space of having to do it.

Belief: "Daily hassles are traps."

Alternative answers:

- "Moving away from the reality of the situation, not facing the problem, will not get me what I want."
- "True freedom includes freedom to choose unpleasant activities."

- "This is not a physical trap but one I'm making up in my head."
- "The hassles are not closing in on me, I can always leave."

You may be defensive and move away from others because you fear you'll be trapped. You may not make calls or see people who could help your goals. In truth, your extreme autonomy is keeping you in bondage.

Belief: "I have to protect my domain from invasion by others."
Alternative beliefs:

- "Freedom is the ability to choose whom I want to be close to. If I can't choose anyone, I'm not free."
- "I can't reach all of my goals alone."
- "In reality I can't be invaded and taken over by others."
- "The more I become territorial, the more I restrict myself."
- "I short-change myself by my inability to learn from others."

One scientist avoided contact with other colleagues because he thought they would take him away from his project. This grew out of the belief that they would impede his freedom. However, he missed out by not talking to others—their information and input could have helped him in his work.

You may be able to rely on yourself in a limited area; however, by withholding yourself you'll lack independence in most areas of your life because most of life involves others. Many of your self-goals are forms of self-imprisonment. Like the Soviets, you have rigid five-year programs that must be achieved at all costs.

Belief: "I can't trust others."
Alternative answers:

- "Even though I trust others, I can still dance to my own tune."
- "I miss out on a lot when I believe my ideas are the only ones that are right."
- "I need information from those who have it in order to learn."
- "Not following others' instructions as a symbolic gesture is an adolescent way of acting."
- "I can tolerate others helping me. This doesn't mean they are controlling me."
- "Because most of life is interrelated, I hurt my ability to reach goals by avoiding others."

- "How can I learn from mistakes if I won't listen to others to find out what my mistakes are?"

You may think, "I can't stay in one place." This is a common thought of anxious people as they start more independent activities. Not tolerating one place can hamper your independence and your ability to author your own life.
Belief: "I have to get out of here."
Alternative beliefs:

- "I don't have to, I have a free will to stay."
- "There's nothing inherently dangerous about this place."
- "It's my thoughts, not the place, that's making me feel scared."
- "I'm attributing the fear to external space rather than to the true source, myself."
- "Beliefs like this keep me from making commitments that are needed to be independent across a full range of activities."
- "This belief leads to low frustration tolerance."
- "In fact, I'm not boxed in by events or people. I can always choose to leave."
- "People are not weighing me down or piling things on me. They really can't. Only I can do this to myself."

Vertical space. You may have developed the false idea that how you fare in life depends on how others treat you. You may fear that others will belittle you or put you down. This is based on the idea that people are lined up in a hierarchy with some people being on top of others.
Belief: "I need others to hold me up."
Alternative answers:

- "No one can let me down or push me down, unless psychologically I'm asking them to hold me up."
- "I'm quite capable of holding myself up. I don't need the ride, I only believe I do."
- "In truth, no one is literally up or down. This describes a feeling, not a true spatial situation."
- "I am where I am in life. Calling it up or down is an evaluation, not a fact."

• "Putting others higher than me is the source of my inferiority feelings."

• "Ranking people in order from high to low is an adolescent way of looking at the world."

• "We are all equal and there is no need to make up phony scales of importance."

• "This way of rating people doesn't do any good and leads to feelings of dependency and inferiority."

You may believe you're small and easily controlled while others are large and immovable. One patient, an artist, came to me and said, "It's literally a matter of perspective. I see others or problems as much bigger than they really are and myself as much smaller." He was able to solve this by drawing pictures of others in his life and himself and putting them in proper perspective.

Belief: "Others are too big and I'm too small."
Alternative answers:

• "I inhabit the same space essentially as anyone else."
• "Don't confuse symbolic meaning of size with actual facts."
• "Don't sell yourself short."
• "Don't engage in hero worship or hero fear. I have the same rights as everyone else."
• "I'm the only one that can belittle or shrink my own sense of self."
• "I'm as big as I think I am."
• "Just because someone has more of something—status, money—doesn't mean they are worth more than me or have more rights."
• "It's ridiculous to think everyone else is bigger than I am."

Motion

By motion, I mean how you move toward your goals. You may have a personal goal of being more assertive or independent, or other self-improvement goals such as losing weight or exercising daily. Motion also refers to projects you may want to get moving on, like going into business on your own or writing a school project.

In all these forms of motion, you go through three stages—

your misperceptions on how to proceed can bog you down in any of these stages. The first stage is *initiative*, or the beginning point. Initiative is almost synonymous with independence. When you're dependent, you lack initiative. Second is *choice*, or the middle stage. Here you have to figure out a way to keep going even when your mind is trying to distract you from it. *Ownership* is the final stage. One of Murphy's Laws is that the first 90 percent of a project takes 90 percent of your time and the last 10 percent takes another 90 percent. Many people have trouble finishing projects because they are afraid of owning up to the consequences.

If you have trouble moving toward goals in your life, it's probably because your strategies are based on misperceptions.

Initiative. Lack of initiative prevents you, more than anything else, from getting started. You need to challenge anything that gets in the way of your initiative.

Belief: "I can't start because I'm afraid I will fail."

Alternative beliefs:

- "If I don't move at all, it's an automatic failure."
- "Generally, it's better to err on the side of inclusion rather than exclusion."
- "It's better to endure some frustrations and embarrassment than to miss out on the opportunity or benefit."
- "Where's my evidence that I'll fail?"
- "It's impossible to fail 100 percent because initiation itself counts for something."
- "Failure, if I really see it as such, is often the seed of success."
- "Each time I fail I learn something that I can use to succeed."

Fear stops you from choosing something new. Because of your uncomfortable feelings, you avoid movement. You can start to think differently about fear: see it as a sign to use your initiative in order to get moving.

Belief: "I feel scared about starting something new."

Alternative answers:

- "Anxiety is to be expected when you start something new."
- "The only way not to have any anxiety is not to try anything for the first time."

- "I can accept that the first time is always the hardest."
- "If I stick with it, the anxiety will become manageable."
- "The feelings are just feelings, not predictors of danger or failure."
- "Most people can function relatively effectively even when they are anxious."
- "In order to move, I have to endure these feelings."

Often the problem in getting started is lack of acceptance. As I mentioned before, your mind doesn't want to accept anything that could be unpleasurable, so it makes motion all the more unacceptable by blowing up the discomfort ("I can't stand being alone"). So the first step is to accept the situation as it is, not as the way you want it to be. Accept it the way your body accepts —automatically and without evaluation.

Belief: "There's too much for me to do," or "It's too difficult."

Alternative answers:

- "I don't have to do it all at once."
- "I can focus on one task at a time."
- "I can work on it for a short period of time."
- "There is as much as there is—no more, no less."
- "The word *too* isn't specific enough and implies that I'm not big enough to do it."
- "Don't think about it, just do it."
- "Starting projects usually appears more difficult than it is."
- "I'll feel better once I get into it."
- "It takes more energy to keep from thinking about it than it does to do it."
- "I can just jump in and see what happens."
- "I'm not so weak that I can't tolerate some discomfort."

Waiting for inspiration may seem like the thing to do, but the problem is that it rarely comes. One of the reasons that nothing succeeds like success is that motivation follows action. First you do it, then you feel like doing it.

Belief: "I have to wait until I have self-confidence before I can start it."

Alternative answers:

- "Confidence works backward—you do it first and confidence comes later."

- "Appetite comes with the eating, motivation comes with the doing."
- "Don't put your whole ego on the line."
- "Successful people are able to act without 100 percent assurance of success."
- "The best-kept secret is that experts don't know everything that's going on. They move forward even though they don't have all the information."
- "The second-best-kept secret is that everyone feels inferior at times. I can still function even though I don't feel competent."
- "I have to take some risk if I'm going to get what I want and where I want to go."
- "I don't need to know all the answers to get started. More answers will come as I move ahead."

One of the reasons you may have trouble moving is that you have fantasies that someone will come to your rescue. We're raised on thirty-minute TV dreams where someone always shows up at the last moment to save the person in distress. This isn't the case in real life. You have to get past this fantasy before you can get in motion.

Belief: "Someone will come along and do this for me."
Alternative answers:

- "This is a magical notion that doesn't correspond to the way the world really is."
- "Demanding the impossible to happen will make me give up."
- "If I want to accomplish it I had better start now moving toward it."
- "I can tolerate not having someone to do it for me."
- "I can do it myself."

Choice Stage. It can be difficult to maintain momentum once you get going. It can be frustrating to come back to a task that was going well and find that the pace is gone, that the momentum has left you.

Once you put yourself into motion, you become vulnerable to a host of problems. For example, because you usually feel good about initiating something, you'll be tempted to let up on your efforts once you get moving. This is caused by the false belief that you have your task or goal completely under control.

Belief: "Now that I'm moving on it, I know I'll change."
Alternative answers:

- "This is a trap that I've fallen into before."
- "If I stop now I'll have to go through the whole starting up again."
- "My mind is trying to trick me into thinking I've reached my goal when I haven't."
- "I can keep working although I'm not getting any rewards right now."
- "Good moods as well as bad moods can get me off track."
- "Stick with this until it's done."
- "My mind always tries to get me to move off target—I have the choice not to do this."

Often after you've started a project you encounter frustration and discomfort. This is the time you have to focus on the fact that you really want to finish it or you wouldn't have started it.

Belief: "I don't want to do it."
Alternative answers:

- "This is irrelevant right now."
- "I've done many things I haven't wanted to do."
- "So what? I can still do it."
- "In the bigger picture I do want to do it."
- "I do want to finish—I just don't want to do it."
- "See if you can get some fun out of it."
- "This is just your mind trying to take you away from reality."

A typical pattern is to set high standards and then, when you run into an obstacle or make a slip, you tell yourself you've blown it. You have to get past this point to finish projects.

Belief: "I've messed up now so why go on with it?"
Alternative answers:

- "Think averages—some aspects will be better and some will be worse—it will average out."
- "I can learn to tolerate slips."
- "Keep my eyes on where I'm going."
- "Use these slips as cues to stay with the program."
- "This is either/or thinking."
- "Don't make a trauma out of this slip, just get back with the program."

Often when you're in motion, you start to feel it's not the real you. You may feel like an impostor and that your progress is not a true reflection of you. Then you move forward. You have to endure these feelings.

Belief: "I feel like a phony."

Alternative answers:

- "This is a feeling that comes with all new choices."
- "Don't use feelings as justification for quitting."
- "This seems artificial because it's new."
- "With practice, it will feel more natural."
- "It's a new me."
- "Old habits want to hang on."
- "The best way to get over this is to persist."
- "I don't have to give in to it."

Ownership Stage. When you're in motion but haven't reached your goal, you can have trouble accepting that it's incomplete. This becomes a further drag on finishing it.

Belief: "I should have finished (achieved) this by now."

Alternative answers:

- "The world is as it should be. Proof? It is."
- "Demanding that it be different than it is is grandiose."
- "The gap between what is and what I want is causing most of my problems."
- "Once I accept what is, I can function much better."
- "The requirements for finishing it haven't been met—so it shouldn't be done."
- "This is a demand that the world be different than it is."

You don't reach your goal, so you blame yourself. You begin to believe you're inadequate, lazy and worthless for not getting it done. This has the effect of making it more difficult to be successful.

Belief: "I'm bad for not having finished by now."

Alternative beliefs:

- "Accept that it's not done now."
- "Be task-oriented, not blame-oriented."
- "Keep personal evaluations out of it."

- "You aren't bad for not finishing it, only fallible."
- "Not doing what is in your own best interest has its own natural consequences—why give myself a double whipping?"
- "Guilt is what I feel about something I'm going to do again. (I overeat, feel guilty and then overeat again.) Thus, guilt doesn't help."

As you move toward your goal, your mind will often start cooking up a lot of reasons why you can't take the final steps. You need to overcome these excuses so that you can be successful.

Belief: "I can't reach my goal right now because of ________. (Fill in your favorite excuse.)

Alternative answers:

- "Recognize these as excuses that are covering up deeper fears."
- "I won't fool myself or lie to myself."
- "Move toward reality."
- "What am I afraid of?"
- "I can refuse to listen to these excuses."
- "I'm not going to let these little excuses cripple me."

Fear that you will be evaluated by others or other perceived negative consequences can often stop you. A woman who couldn't enjoy sex was afraid that men would not find her sexy. She learned to confront these fears.

Belief: "Others will see I'm not perfect."

Alternative answers:

- "Anxious people often think that their hat is on fire. In reality, no one notices me or my work that much."
- "Where's my evidence that others will think badly of me?"
- "I'm just projecting my own harsh self-judgments onto others."
- "My shame is self-created. Most people are tolerant of me."
- "Even if others do make immature judgments of me, I don't have to buy into them."
- "Mistakes I make are just another name for experience."
- "I need corrective feedback from others in order to grow."
- "It's their choice how they respond and it's my choice how I respond."

Learning to become intellectually independent is a process, not a goal. The process is found in valuing yourself. In the next chapter, I'll talk more about this.

TABLE 1
TIME AS A SMOKE SCREEN

Smoke Screen	*Reality*
I don't have time.	I'm choosing to do something else instead.
I don't have the spare time.	I'm not making it a high priority.
Time got away from me.	I goofed off.
I wasted my time.	I chose to do X instead of Y.
I need to learn to manage my time.	I need to learn to manage myself.
I'll get over it (change) in time.	I'll get over it (choice) when I decide to.
I have to kill some time.	I don't know what to do with myself.
Time is the one thing you can't change.	I don't want to make different choices.
I don't want to spend the time.	I don't want to do it so I'm holding back.
He wasted my time.	I didn't ask him to leave.

FIGURE 1

THE USE OF SETBACKS TO ESCALATE YOUR GROWTH CURVE

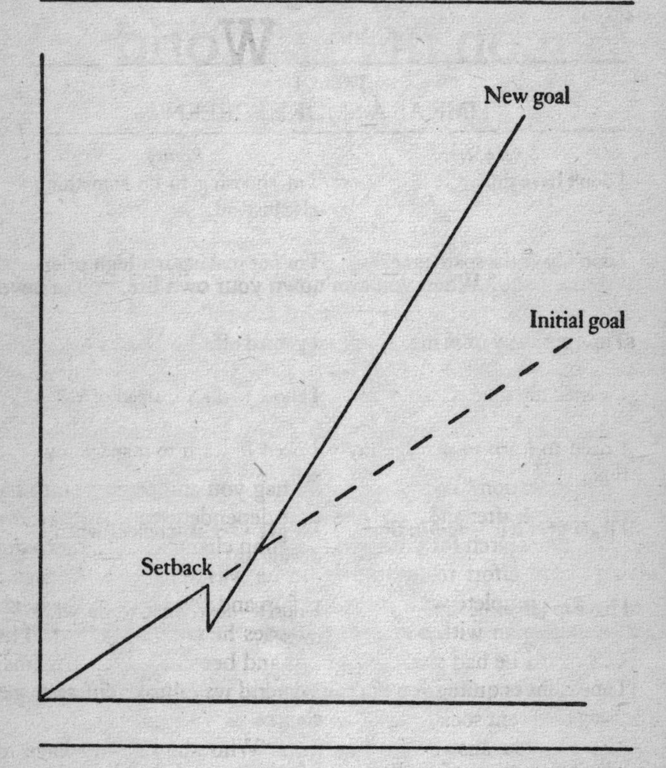

CHAPTER SIXTEEN

The Most Important Person in the World

WHO ARE YOU? When you don't own your own life, you're never sure who you are. Are you your husband's wife? Your father's son? Your boss's assistant? Are you your job? Your work? Your successes? Your failures? When you're dependent, you often try to answer this question by seeing who you're attached to. This fails to answer the question satisfactorily—you know you're more than this.

The question "Who am I?" can nag you and cause you to try on one mask after another. The more dependent you are, the more frantic the search for who you are. John changed costumes regularly in an effort to find out who he was. One year he was a cowboy, complete with boots, pickup and cowboy hat; the next, a businessman with a leased Mercedes he couldn't afford. The last I heard he had shaved his head and become a Hari Krishna. He never was quite sure who he was and was always trying to get lost in different social roles.

Before you answer the question "Who am I?" you have to answer another one: "Who needs to know?" Your parents? Your kids? Your boss? Your wife or husband? Your friends? Strangers in the street? After you think about it, you'll probably conclude that you're the only one who ever needs to know. This is fortunate, because you're the only one who can experience who you are. The question then becomes "To me, who am I?" The answer:

YOU'RE THE MOST IMPORTANT PERSON
WHO EVER LIVED.

The most important person in the world happens to live in your home town and also happens to sleep on your side of the bed. Why you? Well, why not? Someone has to be the most important person in the world, and who better than you?

As a child you knew this and have suspected it at other times. Haven't you at one time thought that the rest of the people in the world were just bit players in your movie? Well, they are. The world, in the whole universe, revolves around you.

When I tell clients "To you, you're the most important person in the world," I get a variety of responses. One woman broke into tears and said, "I was always told by my parents, 'You are not so important.' " One man nodded quickly and said, yes, he knew that. He was raised by indulgent parents and had only learned part of the answer to "Who are you?" He had learned that he is the most important person in the world, but hadn't learned the two important words that go with it: *to me*. To every person, the answer is the same. Each person is the most important person in the world to him- or herself.

You may not accept that you're the most important person in the world. Jerry, a depressed businessman I saw, said, "A lot of people are more important than me. In fact, I'd say just about everyone is more important than me."

Psychiatrist Maxie Maultsby suggests that to prove who is the most important person you push the matter to the extreme. I did this to Jerry.

I asked, "Who specifically is more important than you?"

CLIENT: I don't know . . . Warren Beatty?

THERAPIST: Why is he more important than you?

CLIENT: He's handsome, I'm ugly. He's rich, I'm poor. He has beautiful girlfriends, I'm divorced and don't have even one girlfriend.

THERAPIST: Any other reasons?

CLIENT: Plenty. He's famous, a winner—he has a great career . . . and I'm a loser.

THERAPIST: Then you're saying he's more important than you?

CLIENT: Of course.

THERAPIST: Suppose you were in a room with Warren Beatty and there was only enough oxygen for one person in the room and poisonous gas outside. Would you volunteer to give up your life to save his?

CLIENT: No.

THERAPIST: Why not? If he's more important than you, why wouldn't you give up your life for him?

CLIENT: I just wouldn't. His life's not more valuable than mine.

THERAPIST: Could it be that you're more important *to you* than Warren Beatty is to you?

CLIENT: I see what you're driving at, but I might give up my life for my kids. Wouldn't that make them more important than me?

THERAPIST: You might decide that, but you would be the only one that could decide that, which would still mean that you're the most important person in the world. You're the only one in the world who could make that choice.

If you have doubts about being the most important person, ask yourself who has the power to invent the world you see? Only you can make your adversaries ten feet tall and yourself ten inches high. You're the only one who can assign meanings to your experiences. You're the only one who has the power to control how you think, feel and act. And you're the only one who can have your experiences.

Implications

Accepting that you're the most important person has significant implications as far as owning your own life goes.

You Have No Need for Comparisons. You no longer have to make the insidious comparisons that caused you to be depressed and envious. No matter what others accomplish, you'll always remain more important. Once you stop making social comparisons you become independent from others' achievements. You become freer and lighter.

You Stop Demanding Perfection from Yourself. Once you realize you're already the king, you don't need to be a slave to perfection. Perfection is only a pretender to the throne. You become independent from the tyranny of your unrealistic high standards. Once you're free of this excess baggage, you can move faster and farther.

Your Fear Goes Away. When you believe falsely that your importance comes from others, you're always afraid that your importance will lessen—that others will somehow take it away from you. However, you can never, in reality, become less than the most important person in the world. Even if you're living on handouts and sleeping in a cardboard box, you're still the most important person who ever lived *to you*. When you choose not to tie your importance to others' opinions of you, people no longer have the whammy on you.

You stop becoming a pleaser. You don't believe you have to get the approval and recognition from others whom you believe are more important than you are. When you give more power to others and hold them up as your betters, you become afraid to cross them. However, when you know you're the most important person, you're willing to stand up for yourself. You don't discount yourself or let others discount you.

You'll Stop Trying to Be a Big Shot. When you really believe you're the most important person, you stop going around trying to convince others how important you are. Bragging makes you feel less important and causes you problems with people.

Once you realize you're already on the top of the heap—that it's your birthright—you free yourself of having to try to impress others. Why would the most important person who ever lived need others' worship?

Your Relationships with Others Will Improve. Once you realize you're already the most important person, you can forget about your worth and social standing; you can start to make contributions to others. When you see that the two crucial words *to me* are added, you'll respect others more.

You start to realize that all people are the most important person in the world to themselves. You stop trying to get them to think you're more important than they are. You realize that if they believe this, they are kidding you and themselves. You become truly democratic and stop believing others are more or less than you: your judgments go away—young, old, rich, poor, beautiful, ugly—each is still the most important person to him or herself. You feel equally at home with all people.

You Begin to Operate in Your Own Best Interest. Seeking your importance outside yourself sends you down blind alleys (hero worship, expensive status items, workaholic behavior). You know that you can't become *more* than the most important person. You don't *need* more money, success or recognition to validate yourself. This frees you to work in your own best interest. You don't have to achieve to prove to others how important you are; you achieve because this is what you want to do for your own best interest.

You Can Make a Contribution to Others. When your self-respect is high, you feel free to help others. Even more, you have a desire to help others. When your self-respect is down, you have a desire to bring others down. After you see that everyone is a king and that there are no inferiors, you can be the king who picks up his or her own socks. Once you know you're the most important person, you can carry yourself with a quiet dignity. You can afford to give others a break. You can be the benevolent ruler who gives of yourself, rather than one who beheads people you fear.

You Treat Yourself Well. You take care of health and treat the most important person in the world with respect. You don't put yourself at the end of the line, waiting for handouts. You fasten your seatbelt and keep yourself in good physical condition. One of my clients had three children and a demanding husband. The first few times I saw her, she looked terrible. Her hair and clothes were out of date and she was twenty pounds overweight. The change that came over her as she began to accept that she was the most important person in the world was remarkable. She began to lose weight and had her hair styled. She rewarded her weight losses with new clothes. She said, "I've spent twelve years being last in line in my family. Now, I treat myself as the important person I am. Amazingly, my family seems to like me much better."

You Open Up Your Potential. The vast majority of your perceived limitations are illusions; you place them on yourself because you don't realize your importance. With your new knowledge you can become independent of your illusions of inadequacy, helplessness and hopelessness.

You Start Applying the ACT Formula Automatically. You *accept* yourself. You're free to *choose* to be independent. You *take action* that's in your best interest. You don't need temper tantrums, the strategy of the weak—you can ask for what you want. You don't need to chase the elusive white rabbit to become important—you already are important.

Enlightened Indifference

Once you own your own life you reach a point of enlightened acceptance. You start using the ACT formula in more and more of your life; you start to let the RAT formula (*R*esisting reality, *A*llowing dependence, and *T*aking dependent action) go. Following is the type of dialogue you have with yourself after you have chosen enlightened acceptance over dependency.

Dependency: "If I accept the unacceptable (it might rain), it'll happen."

Enlightened acceptance: "In reality, accepting or not accepting the unwanted has nothing to do with it. The rain will come whether you like it or not."

Dependency: "Because this is so important, it has to be taken seriously. It's no joke."

Enlightened acceptance: "Because you can accept whatever happens, you don't have to take life that seriously. Life in many ways is a practical joke. It only hurts if you take it seriously."

Dependency: "But what I'm worrying about really does make a difference."

Enlightened acceptance: "Will the things you're worrying about now make any difference in ten years? Did the things you worried about yesterday, last week, last year, ten years ago, make any difference?"

Dependency: "My past was a tragedy, the present and my future is terrifying."

Enlightened acceptance: "So what?"

Dependency: "But this problem is serious and important."

Enlightened acceptance: "The sun is slowly burning out. In a few billion years the earth will be gone."

Dependency: "But you don't understand. I'm really in a bind *now*."

Enlightened acceptance: "Sometimes you ride on top of the horse, sometimes you ride under it. The only difference is the view."

Dependency: "If I accept what I don't want, I'll never be able to change it."

Enlightened acceptance: "Only after you accept what you don't want are you free to make different choices. You have to accept that your arm is broken before you can fix it. As long as you won't accept that it's broken, you can't do anything about it."

Dependency: "I won't have any motivation if I get rid of my expectations."

Enlightened acceptance: "Negative expectations lead to self-fulfilling prophecies, overly positive expectations lead to disappointment and no surprises. Better to keep your expectations low (what happens you can accept) and your motivation to stay out of the rain high."

Dependency: "People who don't do what I think is important are bad and should be punished."

Enlightened acceptance: "You can accept what others do. It's their choice. If it affects you, try to stay out of the rain if you can. Tolerance plus common sense = enlightened acceptance."

Dependency: "What I want (that is, sunshine) is crucial to my happiness."

Enlightened acceptance: "In the final analysis, it doesn't matter if it rains or shines. You'll be wet or you'll be dry. So what?"

Dependency: "If I don't care very much, I'll get into trouble. I'll be in the rain forever."

Enlightened acceptance: "Enlightened acceptance means acceptance plus common sense. Common sense says that you should come in out of the rain. If you can accept being wet or dry, why not be dry?"

Dependency: "I must have more of what I think is important."

Enlightened acceptance: "More of anything is seldom desirable. Believing you always need more money makes for a frightened miser. And believing you always need better health makes for a frightened health nut. You quickly reach a point of diminishing returns; more makeup soon makes you ugly."

Dependency: "This is really important. I can't let it go."

Enlightened acceptance: "Years ago you stayed up all night worrying about something you thought was important. Like a thousand other nights in your past, you can't even remember now what you were worrying about."

Dependency: "I have to work hard at getting everyone to do what I want them to do—or they won't do it."

Enlightened acceptance: "The harder you try to get people to do what you want them to do, the less likely they are to do it. Tell people twice what you would like them to do and let it go. Also, tell them you're only going to tell them twice."

Dependency: "If what I think important doesn't come to pass, this will be terrible for the future."

Enlightened acceptance: "Nothing is frozen in time. Like a dream, everything seems important right now, but when you look back on it, you'll see that it has no permanence. It lasts only in your imperfect memory of it. A dream seems real at the time, but like other events, all you have afterward is a fuzzy memory of it. The wheel will always turn—the good patch leads to the bad patch leads to the good patch . . . and so on."

Dependency: "Because everything is so important, I have to worry about the future."

Enlightened acceptance: "Because you can accept whatever happens, worrying about the future is unnecessary. Whatever happens will happen—if you worry about it or not."

Dependency: "There is such a thing as 100 percent bad luck and 100 percent good luck."

Enlightened acceptance: "Everything is black *and* white. Nothing is all black or all white."

Dependency: "The best and easiest way to get something I really want is to consider it very important and to really want it."

Enlightened acceptance: "It's much easier to get something if you don't care if you get it or not. Wanting something too much creates anxiety in yourself and resistance in others."

Dependency: "Because I'm special, I must have everything go my way."

Enlightened acceptance: "Everyone is special. You don't have to have everything go your way to be happy. The cosmos doesn't really care if things go your way or not."

Dependency: "The more things (health, wealth, fame, success) I believe are important to me, the happier and saner I'll be. My fetishes (desires) make me happy."

Enlightened acceptance: "The fewer things you believe are important to you, the healthier and happier you'll be. Your fetishes lead to your phobias, that is, fears of losing them."

Dependency: "I can't accept what is unacceptable to me."

Enlightened acceptance: "Not accepting what is leads to pain. Accepting it removes the pain, that's all."

Dependency: "I need more of what I think is important (security, approval, love)."

Enlightened acceptance: "You can never get enough of something you think you need but in fact don't."

Dependency: "Why did I get into this fix?"

Enlightened acceptance: "You're in the fix because you're in the fix. Instead of asking why you're in the rain, ask yourself, 'How can I get out of it?' "

Dependency: "Why me?"

Enlightened acceptance: "Why not?"

Self-worth. Enlightened acceptance means that you separate your basic self-worth from your good and bad patches. When you buy a ticket that equates your worth with your place in the world, you put yourself in a passive, dependent position. You're in the back seat. You're forever chasing after the eternal good patch (the perfect lover, the perfect career). You're constantly looking for outsiders to punch your ticket and thus prove your worth, once and for all, to yourself and to others. But in the end all you get is a ride on an emotional roller coaster that's out of your control.

The way to get off the roller coaster is to separate your basic self-worth from your life experiences. Your basic self-worth is a given. You don't have to prove it. You can't prove it. It just is. You can call this your essence, your soul, or ninety-eight cents worth of chemicals. Whatever you want to call it, it's a given. It starts when you're born and stays with you until you die. It's the same for everyone—kings, beggars and poets. Neither you nor anyone else can ever subtract from it. It's money in the bank. Similarly, you can never add to it—it's a constant.

Gordon Overbo, a retired farmer from North Dakota, considers your self-worth a straight line that never ends. This is a good analogy. As long as you keep this straight line in mind as a given, you'll be all right. However, when you fuse it with your good and bad patches, you're back on the roller coaster. In *Figure 1*, I've shown the dependent and the independent ways of looking at your self-worth.

FIGURE 1
SELF-WORTH

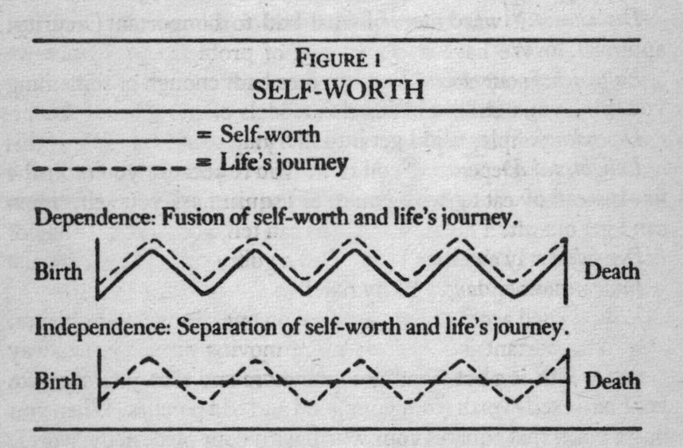

In separating your self-worth from your external validation, it's helpful to keep your uniqueness in mind. There never has been and never will be another person exactly like you. Everything about you is unique. No one, for example, has ever had eyes, hair or hands exactly like yours. And even more telling is that little voice you've heard inside your head ever since you were a child. No one else has a little voice exactly like yours. This little voice will be with you the rest of your days and no one else will ever be able to hear exactly what it sounds like. This is always 100 percent yours.

Once you stop confusing your worth with your good and bad patches, you stop taking your ups and downs seriously. You brag and complain less. You start to look at your life as a journey that's not good or bad, just more interesting at times and less interesting at other times. You start to see that the valleys are often more interesting than the peaks.

In the final analysis, enlightened acceptance means you stop judging your experiences as good or bad—you just accept them as they are. The more you label events as good or bad, the more nonacceptance you have of your life and thus the less you own it.

Most of our troubles with acceptance started with Adam and Eve. They were in Paradise before they ate from the tree of the knowledge of good and evil. Like animals and small children, they didn't know it was shameful and bad to be naked. They just accepted it. We have had all kinds of problems ever since we started calling our experiences good or bad.

Animals and children are good models of enlightened acceptance. For example, my cat is always trying to eat my bird. Is this good or bad? Depends on whether you're the cat or the bird. I don't want my cat to eat my bird, so I squirt her with water when she goes after it. The cat, as far as I can tell, accepts my behavior and doesn't stay awake at night with a guilty conscience. She just waits for another day to get the bird.

Enlightened acceptance is an ideal no one completely achieves. What's important is whether you're moving toward it or away from it. This is a process of owning more and more of your own life.

Walk, Don't Wait

When you don't own your own life, you spend most of your time waiting. You wait for others to change so you can feel good.

You wait until you feel big enough to step up and ask for what you want. Like Sleeping Beauty, you wait for that special person or event to bring you to life. You wait for the phone call, letter or chance meeting that will release you from the pain of waiting. You wait for the right time to start the big project you've been putting off.

Your waiting is not all in the abstract. Daily, you wait for those you're the most dependent on. You wait for over an hour for your friend to take you shopping. You wait for your husband to come home, or at least to call. You wait for your wife to fill out the insurance forms. You wait for your boss to read your report. Will he give you a pat on the head or not?

Much of what you wait for turns out to be like *Waiting for Godot*, a no-show. The epitaph on your tombstone could read "Wait until next year."

Once you own your own life, you stop waiting. You start feeling good without needing others to change. You decide to live for the present instead of for tomorrow. Your motto becomes "Now is as good a time as any to get what I want." Rather than wait for others to do your housekeeping for you, you do it yourself.

By choosing to own your own life and by acting now, you can start to lead a freer and more self-determined life. Your waiting can be over.

Recommended Reading

Beck, A. T. *Cognitive Therapy and Emotional Disorders* (New American Library, 1979).

Beecher, Willard, and Beecher, Marguerite. *Beyond Success and Failure* (Pocket Books, 1981).

Burns, David. *Feeling Good: The New Mood Therapy* (New American Library, 1981).

Dwyer, Wayne. *Your Erroneous Zones* (Funk and Wagnalls, 1976).

Ellis, Albert, and Harper, Robert. *A New Guide to Rational Living.* (Prentice-Hall, 1975).

Emery, Gary. *A New Beginning: How You Can Change Your Life Through Cognitive Therapy* (Simon & Schuster, 1981).*

Emery, Gary. *Controlling Your Depression Through Cognitive Therapy: Audio Tape Series and Workbook* (BMA Audio Cassettes, 1982).*

Emery, Gary. *A Guide to Self-Reliance: Audio Cassette* (Los Angeles Center for Cognitive Therapy, 1982).*

* Available from the
Los Angeles Center for Cognitive Therapy
630 South Wilton Place
Los Angeles, California 90005
(213) 387-4737

APPENDIX

Independence Rating Scale

YOU CAN USE THE *Independence Rating Scale* to take stock of yourself. The scale is made up of descriptions of ten different levels of independence; the levels go in ascending order from least to most independent. You can use this scale as a guide to determine your present level of independence.

You can use this scale to make an independence rating of yourself. The scale gives you an independence score from 10 to 100. To determine your score, first read through all of the levels; then go back and determine which level best describes you. If you find yourself between 60 and 70, and you're closer to 70 than 60, your score might be 67. Although this rating is somewhat subjective, most people can determine where they fit on the scale.

After you have rated yourself, ask someone else to rate you. This comparison score can be quite insightful. Others often are better judges of your independence than you are. If there is a large discrepancy between the two ratings, you want to find out why. At the end, you can find an evaluation of your score.

Levels of Independence

Level 1 (10). People at this level are totally dependent on others to meet their needs. Without help the person would die. You were at this level as an infant. Others at this level include those with severe brain damage, the seriously retarded and the gravely ill. People at this level need others to dress, feed and protect them.

An example is Mrs. White, eight-seven. She led a full and active life before she became senile in her early eighties. Her family was unable to take care of her and she had to be placed in a nursing home where she receives twenty-four-hour care.

Level 2 (20). The person at this level has lost some contact with reality and is dependent on others to manipulate the environment to meet his or her needs. The person is often in an institution or operates at a minimal level on his or her own. Tom, forty-seven, has been hospitalized eight times for paranoia schizophrenia. Currently, he has delusions of being a five-star general who designs jet airplanes. The cutbacks in mental health funds have forced him to live in the streets. He is dependent on what others give him or what he can find in the garbage to provide for his needs. He makes no contribution to society and lives off society's leftovers.

Level 3 (30). People at this level are primarily dependent on outside forces. They may live on their own but count on others to provide their sustenance. They are almost never financially self-reliant and are dependent on welfare agencies, friends, parents or other relatives to pay their way. An example is Alice, twenty-seven, who lives in a small apartment that her parents pay for. Her mother brings over groceries each week. She has two children who live in foster homes. She hasn't held a job for three years and has a history of problems with alcohol and drugs.

Level 4 (40). People here get along only marginally. They are often able to make a living but they have trouble with people and difficulty in reaching their goals. Sam, thirty-three, is a handyman. Although he makes his own money, he is always in debt. His appearance is unkempt and dirty, and he keeps his apartment the same way. Over the last ten years he has lived in five different cities on the West Coast. He has a number of unrealistic daydreams. Currently he talks about becoming an actor, but takes almost no steps toward this or any of his other goals. His main problem is not being able to form close relationships with others.

He is often angry and puts others down frequently; as a result, most people avoid him.

Level 5 (50). The person functioning at this level has decided to settle for quite a bit less in life. He or she has chosen to take the path of least resistance by not facing the anxiety that comes with growth. Judy is thirty-three and works at a job that is considerably below her competence and education. She has no close friends and only a few acquaintances. Because of a fear of being hurt, she has decided not to pursue close relationships. She lives with her aged mother who dotes on her. Her mother gets on Judy's nerves, but she is afraid of living alone. Although she causes society no trouble, she has decided not to endure the pain of growth.

Level 6 (60). People at this level have made some movement toward personal and social adjustment. They have (or have had in the past) jobs they like and satisfying relationships. They have problems, however, with emotional independence and are bothered by anxiety, depression and anger *management*. An example is Barbara, thirty-eight, who is married with one child. She is overly dependent on others' opinions of her. In her desire to be liked, she comes across as nonassertive and passive. She wants others to be nice to her; as a result, she is bothered by social anxiety and has had severe bouts with depression in which she feels unaccepted and unloved.

Level 7 (70). People at this level have many successful areas of their lives. They have done what society has asked them to do. They may have gone to school, gotten a job, been married and had kids. However, they have overbought many of society's ideas of what is right for a person. They are taken with status, success and what others think of them. They are easily impressed by those in higher social positions. An example is Gene, who works for a large insurance company. He hasn't advanced as high or as fast as he might have. He's afraid of rocking the boat. He doesn't give his true opinion on matters and, as a result, he is thought of as lacking initiative and creativity. He has made a good material life for himself and his family. He is geared to thinking of enjoying himself in the future. He's now forty-nine and looks forward to retirement when he reaches sixty.

Level 8 (80). People here have a high degree of independence in many areas of their lives. They aren't afraid to state their opinions to others and are more interested in pleasing themselves than others. They keep their word and are reliable. They are often intolerant of others' shortcomings. Their dependence shows up in two ways. First, they tend to rebel against what they are dependent on, their job for example; and second, they don't take risks in the areas that are important to them. An example is Ruth, twenty-nine, a psychiatric social worker. She is happily married to her second husband. Something of a perfectionist, she is well thought of at work, a large hospital. She is unhappy with the administration and would like to start her own private practice, but she is afraid to take the risk.

Level 9 (90). People at this level stand out by their ability to think for themselves. This is a form of integrity that is not swayed by praise or blame. They don't blame their bad experiences on others or on themselves. They can show great concern for others, yet don't take responsibility for others' emotions. People seek them out for their integrity and honesty. They have a minimum of ideological axes to grind. They do have some areas of their lives where they still are dependent and, under stress, they can revert to a lower level of functioning. An example is Brian, fifty, a newspaper editor. He is known for thinking for himself and tells people what no one else will. He is happily married and is only occasionally bothered by dark moods. He is dependent on his wife to think about what to do with the children; he agonizes and has to push himself when he knows he is taking an unpopular stance.

Level 10 (100). People at this level operate at their peak potential. Throughout history there have been small numbers of people who have made a big difference in the way we think and live.

These individuals can be found leading the progress of science, religion, philosophy, government and literature. They have developed a degree of independence that allows them to transcend what they were told was the truth about the world. While they may not have operated at this level throughout their entire lives, they were able to do it long enough to make a significant contribution. The more self-reliant the person, the bigger the contribution. An example of someone at this level is Ralph Waldo Emerson. His writings and observations changed the course of American literature and made significant contributions to philosophy and psychology.

Keep in mind that where you fall on this scale is not fixed. When events are going well for you, you'll probably move up. When you're under stress, you're more inclined to move down.

RESULTS
INDEPENDENCE RATING SCALE

SCORE	
40 and below:	You have a severe dependency problem. In all likelihood, you'll need outside help in becoming more independent.
40–60:	Your dependency is a major problem in your life. To improve, you'll have to make independence training a top priority and work hard at it.
60–80:	You can benefit from independence training the most. You have both the ability and capacity for improvement.
80 and above:	You're operating at a high level of independence. You can benefit by working specifically on areas where you're still dependent.